Liverpool Studies in Europ

No Heavenly Delusion?
A Comparative Study of
Three Communal Movements

LIVERPOOL STUDIES IN EUROPEAN AND REGIONAL CULTURES
Series Editors: Ullrich Kockel and Máiréad Nic Craith

This series presents original research on the regional dimension of Europe, with special emphasis on regional culture, heritage and identity in the context of socio-economic development. It offers an interdisciplinary and comparative perspective on the management of cultural resources, examining the diversity and similarity of regional cultures in Europe, and identifying potentials for inter-regional co-operation and experience interchange.

OTHER TITLES AVAILABLE IN THIS SERIES

Culture, Tourism and Development: The Case of Ireland
ed. Ullrich Kockel, Volume 1, 1994, ISBN 0-85323-369-1

Landscape, Heritage and Identity: Case Studies in Irish Ethnography
ed. Ullrich Kockel, Volume 2, 1995, ISBN 0-85323-500-7

Borderline Cases: The Ethnic Frontiers of European Integration
Ullrich Kockel, Volume 3, 1999, ISBN 0-85323-520-1

Watching One's Tongue: Issues in Language Planning
ed. Máiréad Nic Craith, Volume 4, 1996, ISBN 0-85323-611-9

Watching One's Tongue: Aspects of Romance and Celtic Languages
ed. Máiréad Nic Craith, Volume 5, 1996, ISBN 0-85323-621-6

The Irish Border: History, Culture, Politics
ed. Malcolm Anderson and Eberhard Bort, Volume 7, 1999, ISBN 0-85323-951-7

Networking Europe: Essays on Regionalism and Social Democracy
ed. Eberhard Bort and Neil Evans, Volume 6, 2000, ISBN 0-85323-942-X

The Mediterranean Passage: Migration and New Cultural Encounters in Southern Europe
ed. Russell King, Volume 9, 2001, ISBN 0-85323-646-1

NO HEAVENLY DELUSION?

A Comparative Study of Three Communal Movements

Michael Tyldesley

Liverpool University Press

First published 2003 by
Liverpool University Press
4 Cambridge Street
Liverpool L69 7ZU

British Library Cataloguing-in-Publication data
A British Library CIP record is available

ISBN 0-85323-608-9

Typeset by Servis Filmsetting Ltd, Manchester
Printed and bound in the European Union by Alden Group Ltd, Oxford

So we do not have to first create a world view for the people; that would be completely artificial, transitory or weak, or even romantic and hypocritical, and today would in fact be subject to fashion. We have the reality of the living, individual communal spirit in us and we must merely let it emerge creatively. The desire to create small groups and communities of justice – not a heavenly delusion or a symbolic form, but earthly social joy and readiness of individuals to form a people – will bring about socialism and the beginning of a real society.

Gustav Landauer, *For Socialism* (*Aufruf zum Sozialismus*), 1911

For Kath, Bert, and the memory of Jean

Contents

Acknowledgements

I wish to acknowledge the assistance that I have received from various sources in the researching and writing of this book. The first acknowledgement must be to my series editor, Professor Ulli Kockel. I hope that the final product repays his faith, patience and generosity. I would also like to thank Andrew Kirk at Liverpool University Press for his editorial work.

In respect of the various movements considered in the book, a number of people need to be thanked. From the Kibbutz, I would like to record my gratitude to Chaim Seeligmann, Professor Yaacov Oved and Ruth Sobol, who assisted me enormously both when I visited Yad Tabenkin in spring 2000 and at other times. Professor Avraham Yassour was also an important source of material used here. David Merron should be mentioned in this context; he helpfully spoke to me in London in spring 2001, and has allowed me to quote from an unpublished paper. I must also thank James Grant-Rosenhead of Kvutsat Yovel in Jerusalem. Unfortunately, we have only managed to communicate via email and the telephone, but his help has been invaluable.

Regarding the Integrierte Gemeinde, in the summers of 1999 and 2000 a number of members in the Munich and Walchensee areas of Bavaria generously spoke with me, for which I would like to place my thanks on record. At the Bruderhof, over the years working on this and previous pieces of work, many members have had conversations with me. I must mention with thanks Sophie Loeber and Hugo Brinkmann, with whom I talked in summer 1999. I have frequently spoken with Dave and Fiona Hibbs, and have learned much from them. I must also put on record my debt to the late Walter Hüssy. Although only mentioned in passing in this work, Walter opened my eyes to the meaning of the Bruderhof and also the meaning of the German-Jewish socialist tradition whose most important representative was Gustav Landauer.

I have spoken to a number of other people in connection with this work. Not all of these conversations are directly mentioned in the book, but all have been important and need acknowledgement. In order to attempt to overcome my ignorance concerning Roman Catholicism I imposed on the time of Father Gerry Hughes SJ and Father Edmund Adamus. The connection with Fr Hughes came from the assistance of Father Jack Costello SJ, who helped in a number of other ways as well, as did Paul McPartlan of Heythrop College. I also had a very interesting discussion with Frank Johnson of the Focolare movement about that movement and the 'new movements' in Catholicism generally. I discussed the Youth Movement and the Kibbutz with Professor Walter Laqueur in London in autumn 2000, and must register my thanks for his kindness in speaking to me. In the summer of 1999 I met and talked with Thomas Keller, now of the University of Aix en Provence, in Alsace. While this was not structured and not particularly a discussion on any specific theme of this book, Thomas sparked a number of chains of thought that have been of use to me. Andrew Bolton, of the Harvest Hills Community in Independence, Missouri, has long helped me in my work, and he spoke with me at length in summer 2001. As ever, this discussion was stimulating, useful and enjoyable.

I would also like to thank Lawrence Black and Mark Minion for sending me copies of their work related to Leonhard Nelson and his successors. Paul Ingram of Columbia University graciously allowed me to cite an unpublished working paper. Thanks are also due to Kevin Mahoney and Andy Phillips for assistance they have given. Finally, Roland Crump assisted with some German material when time was pressing, for which all due thanks.

In my own institution, Manchester Metropolitan University, I wish to thank Kirsten Burke, who helped with typing on a number of occasions. I would also like to thank Professors Martin Bell, Neill Nugent and Peter Barberis, and Dr Geraldine Lievesley in my own department for their assistance in helping me obtain funding for aspects of the work involved in this book, and for sabbatical leave in the autumn of 2000. Dr Phillip Hodgkiss of the Department of Applied Community Studies has provided invaluable assistance, in the form of a number of long discussions of some issues involved in the final chapter. He will receive his full reward in the Nawaab, Bradford, in due course.

The usual disclaimer applies: I am solely responsible for any errors, misunderstandings or the like.

Mike Tyldesley
Manchester, Easter 2002

Chronologies

THE KIBBUTZ

1904–1914	Second Aliya
1910	Formation of Degania, the first kibbutz
1918–1923	Third Aliya
1920	Formation of Gedud Ha'avoda (the Labour Battalion)
1920–1921	Betanya, first Hashomer Hatzair kibbutz, in existence
1927	Formation of Kibbutz Me'uhad federation and of Kibbutz Artzi federation
1929	Formation of Hever Hakvutzot federation
1935	Formation of Kibbutz Dati federation
1936–1939	'Wall and Tower' period
1941	L'Ahdut Ha'avoda leaves Mapai
1948	War and formation of State of Israel
1951	Split in Kibbutz Me'uhad. Merger of Me'uhad minority with Hever Hakvutzot to form Ihud Hakvutzot Hakibbutzim federation
1968	Mapai, L'Ahdut Ha'avoda, Rafi merge to form Labour Party
1977	Likud Party forms government
1981	Me'uhad and Ihud merge to form Takam (United Kibbutz Movement) federation
1985	Economic crisis hits the Kibbutz
1988	Tamuz, urban kibbutz, founded
2000	Artzi and Takam merge to form 'The Kibbutz Movement'

THE INTEGRIERTE GEMEINDE

1948	The Junger Bund leaves the Heliand Bund
1953	The property that will eventually become the 'Marlene Kirchner Haus' bought in Urfeld
1954	Walter Cohen joins, but soon leaves and subsequently dies

1966	Death of Marlene Kirchner
1968	Exit of Dr A Goergen, priest
1969	Community becomes known as the Integrierte Gemeinde (Integrated Community)
1976	The 'Cathedral Protests'
1977	Meeting with Bishop Christopher Mwoleka, which leads to the community's work in Tanzania
1978	Official recognition by the Roman Catholic Church as 'Apostolic Association'
1995	Formation of Urfeld Circle with Bruderhof (for brief period) and, on a more permanent basis, kibbutznikim

THE BRUDERHOF

1920	Foundation at Sannerz
1922	Split. Refoundation with seven members
1927	Move from Sannerz to the Rhön Bruderhof
1930–1931	Eberhard Arnold visits Hutterites in North America. Result is the merging into Hutterianism of the Bruderhof
1933	Nazis take power
1934	Alm Bruderhof started in Liechtenstein
1937	Move to Cotswold Bruderhof in England
1940–1941	Migration to Paraguay
1942	Formation of Wheathill Bruderhof in Shropshire, England
1952	El Arado Bruderhof founded in Uruguay
1954	First North American bruderhof, Woodcrest, founded in New York State, USA
1955–1956	Attempts to restart in Germany with the Sinnthalhof
1957	'Forest River affair' finally ends unity with Hutterites
1958	Bruderhof acquires Community Playthings
1961	'The Crisis' in the movement
1961–1962	Regrouping in the NE USA, completed 1966 with end of last British bruderhof
1971	Darvell, new British bruderhof started
1974	Re-unification with the Hutterites
1989	Michaelshof, new German bruderhof started
1990	Two of the three Hutterian 'leuts' sever ties to Bruderhof
1992	Palmgrove venture in Nigeria
1994	Bruderhof ends ties with Palmgrove
1995	Third Hutterian 'leut' ends ties with Bruderhof
1995	Michaelshof shut down
2000	Australian venture commences

Introduction

This book examines and compares three communal movements whose origins can be traced, in some measure, to the German Youth Movement. At the outset, let us consider what is meant here by the term 'communal movement'. Specifically, what does 'communal' mean? Moreover, why are these bodies 'movements'? Taking up the first question, the obvious answer is that all three movements live what could be termed a 'common life'. However, they do not live the same type of common life. The Kibbutz movement and the Bruderhof communities take the form of 'communes'. In these communities, the population mainly lives and works together in the commune, where the actual site, buildings and means of production and consumption are owned collectively by the members of the community. There are some caveats to be entered here. The members of the Bruderhof generally take the principle of common ownership rather further than those of the Kibbutz. Also, there is a small but growing trend to the formation of urban kibbutzim. In the urban kibbutzim it is not the general practice for members to work in departments of the kibbutz, but rather to work for outside bodies. (There may be minor exceptions connected with educational work.) In fact a substantial section of the membership of the traditional kibbutzim now also works outside the commune, but this is a departure from traditional practice.

By contrast, the Integrierte Gemeinde do not live in communes; rather, the members belong to small 'table communities' which meet to eat and talk regularly several times a week. They also belong to 'geographical' communities, with a maximum of 120 members, who meet weekly for 'assemblies'. Members retain ownership of their own money and other property, but statements by leaders make it clear that there is an expectation that members' money will be available for the common tasks of the community. Members may live in 'integration houses' that effectively form part of the movement, and may work in enterprises that are seen as expressions of the movement's economic activity, although formally these belong to one or more of the movement's individual members rather than the community as such. This is clearly a more complex structure than the fairly straightforward commune system adopted by the other two movements. However, it does allow for the development of a common life that is every bit as solid and real as that of the other movements. Because of the structures adopted by the Integrierte Gemeinde this book will use the term 'communal' movements rather than 'commune' movements.

There are two main reasons for the use of the term 'movements' in this book. The first is that all three of these organisations are composed of a number of individual units. The Kibbutz, by a long way the largest of the three, is composed of over 200 separate kibbutzim. The Bruderhof has ten separate communes or bruderhofs, and the Integrierte Gemeinde has ten 'geographical communities' along with a number of smaller units. Both the Bruderhof and the Integrierte Gemeinde are international bodies. The Kibbutz is based in Israel, mainly inside its pre-1967 borders but with a small number of communities in the West Bank, Gaza and – more significantly perhaps – the Golan Heights. The individual units in the Kibbutz have a higher degree of autonomy than in the other two movements. The Kibbutz additionally has been divided into a number of separate federations, although the main ones merged in 2000. The federations had, in recent times, lost a degree of the power they once held vis-à-vis the individual kibbutzim. (The newer urban kibbutzim were linked to these federations, and now to the main federation.) Both the Bruderhof and the Integrierte Gemeinde are unified bodies, which could be seen as practising what was once known in one section of the Kibbutz as 'ideological collectivism'; in other words, they arrive at a movement-wide view on questions and issues that they are faced with, a practice which seems to have declined even in those sections of the Kibbutz that formerly did adopt it.

The second reason that these bodies are seen here as movements is because they are, in differing ways, active in trying to change the world. The Kibbutz is theoretically committed to two aims, Zionist realisation and the construction of a socialist society. By Zionist realisation the movement means the building of a national home for the Jewish people in the land of Israel, and it sees many of its activities in this light. (The formulation adopted here is deliberately wide, as there were differences within the movement on these issues.) In regard to the construction of a socialist society, this was reflected in the form that the Kibbutz movement adopted and refined during its history. As we have seen, this form was basically that of a commune, but again there have been a number of debates on this question in the movement's history. The Kibbutz can broadly be seen as a socialist Zionist institution.

The Integrierte Gemeinde's commitment to world-changing action can be found in its statutes. Statute paragraph 2 deals with its Purpose, and states '[t]he Integrated Community tries in a world estranged from the Church to make the Gospel present in such a form that also those who have no contact with the Church can find access to the faith of the Catholic Church again.' Statute paragraph 4 deals with Form of Life, and section (2) states '[t]he form of life of "Integration" shall enable them – also those with a family and a profession – to take on the mandate of spreading the Gospel, given by Jesus, more intensively and thus live as followers of Christ under the conditions of the secular world. Through this form of life a new "family" shall come into being' (Integrated Community 1996, 108). Although this is couched in much more religious terms than would be found in most sections of the Kibbutz, both of these commitments indicate a desire on the part of the community and its members to make themselves present in the world outside their community, and to be agents of its transformation.

The Bruderhof has similarly signalled clearly its commitment to involvement in world-transforming activities. In its magazine, *The Plough Reader*, it indicates why it is involved in publishing activity in a short statement printed in each issue. 'The goal of our publishing program is to challenge the assumptions of institutional Christendom, to encourage self-examination, discussion, and nonviolent action, to share hope, and to build community' (*The Plough Reader*, Winter 2002, 2). The Bruderhof, like the Integrierte Gemeinde, is a self-proclaimed Christian community. This means that the two movements couch their world-changing aims in 'religious' language. It also means that they will see limitations on the ability of human beings individually, and even collectively, to change the world. However, in both cases the fact that the goals are stated in less obviously 'political' language than most kibbutznikim might use should not lead us to conclude that world transformation is not an intention on the part of these communities.

All three bodies can be seen as movements, then, because they are not simply examples of lone communes, and also because they have aims that involve the changing of the world. In fact, we could adopt and slightly adapt the terminology Rosabeth Moss Kanter used in her considerations of American communes and call them 'Communities with Missions' (Kanter 1972, 191). Indeed, Kanter gives us a framework of comparison for thinking about communes that is useful for situating the three movements. She noted that in the America of the time she was writing and researching – broadly the mid- and late 1960s and early 1970s – there had been a 'rise of nonutopian communities', these being seen as communities that while having common property and the like 'lack ideology or programs for social reform' (Kanter 1972, 167). Although we need to be careful about the way in which we characterise the programmes for social reform advanced by the Bruderhof and the Integrierte Gemeinde (and neither may be happy with this type of terminology), it is clear that the three movements we are considering are 'ideological' in the sense that Kanter used the term, and have social goals. They do not fit into her category of the 'nonutopian' community, a point that is vividly made by the fact that she suggested that the Bruderhof was, in fact, one of the few examples of a strong utopian community extant at the time she was writing (Kanter 1972, 168). For various reasons, it is likely that the neither the Bruderhof nor the Integrierte Gemeinde would like to be characterised as 'utopian'. However, in Kanter's terms, we are looking at 'utopian' rather than 'nonutopian' communities.

A rather less charged terminology was provided by Yaacov Oved in a short paper which gives a very sharp summary of some of the results of his extensive research into communes and their history. Oved considered the question of the relationship of communes to the outside societies from which they have withdrawn and pointed to an apparent dichotomy.

> On the one hand, there were those communes founded in order to make possible the withdrawal and separation from a society they totally rejected and considered as rotten and doomed to disappear. On the other hand were the open, involved communes, which, while criticising society, did not cut themselves off; they were not running away from society in order to be alone – rather they felt a sense of responsibility for the future, and wanted to work at putting things right. (Gorni et al. 1987, 149)

Oved suggested that comparing these two spiritual worlds, as he put it, revealed complete opposites. However, considering aspects of their lives other than ideology 'it became clear that in all the communes I studied, both secluded and involved, there were situations which created an ambivalence of attitude to the outside world' (Gorni et al. 1987, 150). This was true for the 'secluded' communes, because there were times when they came into contact with the outside world whether through choice or through necessity. These contacts could be economic, neighbourly, legal, or the like. However, it was also true for the 'involved' communes. They may have started with the intention of being open to the world, for whatever reason, 'but as they were small communities in isolated areas, and became obliged to put all their efforts into the building of a communal group objectively removed from the society they wished to change, so the basis of separation and the barriers of estrangement grew, and as time passed a whole network of ambivalent relationships came into being' (Gorni et al. 1987, 151).

Oved comments, 'I realised that this ambivalence developed in all communes, whatever their motives' (Gorni et al. 1987, 150). Moreover, the pervasiveness of this phenomenon led Oved to the view that it was justifiable to investigate it in the context of the Kibbutz, a classic example of the involved commune (Gorni et al. 1987, 151). Oved presented an alternative terminology to that of Kanter: for utopian read involved, and for nonutopian read secluded. However, he did more than that; he showed the limitations and ambiguities of this dichotomy, and pointed to the necessity for a concrete examination of these issues in any given case.[1]

QUESTIONS

This is clearly relevant in considering the first of the two questions that this book will return to in the case of all three of the communal movements: What impact have the movements made upon their host societies, and more generally, how can their interactions with their host societies be characterised? Oved's analysis shows that this is by no means a straightforward question, and the ambiguities need to be teased out in each case. We have established that all three of the movements are 'involved' communities in that they feel they have something of relevance to say to the people of their host societies. Oved's work suggests that we may need to be careful in checking for ways in which they may separate and isolate themselves from the society around them. It should be noted at this point that whereas the Kibbutz has clearly made an impact on Israeli society at the national level, the same is far from true of the Bruderhof and the Intergrierte Gemeinde. In these cases, the influence has tended to be a more local and regional matter, although there has also been some more general impact within specific sectors of the host societies. (So, for instance, one might posit an impact of the Intergrierte Gemeinde on life in Munich and Bavaria, and also on the Roman Catholic section of German society more generally.)

The second question relates to this latter point, and it is to consider exactly how these movements have gone about constructing an 'alternative society' and indeed alternative economy for their members. All three reject contemporary 'bourgeois' society in various different ways. They have started to live in non-bourgeois ways that they consider to be more adequate and acceptable given their beliefs. This process will be considered. Oved's comments above suggest that it is in the process of the building of an 'alternative society' that he often found the basis of separation and estrangement from society in 'involved' groups, a point we need to keep in mind.

These two questions will form part of the basis for a comparative examination of the three movements, which, despite a common source of sorts, are now profoundly different from each other, despite recognising in various ways their 'family' resemblances.

METHODOLOGY

Turning to methodological issues, this book will generally use qualitative methods. This is not to say that quantitative factors will never feature. On the contrary, in certain parts of the study they will be discussed and considered. However, in the main the qualitative approach will be used. Maurice Punch has argued that '[q]ualitative research covers a spectrum of techniques – but central are observation, interviewing, and documentary analysis' (Denzin and Lincoln 1994, 84). To some extent this means following Howard Becker's injunction, quoted by Punch, to the student who asked which paradigm should be employed in some field research: 'get in there and see what is going on' (Denzin and Lincoln 1994, 83. Incidentally, this is not the same Howard Becker whose work on the German Youth Movement will be referred to in later chapters.) All three of the techniques mentioned by Punch are used in this book; however, there is a problem of a comparative nature that should be mentioned here.

Following Becker's advice is one matter with the Bruderhof and the Integrierte Gemeinde and quite another with the Kibbutz. The Bruderhof and the Integrierte Gemeinde are comparatively small bodies, and they are also unified organisations in which the individual sub-sections, while having specific features, are still subject to certain central norms and guidelines – 'ideological collectivism'. Indeed, they should be seen as parts of a single community in certain important ways. Accordingly, observation and discussion will yield evidence that can be fairly confidently said to have wide application within the movements. This is not the case with the Kibbutz. While there are obvious common features throughout the movement, it has to be said that the Kibbutz is a much wider and more disparate body than either the Bruderhof or the Integrierte Gemeinde.

This means that generalisation on the basis of observation of one or even several communities is far more dangerous in this case than in those of the other two movements. The result of this is that this book relies more on documentary analysis in the case of the Kibbutz than it does in the other two cases. There is also more reliance upon quantitative evidence in the case of the Kibbutz, reflecting the fact that the Kibbutz is many times larger than either of the other movements and its economic activities are more diverse. In the case of the Kibbutz we also have a phenomenon that is not shared with the other movements: the existence of a substantial academic literature produced by kibbutznikim. In general, this book has tended to utilise such material as a matter of preference, not because it is presupposed to be more accurate than outsider accounts, but rather because it represents evidence from within the movement under investigation. Clearly, it represents the viewpoint of the author(s) rather than the Kibbutz as a whole, or even the federation to which the kibbutznik concerned belongs. However, in the present state of the Kibbutz the same can be said about much material emanating from within the movement. This academic literature is thus seen in two ways here; first, as academic literature, and second as part of the self-expression of the movement. This should not be seen as a 'grudging' acceptance of its standing. Some of this material is extremely important; it is unlikely, for instance, that Henry Near's two-volume history of the Kibbutz (Near 1992; 1997) will be surpassed for many years to come as the standard English-language account. One further point on the Kibbutz should also be mentioned. The recent origin of the urban kibbutzim trend has meant that this book relies strongly on the websites developed by such kibbutzim. There can be no guarantee that such websites will still be extant if a reader attempts to access them; accordingly, where possible alternative – if more obscure – means of retrieving the material will be indicated.

As the purpose of this book is not primarily statistical, but concerned in large measure with the ideologies of the movements concerned – taking ideologies in Louis Dumont's sense of a 'set of ideas and values, more or less fundamental, held in common in a group of people' (Dumont 1994, vii) – it seems reasonable to use qualitative methods as specified above. Such methods should be useful in facilitating an understanding of the ways in which members see their movements and the ideologies associated with them.

TERMINOLOGY

Certain terms will be used throughout this book and should be explained. In respect of the Kibbutz movement, 'Kibbutz' (upper case) denotes the movement as a whole, with 'kibbutz' denoting an individual settlement. 'Kibbutzim' is the plural of kibbutz, and 'kibbutznik' denotes a member of a kibbutz. The plural of kibbutznik is kibbutznikim. The only other word that needs early explanation is 'kvutsa' or 'kvutsat'. Initially the more generally used term for what became known as a kibbutz, this word gained a certain ideological meaning during the 1920s with the debate on the appropriate size of communal settlements, kvutsa being used by those who wished to preserve the small scale and agrarian nature of the early movement. Recently the term has been picked up again in the Urban Kibbutz movement that is in its early stages in Israel.

In respect of the Bruderhof, 'Bruderhof' (upper case) denotes the movement as a whole, with 'bruderhof' denoting an individual community. The movement has used a number of titles over the years. Currently it calls itself the Bruderhof Communities. In the past the title Society of Brothers was the best known in the English-speaking world, with Hutterian Society of Brothers a variant on this. Prior to the most recent split with the Hutterites, it used the titles Hutterian Brethren and sometimes Hutterian Brethren (Eastern). None of these titles will be used here; the movement will simply be known, as is generally the case now, as the Bruderhof.

The Integrierte Gemeinde presents fewer difficulties, and the title will usually be shortened to IG. The movement has also had a number of names down the years, reflecting the way in which it has changed in form, a process rather different from the other two movements. It started as the Junger Bund; by the mid-1950s its title had become, in English translation, the Association for the Advancement of Religious Education. In early 1968 it was using the title Institut für Theologische Forschung und Bildung (Institute for Theological Research and Education). The title Integrierte Gemeinde started to be used in 1969, and is the title by which the community is best known. In formal terms at some point between 1996 and 1998 the word Katholische (Catholic) was added to the name, but for simplicity's sake Integrierte Gemeinde will be used in this book except in discussions of the early years of the movement when Junger Bund will also be used.

NOTES

1 Yaacov Oved utilises this analysis to powerful effect in Oved 1988, ch. 23

Chapter 1

The German Youth Movement

INTRODUCTION

The three organisations that form the focus of this book have aspects of their origins in the German Youth Movement, and thus it is an appropriate starting point. The sense in which the term 'German Youth Movement' is used here is that offered by Walter Laqueur when he wrote of 'the youth movement proper, the autonomous groups' (Laqueur 1962, xi). By this he meant that he was examining only those youth groups that regarded themselves as being independent of adult control; in other words, those for whom the slogan 'Youth among itself' (Mosse 1964, 171) was the watchword.

For some writers on the German Youth Movement, notably Stachura, this definition is too narrow, and indeed possibly places too much store on the notion of independence from adult control (Stachura 1981, 3). However, by following Laqueur's usage we can differentiate the German Youth Movement quite sharply from phenomena that arose at around the same time in other parts of the world, such as the Boy Scout and Girl Guide movements, which were not independent of adult control and had no pretension to such independence, and also similar non-independent youth bodies in Germany.

The German Youth Movement arose formally on 4 November 1901 in Steglitz, a suburb of Berlin, with the formation of the Wandervogel movement. This developed from a group of schoolboys based on a shorthand class in Steglitz in 1897, called Stenographia, which had organised rambles as far afield as Bohemia in 1899. The leader of Stenographia was Hermann Hoffmann, and his deputy was Karl Fischer. Fischer was the driving force behind the formation of the Wandervogel as a schoolboy rambling club and can be seen as the founder of the German Youth Movement. Borinski and Milch, in their history of the Youth Movement (an important English-language source, in that Borinski had been a member of the Deutsche Freischar and a leader of the Leuchtenburg Kreis Youth Movement groups), explain that it was no accident that the starting point was a shorthand class. Shorthand, they contend, had a rather esoteric attraction to the young at this time; it was something that adults were not au fait with (Borinski and Milch 1982, 6. Note that this and all subsequent references – unless stated – refer to the English text of this book.)

MEMBERSHIP

The German Youth Movement went through a number of distinct periods: the Wandervogel was the dominant trend from 1901 to 1913; 1913 to 1923 was the period of the Freideutsche Youth; 1923 to 1933 the era of the Bündische Youth; and there was also a sort of 'after-existence' that started in 1933 and continues to the present day. (This conforms closely to the periodisation used in Borinski and Milch 1982.) Before looking at the historical development in more detail, however, it is useful to consider the size and social composition of the Youth Movement, along with its basis and structure. Three of the most important English-language studies of the movement all seem agreed on around 60,000 as the 'headline' membership figure for the movement, with this peak being reached around 1914 and then maintained for some time. Becker suggests this figure as the 'lowest estimate' for just before World War I (Becker 1946, 94). Stachura suggests that there were no more than 60,000 members in the Weimar era (Stachura 1981, 3). Laqueur simply suggests that the Youth Movement's membership never exceeded 60,000 (Laqueur 1962, xi). By contrast, Borinski and Milch give much higher figures. Discussing the post-World War I period they suggest 70,000 to 80,000 members of the various Wandervogel leagues (with 45,000 in the Wandervogel E.V. alone), along with a further 60,000 to 70,000 in the Freie Schulgemeinde (Free School Communities) and the newer Youth Movement leagues, and many tens of thousands of what they call wild Wandervogels, which probably means youth behaving and perhaps considering themselves as Wandervögel, but not holding formal membership in a league. (They give figures for other bodies that are not strictly Youth Movement organisations, but which were at this time close in ideas and practice to the movement.) They point to the circulation of Knud Ahlborn and Walter Hammer's Hamburg Youth Movement paper, *Junge Menschen*, which they give as 50,000 per week (all figures Borinski and Milch 1982, 18). They later suggest a membership figure of 100,000 for the free leagues (including Catholic and Protestant leagues) in 1928 (Borinski and Milch 1982, 32).

A number of important points can be made about the members of the German Youth Movement. There is general agreement that the overwhelming bulk of the members were 'bourgeois' or 'middle class'. Laqueur is straightforward on this point; it 'was almost exclusively "bourgeois" in its social composition' (Laqueur 1962, xi). Stachura agrees and his account shows this to have been the case in different phases of the movement. Of the Wandervogel he writes that it 'was, therefore, solidly middle-class, rather than lower-middle-class in social composition, as Marxist historians have alleged' (Stachura 1981, 21). Stachura shows that the Wandervogel attracted few working-class youths, but also that it attracted few members from the aristocracy or the industrial haute bourgeoisie. Of the later, Bündische Youth phase, he notes that it 'was composed of middle-class youths in sheltered bourgeois surroundings who really did believe that the world revolved around them' (Stachura 1981, 6). Borinski and Milch are also straight-forward on this question; it was a bourgeois movement, and the word 'bourgeois' became a term of abuse in the movement, because it was associated with the world of parents and teachers and their priorities (Borinski and Milch 1982, 6). This point can perhaps be slightly expanded, to show from their account what sort of bourgeois revolt the Youth Movement represented.

> The Jugendbewegung revolted against the dress which had been forced upon it and fought against the opinion that it was through smoking, drinking and flirting that a young man proved his manliness. It turned against the literature and music which had been imposed upon it, it rebelled against the dull routine of daily school life and, in a positive direction, took for its aim the conquest of its own world and the discovery of its own values which were not to be found in the grown-up world. (Borinski and Milch 1982, 5–6)

Perhaps some of these issues would have been less urgent priorities for the youth of the proletariat.

Members were both male and female, although this was the subject of debate and discussion. Once the movement developed beyond Steglitz, it became extremely fissiparous, and one of the issues upon which the Wandervogel group-ings might occasionally split was whether young males and young females should belong to the same groups and undertake activities such as hikes together. One of the first splits, in 1907, was on this issue. Laqueur suggests that by around 1911 most leaders of the movement agreed to the full and equal participation of females, although in many cases there were separate groups of males and females. In the Freideutsche phase he appears to suggest that the movement became less prone to such division (Laqueur 1962, 57, in his chapter on 'The War of the Sexes'). In the Bündische phase most groups were single sex.

In terms of religious background, the Youth Movement was largely based upon the Protestant middle classes in its original phase (Stachura 1981, 20). However, there was a distinct influence of Youth Movement ideas on Roman Catholic youth groupings, which in the post-World War I phases resulted in some extremely important bodies that, though Catholic, can be seen as being part of the Youth Movement. Much more problematic is the question of whether Jews could join the movement. This issue first came to prominence in late 1913 in the aftermath of a branch of one of the Wandervogel bünde in Saxony deciding not to admit a candidate for membership simply because she was Jewish (she had passed all other requirements for membership). A debate broke out in the *Wandervogel Führerzeitung*, a newspaper for group leaders in the movement. This debate climaxed with the notorious 'Jewish edition' of the paper in October 1913. Friedrich Fulda, who edited the journal, was an anti-Semite.

The issue of Jewish membership thereafter became an important one, but it was also a complex issue. There undoubtedly were anti-Semitic elements in the movement, and the accounts of the controversy (Stachura 1981, 30–31; Laqueur 1962, Ch. 9, 'The Jewish Question') indicate the substantial level of support for anti-Semitic views. This often operated under the mechanism of the 'Aryan Paragraph', a section of a group's rulebook allowing only Aryan Germans to join. Equally, there were sections of the movement that were opposed to anti-Semitism, along with sections that expressed rather muddled views on the question prior to World War I. With the subsequent drift to the political left in the Youth Movement following World War I, the issue became less heated.

The complex internal politics within the German Youth Movement around the Jewish issue obviously connect with general social and political issues in the Germany of the first third of the twentieth century. One of the most significant was that of the prevalence of Völkisch thought. The issue is raised quite sharply by the 'Jewish question' within the Youth Movement, which could be posed in the following terms: can Jews be members of the German Volk? If the Wandervogel was a movement of the German Volk, then clearly, if Jews were not members of that Volk, then they should not be members.

This is one way of posing the question, basing the terms on a restrictive and primarily politically rightist discourse about the Volk. This ideology has been examined in some depth by George Mosse (Mosse 1964), and he has commented in some detail about the Youth Movement and its relationship to this brand of Völkisch thought. It is certainly the case that sections of the German Youth Movement were inclined to Völkisch thinking. A caveat should, however, be entered, and this is that Eugene Lunn has criticised Mosse, among others, for tending to overlook the possibility of a more libertarian, leftist and less exclusive variant of Völkisch thinking, which Lunn suggests can be found in the thought of Gustav Landauer (Lunn 1973, 6–7, and see also p. 351 fn 4 for a critical comment on Mosse, though tempered by an assertion that Mosse's later work – e.g. Mosse 1971 – had started a retreat from earlier positions).

However, while this can be considered from the point of view of the German Youth Movement, it also raised very serious issues for young Jews in Germany in the same period. Clearly, some young Jews, like a large number of young Germans of other backgrounds, wanted to have nothing to do with this sort of thing. If, on the other hand, young Jews did want to undertake such activities, then the question as to whether they should join groups consisting of Germans of all backgrounds or exclusively Jewish groups was clearly raised by, among others, young Zionists. Young Zionists might actually have agreed with those in the German Youth Movement who suggested that the Jews were not members of the German Volk. They might have wished to stress the need to renew and rebuild the Jewish Volk, and hence have propounded a sort of

Völkisch thought themselves (see Mosse 1971, Chapter 4 for a discussion of this whole issue).

There was, in fact, a Jewish youth movement in Germany that represented a sort of parallel but allied phenomenon to that of the German Youth Movement, sharing many of its characteristics. This was true even in a comparatively early phase of the period under consideration, with the formation of the Jung-Jüdischer Wanderbund in 1911 and the Blau-Weiß movement in 1912. Stachura notes of the Blau-Weiß that they believed in stimulating Jewish consciousness by understanding the German Volk and transporting its ideals to the Jews. 'In other words, by applying the principles of the Wandervogel, Blau-Weiß sought to transform assimilationist Jewish youth into conscious Jews' (Stachura 1981, 87). For those attempting to set the German Youth Movement in context from a sympathetic viewpoint in the post-World War II period, this Jewish youth movement was of interest. Karl Seidelmann, in his essay 'Der "Neue Mensch"' ('The "New Man"') referred to the reunion of 1,000 Blau-Weiß veterans in Galilee in 1962, and also stated that a competent observer who had been in Israel on a study trip in 1963 argued that 'Israel sei wohl das Land, in dem das meiste an Verwirklichung der Ideen der Jugendbewegung anzutreffen sei' ('Israel is probably the country in which the greatest realisation of the ideas of the Youth Movement is to be found', Korn et al. 1963, 33, fn 13).

The Youth Movement as we are considering it here, in line with Laqueur's definition, can be seen as being not only distinct from movements such as the Boy Scouts which emerged outside Germany. It can also be seen as being distinct from what were called 'Youth Tutelage' groups within Germany – organisations, as Stachura puts it, of political, paramilitary and confessional youth by and large under adult supervision (Stachura 1981, 3). The German-language terms are Jugendbewegung for the Youth Movement as we are considering it, and Jugendpflege for the tutelage bodies. The tutelage bodies were larger, taken as a whole, than the Youth Movement proper (Becker 1946, 105–07 gives a useful survey of them, with some membership figures, and suggests, p. 95, that the ratio of youth tutelage members to Youth Movement members was 25:1). The differences between these two sectors are important, but equally important in some ways is Stachura's point that by 1913 and 1914 some of the ideas of the Youth Movement were beginning to have such an impact on the youth tutelage bodies that, in the post-World War I period, there was a sort of merger of the two youth cultures (Stachura 1981, 36).

THE MEISSNER FORMULA

From October 1913 the Youth Movement did have something that clearly set it apart, not only from the youth tutelage but also from German society as a whole. This was the 'Meissner Formula' (Die Meißnerformel). It was adopted at a meeting on the Hohe Meissner mountain, near Cassell, at which some sections of the by now diverse German Youth Movement met to form the Freideutsche Jugend, and thus initiate the second phase of the movement. Although by no means all the organisations of the Youth Movement were there, the meeting and the formula have retrospectively been seen as crucial in the movement's history. Given its importance, it is necessary to quote it in full in both German and English. One of the key figures in the setting up of the meeting, and subsequently in the whole Freideutsche phase of the movement, was Knud Ahlborn. In his article 'Das Meißnerfest der Freideutschen Jugend 1913' ('The Meissner Festival of Free German Youth 1913', written in 1913) he gave the formula as follows:

'Die Freideutsche Jugend will nach eigener Bestimmung vor eigener Verantwortung mit innnerer Wahrhaftigkeit ihr Leben gestalten. Für diese innere Freiheit tritt sie unter allen Umständen geschlossen ein.'

'Als grundsatz für gemeinschaftliche Veranstaltungen wurde hinzugesetzt: "Alle gemeinschaftlichen Veranstaltungen der Freideutsche Jugend sind alkohol – und nikotinfrei."' (Kindt 1963, 109)

'Free German Youth, on their own initiative, under their own responsibility, and with deep sincerity, are determined independently to shape their own lives. For the sake of this inner freedom they will under any and all circumstances take united action.' (Becker 1946, 100)

'All meetings of the Free German Youth are free of alcohol and smoking.' (Stachura 1981, 33)

Stachura suggests (Stachura 1981, 33) that this formula was written by Ferdinand Avenarius, art historian, editor of the *Kunstwart* journal, and leader of the Dürerbund cultural movement. Avenarius was undoubtedly at this stage a friend of the movement, and spoke at the Hohe Meissner meeting. However, Ahlborn's account suggests a different origin. 'So entstand die Meißnerformel. Der Wortlaut stammt von drei Mitgliedern der Akademischen Freischar: Dr. med. Gustav Francke, Dr med. Erwin von Hattingberg und Dr. med. Knud Ahlborn' ('And so the Meissner Formula originated. The wording is from three members of the Akademischen Freischar; Dr (of medicine) Gustav Francke, Dr (of medicine) Erwin von Hattingberg and Dr (of medicine) Knud Ahlborn', Kindt 1963, 109).

Whoever actually wrote the formula, it remained a touchstone for the movement, although perhaps Laqueur's view that it meant different things to different people (Laqueur 1962, 38), though cynical, contains a degree of truth. Interestingly, two other commentators see the formula in very different ways. For Becker, the formula was nothing more than an explicit statement of the attitudes held by the first Wandervogel some fifteen years earlier, and was accepted at the meeting because it was a virtual platitude. For Stachura, however, 'this was a dramatic, even revolutionary proclamation which asserted youth's demand to be

recognised as an independent estate entitled to self-determination and responsibility. The Formula encapsulated the quintessence of the Wandervogel spirit
and it became a symbol of the free youth movement's sense of mission and
freedom as well as acting as an inspiration for the future' (Stachura 1981, 33).
Stachura's view is certainly the one nearest to the image of the Meissner
Formula held by the movement itself. It is notable, for instance, that a number
of important works on the movement from sources that wished to celebrate its
contribution to society, rather than simply analyse it, appeared in 1963 to mark
the fiftieth anniversary of the Hohe Meissner meeting (e.g., Kindt 1963; Korn et
al. 1963).

THE BUND

As well as a formula asserting their independence, the Youth Movement also
developed an organisational structure which differentiated it from other movements and became the distinguishing feature of the movement's name in its third
phase; the bund. The difficulty of translating this word adequately is perhaps one
reason why historians writing in English have tended to continue to use the
German terminology (*Bund, Bünde, Bündische*). Perhaps the most interesting
example of this tendency is Walter Laqueur, who notes in the introduction to his
history that his origins are German-Jewish, and that he had recollections of the
Youth Movement dating back to his childhood. In his later autobiography
Laqueur makes it clear that he was a member of at least two bünde (Laqueur
1992, 85). One of these was the Werkleute (Laqueur 1992, 136), one of the most
interesting and important of the Zionist bünde. If Laqueur, a veteran of the
Youth Movement, and someone who has written extensively in the English language and held several academic posts in the USA, decided to use the German
terminology, then we can be fairly sure that to put in an English term like
'League' or 'Alliance' might well involve some slippage of meaning.

As the Youth Movement developed, the meaning of the word Bund changed,
and it came to have a rather tighter meaning in the Bündische phase than it had
previously. Laqueur gives a good insight into the structure of the Youth
Movement in a couple of pages early on in his history of the movement (Laqueur
1962, 25–27). He notes that members were usually aged between 12 and 19. After
19 ex-members graduated into rather different types of activity. Group leaders
were usually – though this was not a rule – three to six years older than the followers. The group seems to have varied between around seven or eight members
and 20 members. Groups over 20 were seen as being too large for genuine friendship and coherence. Where there was more than one group in a city, a local
branch would be formed, and all the local branches in a province would form a
Gau. The leader of the Gau was responsible to the national leader of the bund.
Within the lower levels, leaders would meet every few weeks. Full meetings of all
the members in the Gau would be convened and were fairly easy to organise,

given that most Gaus in the movement throughout its history had around 200 members at most. National bund meetings were rare given the technical difficulties of organising them. Laqueur suggests that over time procedures for choosing leaders evolved, although they were never subject to hard and fast rules. He argues that those thought suitable would often be asked to lead a group by the superior leader. All the groups in the movement were selective, but again there were no clear and consistent rules on this. No one became a member at once; there were trial periods in which a candidate would be subject to testing. Some groups evolved rather elaborate hierarchies. The key activities of the movement were expeditions, work at the group's Heim or Nest (its base in the city), sporting contests, singing, amateur theatrical activities and the like. Structures like these are still extant today in the Zionist diaspora youth movement, Habonim-Dror (which had been active in Germany prior to World War II). Children from the age of nine may join the movement, becoming qualified to be leaders at the age of 16. At 18 members go to Israel for a year-long programme, which qualifies them to become senior leaders. Senior leaders leave the movement at 23, by which time in theory they should be building a kibbutz in Israel, although most are not. The crucial point here, however, is that the movement has no outside adult supervision, and as such continues the practice of the Youth Movement.[1]

Laqueur in his autobiography discusses just what it was that the bünde did at their meetings. These meetings were, in the case of the Bund that Laqueur belonged to in the 1930s, weekly and took place in a shack in the garden of one of the members' suburban home.

> The group leader would talk for a few minutes on a topic of his choice; then there would be a discussion or individual group members would talk about their activities or problems they had to confront. Then someone would read a poem or two, the group leader would recommend some books to read, and finally there would be more songs and perhaps a game. Time passed quickly, and after two hours we would disperse. (Laqueur 1992, 78)

Aside from this, there would be hiking, which will be considered shortly. As Laqueur points out in his history, '[s]hared experience and adventures welded a more or less accidental group into a disciplined community. There might be a more intimate friendship between two or more members, but the feeling of comradeship and solidarity extended to every member of the group' (Laqueur 1962, 30). He notes that in the Wandervogel period the group had been a loose association with the emphasis on the individual's development. By contrast, in the bünde as created by Martin Völkel, for instance, at the start of the Bündische period the collective was privileged at the expense of the individual, and there was generally a tighter discipline, with the bund envisaged as a life-long union (Laqueur 1962, 134).

Becker provides us with another perspective on the phenomenon of the bund. He quotes an interesting passage from a Youth Movement magazine that deals with the issue of how leaders changed in groups. This is a sort of fictionalised account by a would-be group leader of his successful challenge to a current group leader, in which leadership change appears to result from a straightforward process of laying down the gauntlet in front of the group. If the group sides with the challenge, the leadership changes, and the ex-leader perhaps leaves with those still loyal (Becker 1946, 60). Becker stressed the importance of the leader principle in the Youth Movement, claiming '[m]any a time I have heard youngsters chorus forth, "Leader, we follow thee" and shout "Yea!" with a passionate intensity that reminded me of camp-meeting revivals' (Becker 1946, 56). Borinski and Milch also throw interesting light on the phenomenon of the bund. Agreeing with Laqueur that the bund of the Bündische period was tighter and more collectively focused than previous efforts, they contrast it most sharply with the Freideutsche period, when, they suggest, there had almost been an 'anti-organisation' ethos. However, in the Bündische period youth 'was now more willing to accept the existence of supra-personal powers, and as the symbol of this tendency the "Bund" came into being' (Borinski and Milch 1982, 28). By this account, what may have been called 'bünde' prior to around 1923 were not 'bünde' in the strong sense of the word thereafter.

PERIODISATION

Wandervogel

After this brief survey of some key aspects of the German Youth Movement, a consideration of its historical periodisation is required. In relation to the communal movements that form the main subjects of this study, this periodisation is important because the movements emerged from different periods of the Youth Movement, and this may be important in considering their specific features. As noted, the movement started with the formation of the Steglitz Wandervogel – technically the Wandervogel, Ausschuss für Schülerfahrten (Wandervogel, Committee for Schoolboy Excursions) – in November 1901. The first phase of the Youth Movement can be seen as the years between 1901 and 1913, and could be called the Wandervogel period. (One of Werner Kindt's books of Youth Movement sources, which covers 1896 to 1919, is called *Die Wandervogelzeit*.)

The word Wandervogel means 'Bird of Passage', although as with many German terms encountered in this book it undoubtedly loses something in translation. Indeed, Becker dispenses with the term altogether, and chooses to call the Wandervogel the 'Roamers', noting 'literal translation would give a false impression' (Becker 1946, vii–viii). Laqueur indicates that the name was discovered by one of the founders – Wolf Meyen – in an inscription on a tombstone (Laqueur 1962, 17). The full original name gives a good impression of what the Wandervogel were about at the time of their formation, and indeed throughout the history of the movement, namely 'excursions'. However, they were not organisers of pleasant days out – quite the contrary.

The type of rambling that the Wandervogel were involved in has been well described by Becker in a section of his book that reflects the considerable amount of first-hand research into the German Youth Movement he undertook in the 1920s and 1930s. This section described the hiking and singing that formed the backbone of Wandervogel activities. His summary of this part of the book is informative.

> Clear it is that this hard primitivism was highly valued and that it took the form of a return to nature . . . Hence the Roamers did not indulge in 'Ohs! and Ahs!' about blue skies and sunsets; there was little passive observation. Instead they found a peculiar beauty and thrill in slogging through a rain-drenched countryside, laughing at torn and sodden clothing until they arrived at a shelter where they could slump and dry out before a roaring fire . . . The sense of fusion, the *Bunderlebnis*, was therefore the cherished outcome of the expedition, not the appreciation of nature as such. (Becker 1946, 81–83)

These passages from Becker stress two things: the first is the central importance for the Wandervogel of the hiking experience, and the second is the result – the formation of a solidarity within the group as the result of the hiking.

A feature of the German Youth Movement in the first and third periods, as considered here (i.e. Wandervogel and Bündische periods), is that it was prone to splintering. This started at a very early stage in the Wandervogel period, with the end of the original Steglitz Wandervogel group in 1904. Opposition had arisen against Karl Fischer, and it solidified around Siegfried Copalle. Stachura presents this as a clash between a more intellectual approach to activities, as personified by Copalle, as against Fischer's more carefree approach (Stachura 1981, 22); Becker writes of the 'hard' (Fischer) and 'soft' (Copalle) variants of primitivism that the two trends represented (Becker 1946, 61–63). Indeed, in his inimitable style, Becker mentions at one point 'Copalle's "Softies"' (Becker 1946, 94). As a result the Copalle group became the Wandervogel (Steglitz) and the Fischer group the Altwandervogel. This was the first of many splinterings, and this is in fact an important point to bear in mind when considering the 'leader principle' issue. The leader principle in a truly voluntary body that one can leave at will is quite different to a leader principle forcibly imposed by a totalitarian state.

Another issue at the heart of a Wandervogel split was that of whether females should be allowed to join the movement as equals. This issue resulted in the secession of the Wandervogel Deutscher Bund from the Altwandervogel, although the issue of abstinence from alcohol and tobacco was also involved. It is hardly surprising that the issue of sexuality should have played a role in the Wandervogel movement, and the question of female participation was not the only issue that arose. In 1912 Hans Blüher, formerly an active Wandervogel (and partisan of Karl Fischer), published *Die deutsche Wandervogelbewegung als erotisches Phänomen* (*The German Wandervogel Movement as Erotic Phenomenon*) and stirred up a hornet's nest around the issue of (apparently only male) homosexuality in the movement. Laqueur indicates that Blüher was an avowed antifeminist, and that he argued that only an association of men (Männerbund) could be creative (Laqueur 1962, 51). Accordingly, he did not regard homoerotic attraction as problematic in the way that many sections of Wilhelmine German society did. (Male homosexual acts only became legal in West Germany in 1969. As in Great Britain, female homosexual acts were never illegal.) Blüher had been influenced by concepts derived from Freud. Laqueur notes that he had been one of the earliest laypeople in Germany to have understood the significance of Freud, and had even been commissioned by Freud to write an article for the journal *Imago* (Laqueur 1962, 51). Regardless of the quality and orthodoxy of Blüher's Freudianism, he had raised an issue that was of some significance. In 1910 the leader of the Altwandervogel, Willy Jansen, had had to resign from his post as a result of controversy regarding his views on homosexuality. The result was the formation of yet another splinter group, the Jungwandervogel. Stachura writes that the 'Jung-wandervogel became somewhat notorious for the prevalence of homosexuality in its ranks' (Stachura 1981, 28). Stachura's summing up on this issue is worth quoting: '[m]ale eroticism did play some part in the ordinary day-to-day life of the Wandervogel, but it would be misleading to conclude on this account that the Wandervogel was a predominantly homo-erotic movement' (Stachura 1981, 28).

Stachura suggests that from 100 members in 1901, the Wandervogel had grown to around 25,000 in 1914, organised in 800 local branches. As we have seen, the movement was spread across a number of different bodies. A reaction to the splintering of the movement arose, and in 1910 the Wandervogel Deutscher Bund, the Bund Deutscher Wanderer and the Deutscher Akademischer Freischar (a body started by Knud Ahlborn at Göttingen in 1907 that consisted of student Wandervögel) concluded the 'Arolser Treaty' as a first step towards greater unity. Resulting from this were the Verband Deutscher Wandervogel (Association of German Wandervogel, formed in 1911) and the subsequent Wandervogel E.V. Bund für deutsches Jungwandern, formed in 1913, and known as the United Wandervogel. This was not joined by all sections, with the Jungwandervogel and sections of the Altwandervogel staying outside (Stachura 1981, 21–22).

Although this book will regard the Wandervogel period as ending in 1913, it needs to be stressed that in the subsequent periods of the German Youth Movement there were Wandervogel organisations in existence. Indeed, there are still to this day Wandervogel bodies in Germany and Austria. The periodisation stresses the key organisational focus in the movement, and it can be suggested that following the Hohe Meissner meeting the focus shifted to the Free German Youth.

Free German Youth
The Hohe Meissner meeting in October 1913 resulted in the formation of what Stachura calls a 'loose federation' (Stachura 1981, 32), the Free German Youth

(Freideutsche Jugend). This body can be seen as the key organisation in the movement until 1923, when a process of disintegration that really started with the end of World War I ran its course. Laqueur indicates a number of the reasons behind the calling of the meeting at the Hohe Meissner. (The ostensible reason was to provide an alternative, unofficial celebration of the centenary of the 'Battle of Nations' against Napoleon.) These included, first, the need to continue trends towards unity in the Youth Movement made even more necessary by the spread of the movement into Austria and Switzerland. A second reason was to deal with the problem of Wandervögel who were over 20 and who were outgrowing the youth groups. Laqueur indicated that among the recently founded student groups there were proposals for a body to unite the older members of all the Wandervogel organisations without distinction. The proposed name was Freideutsche Jugend (Laqueur 1962, 32–33).

After problematic preliminaries to the meeting, and the subsequent meeting itself – attended by rather less than 3,000 Youth Movement members along with adult sympathisers – the Free German Youth proceeded to work along the lines of the 'Meissner Formula'. (Kindt 1963 includes not only Ahlborn's previously cited account, 'Das Meißnerfest der Freideutschen Jugend', but also a 'Festschrift' of the meeting, which includes the calls to the meeting along with some of the speeches made by adult sympathisers. See pp. 91–104.) However, the Free German Youth was not, as Laqueur noted, quite what had been expected. If many of those present at the meeting had expected some sort of union of all the Wandervogel groups under the aegis of the Free German Youth with the possibility that in due course the likes of nationalist and socialist youth would also come on board, then they were to be disappointed. Organisationally, the main outcome was the recommendation of the main Youth Movement bodies that their older members join the Free Germans (Laqueur 1962, 36–37).

What resulted was an undoubtedly much more self-consciously political type of Youth Movement. Stachura suggested that it could be seen as a progressive movement trying to develop an alternative way of life to that of Wilhelmine Germany, but that it was limited by its lack of roots, its minority status and its elitism (Stachura 1981, 33). Its loose unity as a movement was disrupted very soon into its life. The cause was an attack on it in the Bavarian parliament by a Centre (Catholic) Party politician. The focus of the attack was a journal within the movement called *Der Anfang* (*The Beginning*). This journal was perceived as being a mouthpiece for the educational reformer and liberal leftist, Gustav Wyneken. The result of the storm was the expulsion of Wyneken's group from the movement, along with all the affiliated adult sympathising bodies, in March 1914. Wyneken had made one of the crucial speeches at the Hohe Meissner, and his organisations, the Freie Schulgemeinde Wickersdorf (his independent progressive school at Wickersdorf) and the Bund für Freie Schulgemeinden (League for Free School Communities) had been signatories to the calls for the meeting.

Wyneken was undoubtedly at this stage, and also later (as he and his followers were allowed back into the movement in 1917), an important figure in the movement. He was associated with the idea of Jugendkultur (youth culture), which saw youth as something of significance in itself and not as a preparatory stage for adult life. Given this, it is fairly evident why the Youth Movement should have interested him. (Laqueur has an interesting chapter on the two figures of Blüher and Wyneken. Kindt 1963 includes two readings by Wyneken, most notably 'Was ist Jugendkultur?' Phillip Lee Utley has recently produced an in-depth account of *Der Anfang* – Utley 1999 – that shows that it was far from simply being a mouthpiece for Wyneken, and also that through the figure of Siegfried Bernfeld it had an impact on the Jewish youth movement.) Laqueur concluded that the result of the Wyneken–*Anfang* controversy was the formation of left and right wings in the Free German Youth (Laqueur 1962, 37–38). This would be the issue that the Free German movement ultimately foundered upon, but that would come after World War I.

The outbreak of World War I saw members of the German Youth Movement rally to the colours in large numbers. (This was true for the Jewish youth movement too; in this respect p. 11 of Klönne 1993 is instructive, as it consists of reproductions of death notices for fallen members of the Blau-Weiß movement.) The Battle of Langemarck in Belgium in November 1914 became a touchstone for the movement. Here many Youth Movement members lost their lives, and the battle was subsequently commemorated by the movement, a practice later hijacked by the Nazi Hitler Jugend. Not all the movement supported the war, however. A small group around Ernst Jöel produced a journal called *Der Aufbruch: Monatsblätter aus der Jugendbewegung*. Jöel had been connected with *Der Anfang*, and his new journal and the circle around it included some interesting contributors and sympathisers, most notably Gustav Landauer (see Lunn 1973, 249–51) and Hans Blüher. The magazine was published by Eugen Diederichs in Jena, from July 1915, but only lasted four issues before it was closed by the authorities.[2]

With the end of the war, the Free German Youth went into political turmoil that lasted until 1923, when the movement was largely exhausted and was certainly no longer the dominant focus for the Youth Movement. The various accounts of this period paint a confusing picture of conferences and debates that focused around political issues. Three main tendencies formed. The first was a rightist tendency led by Frank Glatzel, which more or less left in 1919 with the (re)formation of the Jungdeutsche Bund. The second was a pro-communist faction, in which figures such as Karl August Wittfogel, Alfred Kurella and Karl Bittel were prominent, and the third a faction around the likes of Knud Ahlborn and Ferdinand Goebel which, though socialist, was not communist. After 1919 the two latter factions fought things out until the Hofgeismar conference of 1920 which according to Laqueur saw the end of the Free German Youth as a viable movement. Ahlborn and Goebel attempted to form Free German organisations (such as the Freideutsche Bund of 1922), and attempted to run a second Hohe Meissner conference in 1923, but this was a failure. Laqueur suggested that there were small Free German groupings around the country thereafter (Laqueur 1962, 127). As with the Wandervogel, the Free German name did not completely die (there remains a Freideutsche Kreis to this day), but the Free German phase had decisively ended.

Bündische Youth
The next phase was that between 1923 and the Nazi seizure of power in 1933. This was the Bündische Youth period, and it is rather difficult to put into order because the Youth Movement scene was characterised by fragmentation at this time. Small bünde proliferated, although some large bodies did come into existence through mergers. These bünde were rather more disciplined and intensive organisations than the bodies characteristic of previous phases of the movement. A useful starting point in thinking about the Bündische phase of the movement is to look at the organisational developments in the bünde. Having previously noted Laqueur's characterisation of Youth Movement structures, it is worthwhile considering his comments on structural developments in the Bündische phase. He noted that the bünde changed with the development of a more segmented structure. For the under-17-year-olds there was the Jungenschaft (the ages in this summary are approximate). The 17- to 25-year-olds formed the Jungmannschaft, with the over-25s forming the Mannschaft. Laqueur indicated that the Mannschaft was not entirely successful, although it was an attempt to implement the idea of the bund as a life-long bond. The Jungenschaft continued the kind of life that was typical of earlier phases of the movement. However, according to Laqueur the really innovative aspect was the Jungmannschaft. In this respect he pointed to the evolution of the notion of voluntary labour service from the summer camps of the Jungmannschaft, an idea subsequently taken over and distorted by the Nazis – though as Laqueur insisted, this was not the necessary outcome of these activities (Laqueur 1962, 142). Stachura also noted the labour service idea, and the various bodies that were involved in it, such as the Deutsche Freischar, the Silesian Jungmannschaft and the Artamanen (Stachura 1981, 52–53). Often – and especially in the case of the Artamanen – these camps took place in the east of the country. One of the few English writers and activists who paid any real attention to the German Youth Movement, Rolf Gardiner, attempted to run something rather similar in Wessex in the 1930s and 1940s (see Gardiner 1943 for an account).

In his general account of the Bündische phase Stachura makes some interesting points. He suggested that Bündische youth was more self-consciously 'masculine' and 'tough' than earlier phases of the movement. The image of the soldier was prominent in its iconography. Like Laqueur, he pointed to the more 'collectivist' nature of the bund, as compared with the rather individualistic aspects of the earlier phases. Leadership, including a leader principle, was a notable feature, and the bünde were selective about who could become members. He also suggested that the need for a 'new man' was important to the Bündische Youth, although this was not explicitly formulated and there appear to have been different views on this idea (Stachura 1981, 46–51). Indeed, the need for the 'new man' appears to have been felt earlier than the Bündische period. Borinski and Milch pointed to the move away from political activity on the part of the bulk of the Freideutsche around 1920. 'Now they were convinced that the "New Man" did not grow up in meeting-halls and street demonstrations, at party conferences and in election battles, but only in the "group", in various forms of new group – and in "Lebensgemeinschaften" (living communities)' (Borinski and Milch 1982, 19). On this account, the quest for the 'new man' takes us towards the communal movements that are the crux of this book.

This phase is also illuminated by the memoirs of Henry Pachter, who joined the Youth Movement (he omits to indicate his precise allegiance) in 1920 as a 13-year-old, becoming a Communist Youth member in 1925 at the age of 18. He suggested that there was a distinctly masculine feel to the movement, noting that from 'the beginning, the youth movement had assumed a flavour of all-male societies, and experience that no mixed company was able to offer' (Pachter 1982, 23). However, set against this, in his account it is clear that at the time of his involvement there were female sections to the movement and that there were occasional interactions. 'We could boast of having beautiful nude meetings with girls' groups' (Pachter 1982, 22).

Despite the arbitrary nature of the exercise, it might be as well at least briefly to consider some 'specimen' examples of bünde from this period. Perhaps the largest of the bünde was the Deutsche Freischar, which emerged in 1926 as a merger of the Neupfadpfinder ('New Scouts') and the Altwandervogel. Other groups also subsequently joined in the bund. Laqueur showed that by 1929 it had around 10,000 to 12,000 members, of whom around 75 per cent were under 18 and around 15 per cent were female (Laqueur 1962, 144). Key figures in the bund included Ernst Buske and Georg Götsch. Götsch was especially important in the musical work of the Youth Movement, and was a leading light in the establishment of the Musikheim at Frankfurt an der Oder in 1929. The Freischar was ideologically diverse, and figures of importance included Eugen Rosenstock-Hüssy (a friend of Rolf Gardiner) and Fritz Borinski, a socialist. Stachura noted that Borinski led a grouping within Bündische Youth that argued for socialism, the Leuchtenburg Circle. He suggested also that Borinski's stand on this was rather lonely, because most Bündische Youth was within the camp of the 'National Opposition', meaning the right and nationalist camp in Weimar politics (Stachura 1981, 63). Laqueur devoted a chapter (Laqueur 1962, Chapter 15) to the Freischar, which given the bund's size and importance is a useful case study.

There undoubtedly existed bünde of the far right. Stachura listed the main examples: Adler und Falken, Die Geusen, Schilljugend, Freischar Schill and the Artamanen, the latter being the most important. The Artamanen was founded in

1924, and held to a 'blood and soil' ideology. Its initial focus was on providing east German farmers with non-Polish seasonal labour, but it developed from this a more rounded focus on settlement on the land in the east and on labour service. Ideologically the closest bund to the Nazi Party, it had members who went on to become important Nazis: Walther Darré, Heinrich Himmler and Rudolf Höss (see Stachura 1981, 62).

The final 'specimen' bund to be considered is the d.j.1.11 – the Deutsche Jungenschaft Eins Elf. This was, in effect, a splinter of the Deutsche Freischar, and its name commemorated its secret founding within the Freischar on 1 November 1929. It was founded by Eberhard Köbel, known as Tusk. Tusk, the subject of a chapter in Laqueur's history, was the main figure in the Youth Movement in the final phase of the Bündische Youth period. The bund itself was a focus within the Youth Movement in the years between 1930, when it came into the open, and 1933. Tusk himself briefly became a Communist, and ended up in exile in London, after a period of arrest under the Nazis in 1934 (see Laqueur 1962, Chapter 17). For Borinski and Milch the importance of the d.j.1.11 lay in its stress on the need to separate the younger members of all the bünde from the 'elders' of the organisations, and unite them into an autonomous body. Despite Tusk's politics, and the generally anti-Hitler stance taken by him and the other leading figures in the d.j.1.11, autonomy of the Youth Movement was their main message. In this, along with their songs and ways of dressing, the d.j.1.11 was influential for a period. Borinski and Milch suggested that this influence was felt in the Freischar, the Catholic Quickborn, and also the Jewish movement (Borinski and Milch 1982, 40).

The Aftermath
With the coming to power of the Nazis, the Youth Movement in a legal sense ended. There are, however, two aspects to its 'after-existence'. The first is its situation under the Nazis. The second is its revival – if that is not too strong a term – after 1945. The question of the political orientation of the Youth Movement will be considered in due course, and so, in looking at how it reacted to the Nazis, issues of political theory need not be considered in detail. With the Nazi seizure of power, elements in the Youth Movement moved fairly rapidly to pledge their allegiance to the new regime. In some cases this was due to genuine conviction; in some cases there may have been an effort to ensure that their bünde would be allowed to continue in existence. Whatever the motivations, most of the bünde were shut down by the middle of 1933, with the remainder being legally dissolved by 1934. Only the Catholic youth held out for any length of time, finally being abolished in 1939. There were, as we have seen, substantial connections between some Bündische youth and the right of politics. That considerable sections of the Bündische youth went over to the Nazi regime is not a surprise; after all, other sections of German society reacted similarly. However, Stachura showed that the bulk of even the most ideologically rightist of the Bündische groups established some element of distance from the Nazi movement (Stachura 1981, 68–70).

In the sense that it was legally banned the Youth Movement died with the coming to power of the Nazis. The only Youth Movement allowed (apart from the Catholics) was the Hitler Youth. Efforts to stay in existence were made by sections of Bündische Youth, and Stachura noted that some resistance to the Nazis was offered in the early years of the Nazi regime by the Nerother Wandervogel group and by the d.j.1.11. That said, and despite the fact that there were a number of trials, he suggested that this resistance was minimal, though he did point to the fact that 131 ex-Youth Movement members lost their lives because of their involvement in resistance activities (Stachura 1981, 136–37). Some details of the trials are given in a pamphlet published in London in 1945 by Hans Ebeling, a former leader of the Jungnationaler Bund, called *The German Youth Movement*. He suggested that 1937 saw three particularly important cases – the Essen case, the Rossaint case, and the Hisch case which led to the execution of a d.j.1.11 member, Helmut Hisch (Ebeling 1945, 23). Borinski and Milch also point out the steps taken against the Youth Movement by the Gestapo, noting that the order forbidding private weekend youth rambling, actually a direct attack on the movement, had to be reissued as late as autumn 1943 (Borinski and Milch 1982, 44).

The second phase of the 'afterlife' of the German Youth Movement started in 1945 and continues to this day. In the wake of the liberation of Germany from the Nazis, efforts were made to restart the movement. Laqueur has a chapter that takes the reader through to 1962, and which points to activities such as the founding of Freideutsche circles (with Ahlborn and Wyneken involved) and the refounding of many of the bünde. As Laqueur noted, lots of the old names reappeared; bodies calling themselves Wandervogel, Deutsche Jungenschaft and the like reappeared, as did other names not yet considered, such as the Quickborn and Neudeutschland among the Catholics (see Laqueur 1962, Chapter 21). To bring this 'afterlife' story even further up to date, celebrations occurred for the fiftieth and seventy-fifth anniversaries of the Hohe Meissner meeting. Further, with the advent of the Internet it is fairly easy to gain access to websites hosted by bodies such as the Youth Movement Archives at Burg Ludwigstein and the Stuttgart-based Verlag der Jugendbewegung. There are also websites hosted by bodies with names such as Deutsche Jungenschaft, Deutsche Freischar and Wandervogel. A small youth movement in the tradition of the German Youth Movement does undoubtedly still exist, enabling today's young Germans to hike and sing in the way their grandparents did.[3]

'SECTORS' OF THE MOVEMENT

Catholic

Having considered the history of the German Youth Movement as a whole, we will now focus on the specifics of three 'sub-sections' in some detail, as these are important in the context of this book. These sub-sections are the Catholic,

Protestant and Jewish youth movements. The first of these sectors to be considered, the Catholic, raises an obvious question: are we considering Jugendbewegung or Jugendpflege organisations? As Thomas Reichardt put it: '[b]ei einer strengen Interpretation der Meißnerformel wäre eine katholische Jugendbewegung gar nicht möglich gewesen, da sich "freie Selbstbestimmung" Katholizität theoretisch widersprechen' ('On a strict interpretation of the Meissner Formula a Catholic Youth Movement was not really possible, as its "free self-determination" theoretically contradicts its catholicity').[4] Although this suggests that the movements we will consider are really tutelage organisations, the reality is rather more complex.

Certain Catholic youth organisations adopted a way of life that was consciously modelled upon that of the Youth Movement. The most notable examples were the Quickborn and the Neudeutschland Bund (there were other bodies and Walker 1970 has a useful summary). Quickborn was started in 1909 as a group of teetotal high school students. (For the early history of Quickborn, see Romano Guardini, 'Quickborn – Tatsachen und Grundsätze' in Kindt 1963, 335–50.) Quickborn's origins may have been as a fairly mainstream Catholic youth tutelage group, but things changed. 'When the groups of young Silesians began to ramble, they came into contact with the *Wandervogel*, and as a result of the experience adopted the dress, activities, and much of the spirit of the autonomous youth movement' (Walker 1970, 22). In 1919 they acquired the Burg Rothenfels castle as the base for their activities. Walker indicated of Quickborn that it 'maintained a creative tension of disparate elements. It was church-sponsored, but led by youth' (Walker 1970, 23).

Quickborn had separate groups for males and females, with groups growing no larger than 15 members. Each of these groups was led by a Quickborn member, but advised by a clerical friend. The male and female groups would occasionally come together for special occasions, but would not hike together (this account mixes elements from Walker 1970, 23 and Guardini in Kindt 1963, 335). It became a large body, with around 30,000 members in the early 1930s, an increase from 6,500 in the early 1920s, when it had almost equal male and female membership (Walker 1970, 23; Guardini in Kindt 1963, 335).

Was the Quickborn a Youth Movement body? An answer in the affirmative may be gleaned from the fact that Kindt's 1963 collection of *Grundschriften* of the Youth Movement includes two pieces of work from the man who was the spiritual focus of the group from 1924, Romano Guardini. (These are the already cited 'Tatsachen und Grundsätze' piece, and also a discussion with Max Bondy on 'Jugendbewegung und Katholizmus' – Kindt 1963, 274–302). Guardini, later in life a Monsignor of the Roman Catholic Church and a priest from 1910, was one of the most eminent Catholic academic theologians of twentieth-century Europe, and, in the words of the subtitle of a book devoted to his thought, a precursor of Vatican II (Krieg 1997). Krieg showed in a section devoted to Guardini's involvement with the Quickborn that it was an experience of some importance to his intellectual development (Krieg 1997, 59–63). Guardini referred to the Youth Movement in one of his most important essays, 'The Awakening of the Church in the Soul', and his references show the importance that he placed on the movement: '[i]n the Youth movement in which the springs of the new age must be sought' (Guardini 1935, 22).

The other Catholic organisation mentioned was the Neudeutschland Bund. This originated as a Catholic boys' club in 1919. It spread from its base in Cologne, but was initially a fairly typical Jugendpflege group. However, around 1921 some members went to Burg Rothenfels for a Quickborn conference. The spirit of that movement impressed them. Over the next few years, in a process described by Walker, Neudeutschland became a very distinct Youth Movement influenced organisation; less exuberant than the Quickborn, with a very ascetic approach to life, and a large number of ex-members becoming priests. By 1933 it had over 21,000 members (Walker 1970, 23–25). It was a male organisation, but it did have a female counterpart called Heliand (Integrated Community 1996, 63).

Quickborn, Neudeutschland and Heliand were thus Catholic youth bodies that bore the impress of the Youth Movement. It may even be suggested that the question raised about their being part of the Youth Movement at the start of this account is less difficult to answer than might have been assumed; Laqueur suggested of Quickborn and Neudeutschland that '[b]oth groups paid lip service to the Meissner formula' (Laqueur 1962, 71). That said, it is also worth remembering that Guardini made the point that Quickborn members were Catholics first and Youth Movement members second, as Stachura noted (Stachura 1981, 75). There was a real tension here. A recent book, *Was Wißt Ihr Von Der Erde*, published by the Verlag der Jugendbewegung, and edited by Catholic priest Hans Böhner and the German Youth Movement historian Arno Klönne (Böhner and Klönne 1995), is a useful source book for the Catholic Youth Movement from around 1919 until around 1940; it is composed of readings, mainly from Quickborn and Neudeutschland sources.

It remains only to make two further points about the Catholic youth movement. The first is that, as Laqueur described, the bodies we have looked at were revived in the post-World War II period (Laqueur 1962, 219). He actually only mentioned the Quickborn and the Neudeutschland, but Heliand was also revived. The second is to note that the German student resistance group active in Munich, the Weiße Rose (White Rose), was partially composed of Catholics and had Youth Movement connections. These links were embodied in the main Catholic member of the group, Willi Graf. Graf had been a member of the Neudeutschland and also of the illegal Youth Movement body, the so-called 'Graue Orden' (Siefken 1994b, 21). Hans Scholl, another member of the group and identified as Protestant by Siefken, had been involved in underground d.j.1.11 activities. Both Scholl and Graf were tried, independently of each other in 1937 and 1938, for 'Bündische Umtriebe', and freed as a result of an amnesty in 1938 (see Scholl 1983, esp. 13 and also, notably, Holler 1999 for Scholl's d.j.1.11 activities. For

Graf, see the fascinating 'Weg-zeichen Willi Grafs' by a fellow 'Graue Orden' participant Günter Schmich, in Böhner and Klönne 1995, 200–06.)

Protestant

There were Protestant groups that bore a similar relation to the Youth Movement as the Quickborn, Neudeutschland and Heliand did. Stachura mentioned a number of such bodies: the Bibelkreise movement, the Bund der Köngener, and the Bund deutscher Jugendvereine, whose leading figure was Professor Wilhelm Stählin. Stachura suggests that Stählin was the only Protestant figure comparable to Guardini (Stachura 1981, 82). This sector of the Youth Movement does seem to be notable for its tendency to far-right political views. The leader of the Köngener, Professor J. W. Hauer, also headed the pro-Nazi German Faith Movement. The Bibelkreise seems to have been particularly inclined towards the Nazis (Stachura 1981, 82–84).

From our point of view, however, the most important of the Protestant bodies is not mentioned by either Stachura or Laqueur in their 'round-ups' of the Protestant youth groups, but it is one that they are both aware of: the Neuwerk movement. This movement originated in 1919 (Baum 1998, 111 et seq.) and quite quickly became an important junction point for radical Christian socialism and the Youth Movement. At least two communes were established by members of this movement: the Habertshof and the Bruderhof. (The Habertshof became an adult educational institution and ended its effective existence under the Nazi regime.) Stachura suggests that Neuwerk was influenced by Karl Barth (Stachura 1981, 52). Laqueur suggests the same, noting also some degree of influence by the ideas of Paul Tillich (Laqueur 1962, 118–19). To some extent this is correct, but a major caveat must be entered. This is that the leader of the Bruderhof, Eberhard Arnold, debated with Karl Barth at the Tambach conference of summer 1919 (Baum 1998, 106–08). This conference took place just before Neuwerk was formed, and some of the organisers went on to participate in the movement. Baum appears to suggest that to some extent later differences in the movement arose when associates of Arnold started to contend with the Barthian line (Baum 1998, 130). Arnold withdrew from Neuwerk in late 1922.

As to Paul Tillich's influence, this is to be expected, given that Tillich was a member of the Berlin Neuwerk group in the 1920s (Baum 1998, 261, fn 9). The major figure in Neuwerk in the period after Arnold's withdrawal was one of the Habertshof group, Emil Blum. Blum wrote the group's history (*Die Neuwerk Bewegung 1922–1933*, 1973), as did the Green politician Antje Vollmer, in the form of a doctoral dissertation ('Die Neuwerkbewegung 1919–1935', 1973). Neuwerk even featured in Becker's book, in the form of a 'reportage' (a feature of the book; see the footnotes to his Chapters I and VI) in which a Bürgermeister discusses the movement and Habertshof. Two of his children had joined the movement, and he provides an interesting sidelight on it from an unsympathetic though fair-minded perspective (Becker 1946, 121–24).

28   *No Heavenly Delusion?*

Jewish

The Jewish youth movement in Germany has been examined in the general histories of the Youth Movement that have been used as sources in this chapter. It
is also the subject of a detailed literature in English, much of which is to be found
in various volumes of the *Leo Baeck Institute Yearbook.* There is also a growing
German-language literature produced by circles connected with the continuing
Youth Movement in contemporary Germany, notably the Verlag der Jugendbewegung.

An introductory consideration in thinking about the Jewish youth movement
is that there were, according to Chanoch Rinott, three trends into which Jewish
youth bünde can be divided. These were, first, German-Jewish bünde, second,
bünde whose core was Judaism, and, finally, bünde whose core was Eretz Israel
(the land of Israel), in other words Zionists. Rinott gave some pointers about
these three kinds of bünde. The first, German-Jewish type affirmed the duality of
being German and being Jewish, searching for a symbiosis, in Rinott's word, of
the two. Whether the accent was on the 'Germanness' or the 'Jewishness'
depended upon the bund, or could even differ within the bund. The second type
of bund aimed to synthesise a positive view of life in the diaspora with national
and religious Jewish views, allied to a growing commitment to Eretz Israel. The
third type of bund placed varying degrees of emphasis on Aliyah (emigration to
Eretz Israel, as Zionists called Palestine) and realising the aims of the Chalutz
(pioneer) movement. These movements focused on kibbutz life and were influenced by the various kibbutz movements in Eretz Israel. (For this typology and
the expansions on it, Rinott 1974, 77. Rosenstock accepted Rinott's typology
[Rosenstock 1974]. It is evident from the first paragraph of Rosenstock's article
that these authors were Youth Movement veterans from different 'types' of
bünde.)

Some suggestions might be made as to examples of the organisations Rinott
had in mind. For the first, German-Jewish type, Rosenstock's bund, the Deutsch-
Jüdische Jugend-Gemeinschaft, is a useful example, because it is documented in
English, although it was small. The Kameraden is another example, from foundation in 1916 until its disintegration in 1932, and following that disintegration
the Schwarzes Fähnlein provides a final example, also documented in English.
(For the Kameraden and the association with it of the philosopher Franz
Rosenzweig, see Mendes-Flohr 1991. For the Schwarzes Fähnlein see Rheins
1978 and Schatzker 1987, 177–79.) Of the second group, the Esra movement,
founded around 1916, is a good example. This eventually became part of the
Agadut Israel movement, a still existing orthodox movement within Judaism that
functions in the diaspora and in Israel. Of the third type, the 'chalutzo-Zionist'
movements, a good example would be Habomin Noar Chaluzi, its German
branch founded in 1933 from a merger of two earlier Zionist bünde, one of which
was the Jung Jüdische Wanderbund/Brith Haolim, itself the product of a merger.
Evidently, the Jewish youth movement was no less prone to splits and splinters

than the German Youth Movement, even within the 'types' laid down by Rinott. (See Klönne 1993, 44–45 for chronologies of some of the key bünde.) In his summary on the Jewish youth movement, Stachura argued that the first organisation that took the forms associated with the German Youth Movement was the Blau-Weiß, Bund für Jüdische Jungwandern. This was founded in 1912 in Breslau. (Some accounts, as noted above, suggest that the Jung Jüdische Wanderbund predated it by a year.) It disintegrated in 1926. As its name implies, it was Zionist, and Stachura suggested that in its early phase it could be seen as a sort of 'Zionist Wandervogel' (Stachura 1981, 87). (An account of the Blau-Weiß by Hans Tramer can be found in the 'celebratory' collection of essays, *Die Jugendbewegung, Welt und Wirkung*, published in 1963. See Korn et al. 1963, 202–20.)

Stachura notes that '[i]f the 1920s had seen a decisive penetration of Zionist and socialist concepts into the Jewish youth groups, albeit in non-party political form, the early 1930s witnessed the ascendancy of these concepts and their prosecution with greater enthusiasm than ever before' (Stachura 1981, 90). What this meant, as well as the growth of the chalutzo-Zionist groups, was that groups from Rinott's other categories (German-Jewish and Judaic) moved over, or saw large sections of their members move over, into the Zionist camp. Given the politics of Germany in the early and mid-1930s this is understandable. A good example of a German-Jewish movement that made such a move in this period is the Werkleute. In 1932 this was founded, out of the ruins of the Kameraden Bund, as the Werkleute, Bund deutschjüdischer Jugend. In 1933 it changed its subtitle to Bund jüdischer Jugend. By 1938 its two kibbutzim in Palestine and indeed the movement as a whole became part of the Hashomer Hatzair movement, a Marxist-Zionist group that originated as a youth movement in Galicia in 1913, and which was affected by the ideas of the Youth Movement (Margalit 1969, 31). However, 'in the last two or three years before 1933 *Werkleute* were nationalist, but still non-Zionist' (Moaz 1959, 172).

An example of the shift from the Judaic bünde towards Zionism can be found in the Esra Bund. In 1928 a Zionist tendency seceded from the bund and became part of the Brith Chalutzim Datiim, or Bachad (the name meant League of Religious Pioneers, Brith being the Hebrew equivalent of bund). Bachad fed directly into the movement today known as Kibbutz Dati, the 'religious' kibbutz federation. Interestingly, even anti-Zionist members of the Esra Bund ended up forming a kibbutz in Palestine. Klönne suggested that some of them formed a kibbutz that became part of what is today Kibbutz Chafez Chaim (Klönne 1993, 25). Chafez Chaim is one of the two kibbutzim today affiliated with the Poalei Agudat Israel 'ultra-orthodox' movement, the smallest sector of the contemporary kibbutz movement.

Further consideration of the Jewish youth movement in this book will focus on the chalutzo-Zionist movements and their connections to the Kibbutz. Perhaps even more than the Catholic and Protestant 'sub-sections' of the

German Youth Movement, the Jewish youth movement forms an extensive field of study in and of itself. The focus on the Zionists should not be taken as indicating that the other types of movement are not of interest. As a fine example of a study of one of the German-Jewish movements that brings out many interesting topics and questions, Rheins' consideration of the Schwarzes Fähnlein (Black Squadron) should be mentioned (Rheins 1978).

IDEOLOGY

General

Although the German Youth Movement was, as has been shown, a diverse phenomenon, something should be said about ideology in connection with the movement. The first point to make is that the Youth Movement can be seen as a part of a wave of neo-Romanticism that swept Germany. This argument has been made from a Marxist standpoint by Michael Löwy. He has been concerned with categorising Romanticism and one of his categories is Anti-capitalist Romanticism. This is where he places the Youth Movement.

> The Romantic anti-capitalist world-view was present in an astonishing variety of cultural works and social movements of this period: novels by Thomas Mann and Theodor Storm; poems by Stefan George and Richard Beer-Hoffmann; the sociology of Tönnies, Simmel or Mannheim; the historical school of economics; the *Kathedersozialismus* of Gustav Schmoller, Adolph Wagner or Lujo Brentano; the philosophy of Heidegger and Spengler, the Youth Movement and the *Wandervogel*, Symbolism and Expressionism. United in its rejection of capitalism in the name of nostalgia for the past, this cultural configuration was totally heterogeneous from a political point of view: reactionary ideologues (Moeller Van der Bruck, Julius Langbehn, Ludwig Klages) as well as revolutionary utopians (Bloch, Landauer) could be characterised as anti-capitalist romantics. (Löwy 1992, 28–29. Kevin Repp has examined in detail quite a number of the figures named by Löwy, most notably Tönnies, Simmel, Schmoller, Wagner and Brentano; Repp 2000.)

Löwy, in another work, argues that '*Neo-romanticism*, as a moral and social critique of "progress" and of modern *Zivilisation* – in the name of a nostalgic loyalty to the traditional *Kultur* – became the dominant trend among the German intelligentsia from the end of the nineteenth century to the rise of fascism' (Löwy 1993, 143).

Löwy's work (see also Löwy and Sayre 1992) represents an interesting original intervention in contemporary leftist politics as well as historiography. From the point of view of this book, however, the crucial points to be taken from his work are these: first, the Youth Movement can be seen as part of the gale of neo-Romanticism that blew through Germany in the first third of the twentieth century. Second, this cannot, if we take Löwy seriously, allow us simply to 'read off' a political position. Löwy makes clear the political heterogeneity of Romantic anti-capitalism or neo-Romanticism. To say that the Youth Movement was part of this neo-Romantic wave is to pose a question about its relation to politics or, more strictly, the relations of its various manifestations to politics, and not to answer one. Before moving on to the question of the relationship between the Youth Movement and politics, however, it is worth registering the extent to which Löwy's argument can be supported by reference to commentators on the Youth Movement.

Laqueur's concluding chapter appears to bear out Löwy's thesis. He noted of the movement that '[i]t tended, like the Romantics before them, to venerate the Middle Ages in contrast to the modern world' (Laqueur 1962, 236), which certainly connects with Löwy's stress on nostalgia. However, Laqueur noted a difference with neo-Romantic literature, and this is that the movement was most definitely not individualistic. In this sense, Laqueur pointed to the '*sui generis*' (Laqueur 1962, 233) nature of the movement, an important counter-balancing point to Löwy's attempt to tie the movement in with other trends, but not one that necessarily negates Löwy's argument, rather highlighting the limits of his observations. It is interesting that several of the authors picked out by Löwy also featured in Laqueur's account. Julius Langbehn is mentioned as one of Karl Fischer's favourite authors (Laqueur 1962, 34). Laqueur also suggested with regard to the idea of the bund that 'the central impulse as far as the youth movement was concerned undoubtedly came from Stefan George and his circle' (Laqueur 1962, 135. George 1944 includes some translations from the most important of George's collections from this point of view, *Der Stern des Bundes*.) Becker's book is less a history and more a sociological analysis of the movement, but it could be suggested that the whole first part is an extended illustration of the Romantic nostalgia of the Wandervogel.

Why is this issue of Romanticism important? A comment from John Macmurray clarifies: 'But in Germany the Romantic movement became the starting-point of an indigenous culture, and a major factor in the creation of the German nation' (Macmurray 1995, 40). Macmurray was referring to the first phase of German Romanticism – pointing to Lessing, Hamann and Herder – in contrast to Romanticism in other cultures. Nonetheless, his point is important, because neo-Romanticism as discussed by Löwy is obviously in part an attempt to revive aspects of the original. Macmurray's comment suggests that, more than anywhere else, Romanticism had a resonance and importance in Germany.

Politics

This discussion of neo-Romanticism has implications for a consideration of the relationship of the Youth Movement and politics. This is a highly controversial area. Some writers see the Youth Movement as a precursor of Nazism, or at least aspects of it. Some suggest very strongly that this view is incorrect, and indeed a distortion. The purpose of these brief comments is not to 'tot up' the overall 'score' among commentators and give the reader guidance on that basis. For what it is worth, of the four main English-language works, Becker is in the first camp, with qualifications, and again with qualifications, Laqueur and Stachura in the latter. Borinski and Milch are quite strongly in the second camp, ending their book with three points which they say outsiders might miss, the second being a strong assertion that the movement was not a precursor of Nazism. The Meissner Formula remained its creed, and clearly conflicted with Führer-worship. The third of the points is a statement that Hitler well understood this, and so dissolved the leagues.

One writer who argued strongly for the thesis that the Youth Movement represented a precursor of the Nazi movement was G. R. Halkett, in his autobiography *The Dear Monster*, which dealt with the years between the turn of the twentieth century and the mid-1930s. Halkett, whose father was German and whose mother had Scottish and Dutch antecedents, was not really making the argument that the movement (of which he had been quite a long-standing member) prefigured the actual policies of the Nazis. Indeed, at one point he suggests that '[i]t is terrifying irony that so many unpleasant and dangerous things should come out of something as lovable [sic] as the Youth Movement' (Halkett 1939, 97). Halkett argued that although Hitler was never a member of a Youth Movement group, he and his party had to be seen as part of it. This was because of what he calls the symptoms that determined if one was a member. Hitler, he claimed, showed these symptoms.

> As far as there is something which might be called German mentality, the Youth Movement was its closest expression; i.e. that part of the German character which makes it distinct from the character of other peoples, can be seen clearly in the attitude, spirit and habits of the Youth Movement. If you want to understand Herr Hitler's and the German people's mind, you have to study the specific type of German reformer and *Schwärmer* as you would have found it in the Youth Movement's groups and *Siedlungen*. (Halkett 1939, 130)

He gave a clue to his meaning in the following; writing of the Youth Movement he argued that '[h]ere the phraseology was invented which was later taken up by the Hitlers and the Goebbelses. No Politics. No System. Feelings. Blood. Faith. Enthusiasm. Above all: *Gemeinschaft*, which literally means Community, but which sounds deeply mystical and supernatural to a German ear' (Halkett 1939, 94). Halkett's was a harsh indictment of the Youth Movement, and one that chimes in with that developed by, for instance, Becker. However, while it is undoubtedly a point of view that must be considered seriously, and not least because Halkett was a member of the movement and in other parts of his account makes clear some of its strengths, it is only one point of view. Contrast it with that of Borinski and Milch. They were as anti-Nazi as was Halkett (both accounts were written for English publishers after the authors had left the Third Reich). They came to almost diametrically opposite conclusions to Halkett, and certainly Borinski had also been in the movement. Just as Halkett clarified some of the movement's strengths, so Borinski and Milch were clear about some of its weaknesses.

If we move on from the specifics of the 'Nazi question', and consider the relationship between the Youth Movement and politics in general, our starting point must be the fact that there were clear differences in general trends between the periods. If it could be said that the Freideutsche period, especially in the years following World War I, saw a degree of politicisation to the left – notably following the virtual secession of Glätzel's rightist tendency – then it may also be said that the Bündische Youth period saw a predominantly rightist tendency. George Mosse, discussing Revolutionary Conservatism (or 'The Conservative Revolution') suggested that '[b]y the 1920s the largest group in that movement, the Bündsiche Jugend, provided some of the most important theoretical expressions of the "third force"' (Mosse 1971, 122).

This seems a reasonable statement. What does seem rather problematic is the type of judgement expressed by Stachura when he states that '[e]ntirely missing from Bündische Youth was a radical leftist contingent' (Stachura 1981, 59–60). Not only does this ignore the Leuchtenburg Kreis around Fritz Borinski, which he himself mentions – although admittedly noting its isolation in Bündische circles, it also ignores Leonhard Nelson's Internationaler Jugend-Bund, called after 1925 the Internationaler Sozialistischer Kampfbund. This non-Marxist socialist organisation, alluded to by Stachura and mentioned in Laqueur's chapter 'Panorama of the Bünde', was in the 1920s and 1930s a fiercely left-wing body. Its afterlife as the originating organisation of the journal of the post-World War II British Labour Right, *Socialist Commentary*, is another story (see Black 1999 and Minion 2000). Stachura's argument also excludes from consideration Borinski and Milch's view, and admittedly they were *parti pris*, that the bünde embodied socialism in their structure to some extent. Writing about the selection of leaders in the bünde, they noted that these bodies were selective. 'On the other hand this selective principle was combined with a complete system of democratic self-government and socialist fellowship' (Borinski and Milch 1982, 29). Generalisations are suspect on this issue, which is what one should expect from the extended quotation from Löwy. He flagged up the fact that the stream in which the Youth Movement swam contained political 'fish' of very different types. Not only was Romantic anti-capitalism heterogeneous; so too was the Youth Movement. The failure to note this mars even such a fine work as Fritz Stern's study of Van der Bruck, Langbehn and de Lagarde, *The Politics of Cultural Despair.* That said, the tendency in the Bündische period was rightist. However, as shown, this statement taken on its own obscures much, as would generalisations about the earlier periods.

The heterogeneity of the Youth Movement and its neo-Romanticism can also be seen in an examination of the political term that sections of the Youth

Movement proposed as an answer to the ills of Germany; the bund. The bund was, for some, not simply the type of organisation that composed the Youth Movement, but it was also a political term or perhaps even project. Stachura noted that although

> some members may have viewed the group [in this context, bund] as only a cultural or educational, or even religious entity, and others simply a convenient organisational form, most saw it as an end in itself, believing that it was a means of communal living far superior to anything offered by atomised Weimar society. The group concept was perfectly appropriate to the youth movement's ethos, for it permitted youth to asset their independent status while simultaneously holding out a blueprint for the future form of German society. (Stachura 1981, 48)

Borinski and Milch also discuss this 'Bündische Politik' (Borinski and Milch 1982, 34). Of the advocates of Bündische political thinking they argue: '[t]heir conception of politics and state were dangerously ambitious and vague, meaning not much more than a state, formed after the model of the league communities and dominated by the men and spirit of the young generation' (Borinski and Milch 1982, 35). They suggested that this was more sober than the earlier, almost anarchistic thinking of the Freideutsche, but at root it remained only a pseudo-realism. This said, they also pointed to efforts within Bündische circles on both the right (notably connected with 'National Bolshevik' tendencies), centre and left (Borinski's own Leuchtenburg Kreis) to formulate realistic political perspectives, which started to see some fruit in the late 1920s and early 1930s. At this time some Bündische activists became involved in failed attempts at new parties such as the Konservative Volkspartei and the Deutsche Staatspartei, and Borinski himself joined the SPD in 1928.

One possible direction bund political thinking could go in was an organicist, conservative direction, predicated on the need for hierarchy and the inequality of members, with each taking their rightful and appropriate place be that high or low. The leader principle would be operative in this type of bund (Mosse 1971, 123–24). However, that there could be a different direction is shown in a comment made by Ulrich Linse in his consideration of the Gemeinshaft/ Gesellschaft (community/society) distinction in German sociological thinking. Discussing Martin Buber, he mentioned the category of Gemeinschaft, passing on to bund, adding in parentheses '(In Landauers, nicht in Schmalenbachs auslesung!)' ('In Landauer's and not Schmalenbach's reading!') (Linse in Kerbs and Reulecke 1998, 164). Schmalenbach was a sociologist who investigated the Sociological Category of the Bund – or communion as his translators called it. His article is most easily available in English in Parsons et al. 1961, 331–47. Becker indicated that he was a member of the Stefan George circle (Becker 1946, 105, fn 5).

What was Gustav Landauer's understanding of bund? Buber himself stated it in the following terms: 'the creation and renewal of a real organic structure, from the union of persons and families into various communities and of communities into associations' (Buber 1958, 48). Landauer and Buber used the term bund frequently, but as Linse hinted, they meant something rather different by it than the meaning indicated by Mosse. The organicism was present, as indeed was an element of traditionalism, bearing out Löwy's viewpoint. However, the leadership principle was not a feature, and arguably the 'glue' that bound this anarchosocialist bund together was, rather, Landauer's concept of 'spirit'. (See Tyldesley 1996, 37–40 for this concept in Landauer.) Landauer's organisation in the years immediately prior to World War I was called the Sozialistisches Bund. Lunn, in his biography of Landauer, provided a translation of the Twelve Articles of this bund (Lunn 1973, 349–50). There was discussion in these articles of 'voluntary union' and the formation of domestic settlements by pioneers, but the words leader and leadership do not appear once. If Landauer and Buber were advocates of a variant of bund thinking, then as the quotation from Buber above hinted, life in community was close to the heart of their variant of this concept. Both Landauer and Buber advocated a life lived in community. The term used by Landauer, widespread in the Germany of the first quarter of the twentieth century, was Siedlung (literally, colony).

Landauer and Buber were both Jewish, and so it is not surprising that their ideas had a degree of impact on the chalutzo-Zionist part of the Jewish youth movement. (See Schatzker 1978 and Menahem Dorman in Gordon and Bloch 1984 for discussions of Buber in this context, with Dorman providing a rather caustic view). However, Landauer and Buber were significant in the wider Youth Movement at certain times. Landauer's involvement with *Der Aufbruch* has already been mentioned. Laqueur quoted at some length a diatribe from a rightist source in 1920 about the Freideutsche leaders leapfrogging among various different sources – Buddha, Jesus, Landauer and Lenin being among the motley crew mentioned (Laqueur 1962, 121).

Communal Living
However, the advocacy of communal living and the formation of Siedlungen was far from being confined to those in the Youth Movement listening to Landauer and Buber. As Stachura noted, '[s]ettlements (Siedlungen), work communities (Werkgemeinschaften) and labour camps (Arbeitslager) became an established and significant feature of Bündische Youth's broader educational experience during the 1920s' (Stachura 1981, 51). This quote is important because the linking of settlements, work communities and labour camps indicates that this was not only confined to the socialist and Christian socialist sectors of the Youth Movement, but that the concepts spread across the spectrum. After all, the work communities and labour camps were activities undertaken not only by the likes of the Deutsche Freischar, but also notably by groups such as the Artamanen.

We noted Borinski and Milch's comment that around 1920 large sections of the Freideutsche moved on from politics and decided that the 'new man' would grow in life-communities. They discuss such communities and point to the importance of them in the Youth Movement of the 1919–1923 period (Borinski and Milch 1982, 20–21). All this evidence goes to suggest that the main subject of this book – movements advocating communal living with roots in the Youth Movement – is far from being a fringe aspect, but rather these movements represent a continuation of one of the central preoccupations of the Youth Movement. Halkett also stressed the Siedlungen, and on his peregrinations through Germany actually met some communitarians who had connections with the Bruderhof, such as Marie Buchhold from Darmstadt (Halkett 1939, 99 et seq.). His comment on Hitler summed up his feeling on the issue.

> When I looked at Herr Hitler's portrait, I knew what Germany would look like once he came into power. It would be the biggest *Siedlung* the world had ever seen, ardent, zealous to convert the surrounding world; it would be shut off from the world and would open its frontiers only to swallow the surrounding parts bit by bit. (Halkett 1939, 322)

'GRADUATION'

What did the members of the Youth Movement do next? None of us stays young forever, so can we point to any specific patterns among the members of the Youth Movement in the way in which they approached their adult lives? First, it might be suggested that some, in fact, did try to base the rest of their lives around the Youth Movement. Bodies such as the Bund der Kronacher were formed to cater for former members of the Wandervogel. When considering the Bündische Youth we noted the idea of the Mannschaft, which, though judged by Laqueur a failure, does seem to have been an attempt to continue the Youth Movement bund on into adult life. One of Becker's 'reportages' involved a comment (by an American observer of the Youth Movement from a student organisation) on this phenomenon. 'Another funny thing: Have you noticed what a big bunch of youth movers you'll find who are getting long in the tooth?' (Becker 1946, 135).

If the 'youth movers', to use Becker's term, did decide not to try to live the rest of their lives out in the movement, one possible career choice that would have allowed them to maintain some of their youthful interests would have been to become some form of professional educator. The Youth Movement, for fairly obvious reasons, was intensely interested in education, and had a significant impact on German education. Educators such as Wyneken were interested in the movement, but perhaps more importantly, movement members went on to work in education in fairly large numbers. Stachura showed in a brief passage the impact of the Youth Movement in the 1920s on education: transformation of relations between pupils and teachers, parental involvement in education, changes in the curriculum which resulted in greater emphasis on cultural subjects and more physical education, the use of school outings and rural facilities, and even the extension of school holidays (Stachura 1981, 55). This educational emphasis should come as no surprise as the Wandervogel arose 'in part as a rebellion against the authoritarian school system' (Stachura 1981, 24).

An important source for information on the impact of the Youth Movement on education in Germany in the period up until around the Nazi seizure of power is the doctoral thesis produced by George Thomson at the University of Glasgow in June 1934. (This was used by Stachura as a source for his book.) Thomson undertook work in Germany in every year between 1928 and 1933 except 1931, and so the thesis is based on a first-hand understanding of German education. Divided into two volumes, the first examines the Youth Movement, the youth tutelage groups, and also the Youth Hostels movement, with the second focusing upon specifically educational questions. Thomson is particularly enlightening on the kind of educational experience that the Youth Movement was in revolt against at the time it started. He suggested that by the time scholars reached the upper levels of the secondary school they found themselves in an 'unremitting grind' that made school 'little better than a prison' (Thomson 1934, II, 194). He suggested that the 'whole atmosphere of the schools seemed to foster morbidity, leading to an introspective weltschmerz rather than to a natural joie-de-vivre' (Thomson 1934, II, 195). Halkett's autobiographical account offered support to these judgements (Halkett 1939, 50 et seq.).

Thomson looked at how change came about in the German school system in the post-World War I period. He described many aspects of this change, from work in experimental schools outside the state system to changes that actually occurred in the ordinary school system. Two crucial points emerge from his account. The first is that the Youth Movement was only one in a number of factors making for change in German schooling at this time. This can make it difficult to be specific about its influence (Thomson 1934, II, 257). A second, general point, made towards the end of his sixth chapter, was his argument that while leading figures in the Youth Movement had views that impinged on education, influence on practice tended not to be asserted by the movement as a whole, but rather through the vehicle of adult leaders, naming the obvious example, Gustav Wyneken. Taken together, these points mean that any attempt to trace the impact of the Youth Movement on educational practice will need to be detailed, and often focus on the Youth Movement backgrounds of people who may initially appear to be 'straightforward' examples of educational reformers.

As the Nazis came to power at a point in German history when reasonably large numbers of people with a Youth Movement background would have been on the scene and looking for work, it is not surprising that some ex-Youth Movement members became Nazi officials. The most notorious example of this emphasises the full horror of the Nazi period: Rudolf Höss. Höss had been a member of the Artamanen, and in his autobiography he talked about that bund, and the fact that he met his wife through it (Höss 2000, 62–64). Höss went on to become the commandant of the Auschwitz extermination camp, having worked in other concentration camps, between 1940 and 1943. After capture by the British he was tried by the Poles, found guilty, and sentenced to death. The sentence was carried out by hanging at Auschwitz. A colleague of Höss's in the Artamanen was the leader of the SS, Heinrich Himmler.

A further way that Youth Movement members might 'graduate' from the movement connects back to the point made earlier about the prevalence of notions of living in community: Youth Movement members might form communes, and with good fortune live out the rest of their lives in community. The rest of this book will examine three groups of people who can be seen as having done precisely that.

NOTES

1 Information supplied by James Grant-Rosenhead of Kvutsat Yovel, Jerusalem, 12 November 2000.
2 *Der Aufbruch* is available in part on the Internet at the Walter Benjamin Research Syndicate Home page, http://www.wbenjamin.org/aufbruch.html
3 Klönne 1990 is an excellent documentation of the Bündische Youth in the immediate aftermath of World War II.
4 Thomas Reichardt, *Geschichte der Deutschen Jugendbewegung, 4. Die Bündische Zeit (1920–1933)*, website http://dpvonline.de/hist_4.html

Chapter 2

Introducing the Movements

THE BRUDERHOF

The Bruderhof was founded in Sannerz, Germany, in 1920, and is now an international movement, with around 2,000–2,500 members living in ten communities. Seven of these are in the northeast United States (New York state and Pennsylvania), two are in England (Kent and East Sussex) and one is in Australia. These bruderhofs are based upon absolute community of goods and work. Full members give over all their worldly goods at the time of joining (baptism). The members mainly work within the community either on domestic tasks (cleaning the 'hof', washing the clothes of the inhabitants, cooking for the inhabitants, mending and making clothes; all these tasks are performed by the women) or in the factory that produces the wooden school equipment (Community Playthings) or equipment for the disabled (Rifton products) that are important sources of the communities' income. (The factory workforce is overwhelmingly male.) There are some other smaller 'branches' in which people can work; bookselling would be an example. A small number of bruderhofers might work off-site.

Although there are ten communities, the Bruderhof is one body, presided over by an Elder. From 1983 until April 2001 the founder's grandson, Johann Christoph Arnold, was clearly the holder of this role. Reports appeared in the bulletin *Keep in Touch*, a journal produced by disaffected former members of the Bruderhof, and a hostile source on Bruderhof issues, in its April–May 2001 issue, indicating that Arnold had stepped down and that Richard Scott had replaced him.[1] The Bruderhof continues, however, as of March 2002 to call Arnold its 'lead pastor'.[2] Each community's full members form a 'Brotherhood' (in which women can be members), and there are ministers called Servants of the Word, a position only tenable by males, in each community. However, there is a common purse shared between all the communities of the movement. The basis for the Bruderhof's way of life is a shared understanding that Christianity requires this form of life, the biblical roots of which are to be found especially in the Acts of the Apostles, with its description of the early Jerusalem Church, and the Sermon on the Mount, a central text for the community. The co-founder and main ideologist of the Bruderhof, Eberhard Arnold (1883–1935), laid down the Bruderhof's understanding of the demands of Christianity, and his life and work represent a continuing inspiration to the Bruderhof.

Arnold was not only a founder of the Bruderhof, but was also a key link between it and the German Youth Movement. This can be seen by considering one of his final letters, written shortly before his death in November 1935 to his son-in-law Hans Zumpe (the leading figure in the movement between 1935 and 1961). Here Arnold wrote that 'I hold firmly to the inward and outward uniting of *genuine old Hutterianism* with the *attitude of faith* of the two Blumhardts and with the life-attitude of the true *Youth Movement* as a real and wonderful providence for your future' (Mow 1991, 109, italics in original). The significance of Hutterianism and the Blumhardts for the Bruderhof will be clarified later. The important point here is that the Youth Movement was sufficiently important to Arnold to feature strongly in his ideological 'last will and testament'. Perhaps if only for this reason it is possible to say that, of all the three movements to be considered, the German Youth Movement is most seen as a living part of its current reality by the Bruderhof. The phrase 'life-attitude' also conveys quite nicely just what it is that the Bruderhof has acquired from the Youth Movement.

Eberhard Arnold actually discovered the Youth Movement at a latish point in his life. According to his biographer, Markus Baum, it was in 1917, when Arnold was 34, that he came into meaningful contact with the movement, then in its Freideutsche period (Baum 1998, 96, 270 fn 3). He attended Freideutsche conferences (and as a result of one changed the style of clothing he wore for good – Baum 1998, 103), members of the Youth Movement were involved in the discussion groups at Arnold's home in Berlin that preceded the formation of the Bruderhof, and Arnold was involved with Youth Movement groups on a continuing basis.

Two examples can be given of the latter point. The first was the involvement of the circle around Arnold (notably his wife Emmy and sister-in-law Elsa Von Hollander, but also others) in the Neuwerk movement. It should be noted that Arnold was involved in editorial and management work on the group's journal (*Das Neue Werk* at the time of Arnold's involvement) prior to the Bruderhof's secession from Neuwerk (Baum 1998, 129–30). The second example is the continuing involvement of Arnold and his co-workers in Freideutsche circles. Arnold's biographer has written about his involvement in the second Hohe Meissner youth conference in 1923. As noted in the last chapter, this was seen as a failure, and came some three years after the Freideutsche had started to run out of steam. Arnold was on the planning committee of this second Hohe Meissner conference. Nevertheless, he continued to be active in the remaining Freideutsche activities, and on Baum's account was a leading figure in a split between the Free German Fellowship, led by Knud Ahlborn, and a Free German Union. This latter was formed in 1924, and was joined by Arnold (who resigned from the

Fellowship) and all the adult members of the Bruderhof (Baum 1998, 161–64). Arnold persisted with the Free German Union until its apparent death around 1930, co-operating closely with Erich Mohr. Mohr, Arnold and Hans-Joachim Schoeps attempted to form a sort of elite grouping within the Union, to be called the Free German Brotherhood, but this seems to have expired with it (Baum 1998, 186–88). The Freideutsche connection was so significant to the Bruderhof that Eberhard Arnold's son, Eberhard C. H. ('Hardy') Arnold said in a speech to a conference devoted to the idea of life in community in Britain in 1937 that '[u]ntil the advent of National Socialism it [the Bruderhof] was regarded as the settlement of the pacifist section of the Free German Youth Movement (Freideutscher Werk-Bund)' (Community Service Committee 1938, 26).

Aside from practical involvement in the Freideutsche section of the Youth Movement it is also significant that the Bruderhof recruited from Youth Movement circles in the 1920s and 1930s. Looking at the historical sources on the Bruderhof, some examples can be found: Hans Zumpe, Arnold's son-in-law, joined up after hearing Arnold talk at a Freideutsche group in Dresden; Georg Barth came to the Bruderhof from a background of activity in the Bund der Köngener (for both examples see Oved 1996, 38). Hans Meier's background was in Swiss religious socialist circles, and he had been in a group called the Freischar (Oved 1996, 73). Walter Hüssy also came from this group (Baum 1998, 185), which was a specifically Swiss Christian youth movement group. Hüssy, Meier and Barth were involved in the Bruderhof from the 1920s and 1930s through to the 1990s; all are now, sadly, dead. They are specific examples of a trend; in a document of 1929, Eberhard Arnold quoted a memorandum produced in 1921 in which the nascent community stated, '[a]ltogether they are twelve of us – most of us from the Youth Movement – who have come together for the *common task*' (Eberhard Arnold 1976a, 13, italics in original). The depths of the Bruderhof–Youth Movement connection are also shown in the *Sonnerherz Buch* (Sunheart Book; the title is a play on the word Sannerz). This was described by Baum as 'recording the communal life in notes and sketches, from the beginning at Sannerz until the move to the Rhön' (Baum 1998, 275). This book, referred to by both Oved and Baum, contains a good deal of material relating to the Youth Movement, trends within it, and the activities of Arnold and others connected with it. For instance in the book there is a copy of an article from the *Frankfurter Woche* from 13 November 1921 describing 'A Week of the Youth Movement' organised by a Youth Bookshop. One event in this week was a session in which lectures were given by Wilhelm Stählin and Eberhard Arnold on issues facing the Youth Movement. The book is unpublished, but a typescript copy is located in the library of Yad Tabenkin. In passing, it is worth noting that at around the same time, in Palestine, young people on a kibbutz were producing a similar type of book, later to be seen as a vital document in the history of the Kibbutz: *Kehilatenyu* (*Our Community*).

Two veteran bruderhofers, Sophie Loeber and Hugo Brinkmann, made it clear in discussion on the subject of the Bruderhof and the Youth Movement that for the Bruderhof communities today certain Youth Movement practices are still alive. These practices include the notion of a simple life, especially simplicity in clothing, and closeness to nature. All the Bruderhof's communities are situated in the countryside, and members wear distinct, plain clothing. They suggested that the Hohe Meissner still represents an ongoing inspiration to them.[3] They also suggested that although the fact that the Hitler Youth took certain forms from the Youth Movement may have contaminated its memory for some, this is not the case for the Bruderhof. For instance, Youth Movement songs – some of which are in the songbooks used by the communities for the mealtime singing that is such a joyful part of their life together – still retain their original meaning for the Bruderhof.

Closeness to nature in the countryside can be seen as a point of contact not only between the Bruderhof and the Youth Movement, but also between the Bruderhof and Gustav Landauer, who advocated a move to rural living for socialists. Landauer was, in fact, an important inspiration for Eberhard Arnold and other bruderhofers (see Baum 1998; Oved 1996; Tyldesley 1996). Moreover, Landauer's friend Martin Buber, another figure of some importance for the Youth Movement, especially parts of the Jewish youth movement, was also known to the community, intellectually – as with Landauer – but also personally (see Tyldesley 1994 for details of Bruderhof–Buber interaction).

THE INTEGRIERTE GEMEINDE

The Integrierte Gemeinde (IG) is primarily German, though with some expansion, notably in Tanzania, Italy and recently Austria. The community has rather more than 1,000 members, most of whom live in cities in urban parts of western and southern Germany. The Bruderhof takes a classical 'commune' form, and the same is broadly true of the Kibbutz. However, this is not true of the IG and it is rather more difficult to describe briefly the form taken by its community life than in the other two cases.

The IG is organised around 'table communities', which are groupings of members who eat and talk together very regularly. This is the basic 'cell' (not a term used by the IG) of the movement. The basis for this format is deeply rooted in the theological thought of the IG. The 'cell' forms the basis for the practice of Integration (hence the IG's name), in which members' lives become lived in common. Some of these units are formed in Integration houses. Examples could be found of four- or five-storey premises in Munich, for instance, in which the ground floor might be used for a chemist's shop run by a community member. The next floor might see some surgeries, in which community members who are doctors practise. The remaining floors could be living accommodation and one or perhaps more 'table communities' might be formed from the people living there.

Unlike the Bruderhof, the members of the IG do not surrender their goods upon joining. In fact joining the IG involves a process designed to enable members to become potentially more economically independent than they might otherwise have been. Most of the institutions associated with the IG are actually owned by members, grouped together in some cases and individually in others. As a concrete example, the Integra Co-operative Bank in Munich is seen as a 'community' institution, and is to some extent presented as such (Integrated Community 1996, 232). However, it is legally owned by a society that consists of a number of IG members along with some non-members. Some aspects of the structure of the IG are reminiscent of another communal movement that emerged from the German Youth Movement, the Bund, Gemeinschaft für sozialistisches Leben, as described by Mark Roseman in his book *The Past in Hiding* (Roseman 2001, especially 269–81). The Bund as considered by Roseman appears to have been primarily a Kantian-influenced socialist group with similarities to the Internationaler Sozialistisches Kampfbund discussed in the previous chapter, clearly having a different ideological stance to the IG's Catholicism.

If this starts to make the IG seem like a rather protean and free-floating community, this would be simultaneously a valid and an invalid judgement. The IG does place a very great stress on the freedom of its members to join and stay with the community. The intention is that its members remain only because they are personally committed to the community. The IG is a Roman Catholic community, and this stress on freedom is at least in part a critique of the extent to which the Church has become bound up in the machinery of the German state, and takes money from it through the taxation system. All the activities of the IG are self-financed. The inference would also be invalid, however, because any interaction with the community and its members makes clear that it is bound together very firmly, albeit in sometimes less visible ways than the Bruderhof and the Kibbutz. One of the strongest binding forces is its theology. Theology is discussed by the ordinary members of the community in conjunction with a group of theologians who work in the community. Some are important figures in German Catholic theology and at least one person gave up an academic position at professorial level to work as a theologian in the context of the IG. The community is also bound together by a number of formal local branches which unite several 'table-communities' and which meet regularly – often for discussions of theology. In the IG's stronghold of Munich there are a number of local branches, which we could regard as 'geographical communities', in that they are based upon grouping members who live in given localities.

The IG's connection to the German Youth Movement is via the Catholic youth movement groups that were considered in the last chapter. Specifically, the IG can be seen as a splinter from the Heliand female Catholic youth movement group. The initiative for the founding of what became the IG came from Traudl Wallbrecher (*née* Weiß). In June 1945 she was appointed national leader of Heliand, a position confirmed by election in the spring of 1946. Wallbrecher, a native of Munich, had been a psychology student and a nurse during the war years. She had contacted the Weiße Rose resistance group through her attendance at Professor Kurt Huber's seminars at the University of Munich (Integrated Community 1996, 63). In its own history of the community, the IG comments that Wallbrecher felt that the war had not just destroyed physical things but also the old forms of Christianity. She felt that the way forward that was favoured in Heliand, especially by the older generation of leaders, was to reconstitute the bund as it had been before 1933. She challenged this view, suggesting instead that things had to change radically in the new situation, which, of course, included the knowledge of what had occurred during the rule of the Nazi Party. The result was that Wallbrecher left Heliand in early 1948, with around 50 to 60 members of the bund and the support of a priest, Fr Aloys Goergen, and founded the Junger Bund. This body is the precursor of what was to become the IG (Integrated Community 1996, 64–66). The IG sees the move out of Heliand as the start of a radical departure from the 'old' Youth Movement. This is crucial to understanding the community. It sees itself as a 'new' thing, and most definitely not a continuation of the Youth Movement – even in its Catholic form. This said, certain connections and continuities can be seen between the community and aspects of the Youth Movement.

The first of these derives from the fact that the IG of today is not a female-only group. Over time the Junger Bund moved away from this aspect of its origins. The Junger Bund started to take in male members or participants and Traudl Weiß married Herbert Wallbrecher in October 1949; Herbert Wallbrecher had actually been involved in Junger Bund from the summer of 1948 (Integrated Community 1996, 71). He had been a member of the Neudeutschland Bund, and this was the case with some other male contacts. Hence the IG drew upon not just one but at least two of the bünde of the Catholic youth movement.

The second connection comes through the figure of Romano Guardini. Father Aloys Goergen left the community in October 1968. The IG's own history describes this separation in the following terms:

> [t]wo weeks before Dr Goergen left, Romano Guardini, whom he called his teacher, was buried. By leaving the Community then, Dr Goergen also abandoned Romano Guardini's vision . . . Romano Guardini had been the spiritual mentor of the Catholic youth movement. He knew neither the 'Junger Bund' nor the Community of that time; Dr Goergen had never introduced these to him. (Integrated Community 1996, 96)

Printed opposite these words is an extract from 'The Awakening of the Church in the Soul' (Guardini 1935), cited previously for its importance as an indication of Guardini's attitude to the Youth Movement. The same history of the IG also gives a sequence of quotations from 'clear sighted Christians and Jews'. One of these is from Guardini's *The End of the Modern Age* (Integrated Community 1996, 19). The inference to be drawn from the comment by the IG on Goergen and Guardini is, clearly, that the IG sees itself as embodying Guardini's vision in the present day.

So, while the IG sees itself as having left behind the Youth Movement, the connections can still be seen. Its initial founders – Herbert Wallbrecher is now dead, but Traudl Wallbrecher is still active in a leading role in the IG – were from the Catholic youth movement. This is true in the 'strong' sense of their coming from the sector of Catholic youth that was most influenced by the German Youth Movement. The IG also, despite its view that it has left the Youth Movement behind, still looks to the ideas of Guardini with respect. Clearly, Guardini was a man of many parts – this is clear from Krieg's account (Krieg 1997) – and his connection with the Youth Movement was not the be-all and end-all of his thought and activity. Yet it is an interesting connection for the IG to make in this context.

THE KIBBUTZ

The Kibbutz movement, now entirely located in Israel, is much the most famous of the three movements, and has been examined in many scholarly and other books and articles over the years. In late 1998 there were 267 kibbutzim with 115,000 inhabitants, 2 per cent of the Israeli population. The Kibbutz is, accordingly, much the largest movement to be studied, both absolutely and proportionally vis-à-vis its host community. If the Kibbutz is widely, and correctly, believed to be in a sort of crisis, it is useful to bear in mind that Kibbutz population peaked as recently as 1992, at around 130,000 inhabitants.

The birth of the Kibbutz is much more difficult to be precise about than that of the IG and the Bruderhof. That said, there is a degree of consensus among writers on the movement that the first kibbutz proper was Degania, and that it can be seen as having been a kibbutz from 1910 (Avrahami 1998, 5; Near 1992). There was, in fact, a very complex process of birth of the Kibbutz movement in Ottoman Palestine, and Near's first chapter (Near 1992) provides some detail about the various aspects of collective and communal agricultural life that the Kibbutz emerged from.

Near gives us some pointers as to what constitutes a kibbutz. It is, he suggests, a voluntary body, administered by its members with no legal sanctions, by the methods of direct democracy in a spirit of community and co-operation. The source of authority in the kibbutz is the general (usually weekly) meeting of all the members. Goods and services within the community are provided on a basis of the Marxian formula of 'to each according to their needs'. Like the bruderhofs, then, the kibbutzim are communes. There is a degree of community of goods, and indeed of work, although at a rather less 'total' level than the Bruderhof. The members are, with very few exceptions, Jewish. However, this is for the most part a cultural or national Judaism, not a religious one (Near 1992, 1). The exceptions here are the 17 kibbutzim of the Kibbutz Dati federation – the religious Kibbutz movement – and the two kibbutzim of the Poalei Agudat Israel (Pagi) movement – the ultra-orthodox kibbutzim.

In present times, Near states, the kibbutzim are economically almost all based upon a combination of agriculture and industry. They have evolved an educational system and they are linked through national federations, each of which has political affiliations (Near 1992, 1). The three national federations that Near alludes to are Kibbutz Dati, the religious Kibbutz federation which has connections to the National Religious Party; Kibbutz Artzi, which in 1995 had 84 kibbutzim and which was historically aligned with Mapam (the United Workers' Party), a Marxist-Zionist party now part of the Meretz alliance; and Takam (United Kibbutz Movement), which in 1995 had 166 kibbutzim and had historical ties to the Labour Party. In 2000 Takam and Kibbutz Artzi merged to become the Kibbutz Movement, with the hope that Kibbutz Dati may consider becoming part of this in due course. This merger appears to be a complex process, with swift movement in certain spheres of activity and rather slower movement in others. That said, at the time of writing it appears to be a step that has now been irrevocably taken, and so references to the three federations should be seen in the context of the merging of the two largest in 2000. The three national federations were the products of long-standing historical trends and forces. The Kibbutz has never been ideologically homogeneous in the way that the Bruderhof and IG have; the separate trends may have been intellectually coherent to a greater or lesser extent, but there have always been different ideas within the Kibbutz about the right way for the movement to proceed.

Near's comment on the combination of agriculture and industry points to the traditional role of the kibbutzim as agricultural bastions of Israeli society. This remains a central fact of Kibbutz life; in 1997 38 per cent of Israeli agricultural land was Kibbutz land, on which 27 per cent of the agricultural workforce produced 33 per cent of Israel's agricultural 'value added'. However, the kibbutzim are increasingly also moving into industrial production, with 360 factories and 11 regional corporations employing 30,000 persons forming the Kibbutz industrial sector in 1996. The starting point was, however, agricultural, and Avrahami stated that 'They aspired to a return to nature, to agriculture and physical labor, typical of the "founding fathers", especially in the 2nd and 3rd *Aliya*, which gave the kibbutzim the character of a rural and agricultural settlement, without its members becoming peasants' (Avrahami 1998, 7).[4] It is not only the rise of Kibbutz industry that is changing this historical picture; there has been a recent pattern of formation of 'urban kibbutzim', and this pattern will be examined in a subsequent chapter.

A final point to be aware of is that there are both kibbutznikim who work outside the Kibbutz, and non-members who work on the Kibbutz. In 1998, of 72,000 employed residents of kibbutzim, 11,000 worked outside the Kibbutz; 91,000 were employed in the Kibbutz, two-thirds of whom were kibbutznikim and one-third Israelis not resident in the kibbutzim. The leaflet produced jointly by the Israeli state Central Bureau of Statistics and Yad Tabenkim from which these and the earlier statistics are taken (Central Bureau of Statistics and Yad

Tabenkin 2000) does not make clear the numbers of foreign workers (many young volunteers from countries in West Europe and North America) or what it describes as 'non-Israeli workers from the Judea, Samaria and Gaza areas' who worked on kibbutzim. The phrasing suggests that the 'one-third Israelis not resident in the kibbutzim' could well include Israeli Arabic workers, but not Palestinians from the West Bank (Judea and Samaria) or Gaza.

Avrahami's comment about the aspirations on the part of the early kibbutznikim to return to nature should indicate that there are ideological connections between the Kibbutz and the Youth Movement. Clearly, the major connections will be with the Jewish youth movement in pre-World War II Germany, and in particular the socialist-orientated 'chalutzo-Zionist' formations within that movement.

Before looking at the connections between the Youth Movement and the Kibbutz, however, it is necessary to note the wider context of its birth and development. While the IG can be seen to have emerged from the Catholic youth movement in Munich in 1948, and the Bruderhof's formation in Germany in 1920 in the context of the Neuwerk movement and the Freideutsche Youth is also reasonably clear, the Kibbutz did not solely owe its origins to persons or groups that we can clearly link to the Youth Movement. Near points to the importance of situating the early Kibbutz in the context of the Second Aliya. On this, he argues that the 'men and women of the Second Aliya (1904–1914) came, like their predecessors, mainly from Russia . . . They created the Labour Zionist movement and laid the ideological and structural foundations of the State of Israel. One of those foundations was the kibbutz' (Near 1992, 11). This important passage highlights the fact that the influence of the German Youth Movement on the Kibbutz has to be seen as only one of a number of streams that flowed into the movement. Indeed, Near points to the wide heterogeneity of ideas that were making themselves felt in the Russia of the early years of the twentieth century, where many of the people of the Second Aliya came to maturity (Near 1992, 13).

Near suggests early in his account that two trends in thought were crucial to the Kibbutz: Zionism and socialism (Near 1992, 1–6). The connections of the Kibbutz to Zionism are fairly obvious; from the start they were Jewish communities in Eretz Israel. Regarding socialism, Near commented that the 'principles of the kibbutz are clearly socialist, and despite some terminological disputes all kibbutz members perceived them as such' (Near 1992, 4). However, there are different types of socialism, and there are also different types of Zionism. Near points to the differences within Zionism that arose from the different 'starting points' of the Zionists. Russian Zionism differed from German, and both in turn differed from Polish Zionism. To some extent the same might be said about socialism. All these factors played their part in the make-up of the Kibbutz, and go to make it a much more complex social formation than the IG or the Bruderhof.

A good example of just how difficult it is to be precise about the Kibbutz is to be found in the person seen by many (within and without the Kibbutz) as its spiritual founder: Aaron David Gordon (1856–1922). Gordon became a legendary figure in the Kibbutz, perhaps due to the fact that he left the Ukraine where he had been a 'white-collar' worker in 1903 at the age of 47 to become an agricultural labourer in Palestine, and a member of the Degania kibbutz. Gordon was notable as a thinker about Kibbutz issues, and is associated with the idea of a 'religion of labour', which argued that manual labour in the land of Israel was a necessity for a Jewish national renaissance (Gordon 1938, Ch IV, 'Labor'). Gordon was certainly a Zionist, but as Eliezer Schweid has noted, he took a negative attitude to the state, and especially the institutions of the police and the army.

> It is not surprising, then, that A D Gordon was opposed to the politicization of Zionism . . . and to attempts to establish a state and to form apparatuses anticipating the state. He saw in these attempts a missing of the true purpose of Zionism, which was the regeneration of the Jewish people from its individuals. (Eliezer Schweid, in Gordon and Bloch 1984, 263–64)

In respect of socialism, Near stated the case clearly: 'Gordon himself objected to the term "socialism"' (Near 1992, 213). A reading of Gordon's essay 'Nationalism and Socialism' (Gordon 1938, Ch. III) bears this out (see Baratz 1954, 79–85 for a memoir of Gordon by one of the founders of Degania, the first kibbutz).

Gordon can be seen as opposing one of Near's crucial ideas animating the Kibbutz (socialism) and representing what was historically a very insignificant sub-variety of the other (Zionism); Gordon's Zionism was pacifistic and anti-statist. Most Zionists supported the formation of a Jewish state, though there were important exceptions, but very few other than Gordon were pacifistic. Even this summary of Gordon's views is perhaps over-simplified, because Gordon was vehemently anti-capitalist and late in life came to appreciate the ideas of Gustav Landauer. He returned to Palestine from a convention in Prague in 1920 having, according to Shmuel Hugo Bergman, 'found his ideas' in Landauer's writings (Yassour, nd, 27 fn 20). Landauer will be subsequently shown to have exercised some influence on the Hashomer Hatzair movement in the pre-1924 period. It is probably fair to say that Landauer was not a Zionist, but equally he was not an anti-Zionist. At the very end of his life he engaged in a correspondence with a group of German Socialist Zionists on the subject of communal settlements, and he was, indeed, to have addressed a conference they had called. His murder in 1919 by the Freikorps in the aftermath of the Bavarian Revolution, in which he had played a prominent part, prevented this. (For the letters and background to them see Yassour, nd.)

Part of the ideological ferment and swirl of ideas and movements that contributed to the Kibbutz were undoubtedly derived from the Youth Movement. Near showed that a number of Jewish youth movements from Germany contributed people to the process of Aliya to kibbutzim in the 1920s and 1930s. Members of the early grouping of the Jewish youth movement, Blau-Weiß, did so (Near 1992, 127). The same is also the case with the Jung-Jüdischer Wanderbund (JJWB), the Brith Olim (Near 1992, 127), the Werkleute and the Habonim (Near 1992, 228–30). In more detail, studies have been published which deepen our understanding of this process. A particularly important example is the work by Fölling and Melzer, *Gelebte Jugendträume* (Fölling and Melzer 1989), which examines the life stories of a group of former members of German Jewish youth movements (mainly JJWB) who went to live at Kibbutz Givat Brenner. Similar ground is covered by another former member of the JJWB, Chaim Seeligmann, who is resident at Givat Brenner, where he has lived since 1935. The fifth chapter of his *Spuren einer stillen Revolution* is on the topic of 'The Jewish Youth Movement – a root of the Kibbutzim' (Seeligmann 1998. This book is composed of speeches to the IG, and is published by their publishing house.) In an earlier piece on 'The Jewish Youth Movement and the Kibbutz Movement' he showed why the Jewish youth movement became a root of the Kibbutz, and in so doing shows how this process links in his mind to the wider German Youth Movement:

> Die Jugendbewegung, die sich als Ganzheitsbewegung ansah – hierin war kein Unterschied zwischen der allgemeinen und der jüdischen Jugendbewegung –, versuchte auch im Stadium ihrer Verwirklichung all die Ideen einer umfassenden Lebensform in die Realität umzusetzen. Dieser Gedanke traf sich auch mit der Auffassung der Gründer der Kibbuzbewegung.

> The Youth Movement, which regarded itself as a movement encompassing a totality – in this there was no difference between the general and the Jewish Youth Movement – tried, in the field of its practice, to transplant all the ideas of a comprehensive life form into reality. This thought also met with the understanding of the founders of the Kibbutz movement. (Melzer and Neubauer 1988, 78)

The connections continued in the period of Nazi rule between 1933 and 1938. As Near notes, '[p]aradoxically, the German Zionist youth movements flourished between 1933 and 1938. In line with the Nazi policy of encouraging Jewish emigration they were allowed to continue with their work, though under strict supervision' (Near 1992, 229). Walk observed that the religious chalutz movement– and his account made clear that this was largely a movement of young people – known ideologically as Torah va' Avodah (Torah and Labour) 'achieved its maximum strength under the Nazi regime' (Walk 1961, 236). This period was the focus of a recent book *Nächstes Jahr im Kibbuz*, by Elihayu Kutti Salinger (Salinger 1998), a book rendered especially important by the fact that Salinger was a participant in the events he describes. (He lives today at Kibbutz Kfar Menachem.) Reinharz's account of Hashomer Hatzair in the years 1933 to 1938 is another useful source on the Jewish youth movement (especially its chalutzo-Zionist section) under the

Nazis (Reinharz 1987). After 1938 or so the activity of the Zionist youth movements had to change radically, and some became involved in armed resistance to
the Nazis. In connection with this period, Rich Cohen's *The Avengers* is a moving
account of three Hashomer Hatzair members from Poland (Abba Kovner, Vitka
Kempner and Rushka Marle) and their resistance activities in Lithuania. It also
contains a useful bibliography of material relating to this aspect of the story of
the youth movements. All three survived the war, the subsequent chaos and the
Israeli War of Independence, and lived on kibbutzim in Israel (Cohen 2000).

One of the most interesting aspects of Youth Movement activity in Europe
(this was not confined to the German groups, originating as it did in Poland in
1925) was the kibbutz aliya, or immigrants' kibbutz (Near 1992, 107). These were
kibbutzim in Europe that formed training schools for those intending to go to
Palestine. A well-documented instance of this phenomenon is the Kibbutz Herut
(Herut means freedom in Hebrew). The group from the JJWB/Brith Olim that
went to Kibbutz Givat Brenner in 1926 came from this kibbutz aliya (Near 1992,
127–28). Material on this kibbutz can also be found in Seeligmann (1998, 109),
Fölling and Melzer (1989, 16, 38), and also in Linse (1983, 293–312), who has a
selection of documents on Herut, which was based in Hamelin. Salinger devoted
a section (part 4, section 2) to descriptions of eight such bodies. He calls them
'Hachscharahkibbuzim', or preparation kibbutzim (Salinger 1998, 179–211). He
also included material containing less detailed comments on a number of other
such kibbutzim (Salinger 1998, 148–57. Note that Salinger's discussion is solely
concerned with the years 1933 to 1943.) This phenomenon continued in the post-
World War II period in Britain, where groups (garin) lived communally in order
to prepare to live on kibbutz in Israel. The British section of Hashomer Hatzair
undertook such activities at Bedford between 1946 and 1950, and subsequently
until the mid-1960s at Bishop Stortford. In this case, most participants worked
off the site.[5]

As this account of kibbutz aliya indicates, there were chalutzo-Zionist youth
movements outside Germany. Given the Jewish population level, Poland was a
particularly important area for such movements, with two important movements emerging, at different times, from Galicia: Hashomer Hatzair (Young
Guard) and Gordonia (named after A. D. Gordon). Internationally, perhaps
the most important movement was Hechalutz (the Pioneer), which represented
a mass organisation of a very different type to the rather selective German
bünde. In Germany, Near suggested that it existed as a technical framework
controlled by the JJWB/Brith Olim (Near 1992, 127). Chaim Schatzker's study
of the relations between the Hechalutz and the Youth Movement in the
Holocaust period bears this argument out to some extent (see Schatzker 1988,
132 et seq.). Schatzker's essay provides a very detailed account of Hechalutz
and the youth movements that goes beyond Near's comments. Salinger also
considers the question of 'Bund or Hechalutz?' in the 1933–1943 period
(Salinger 1998, 81–87).

A second way in which the Kibbutz was rooted in the German Youth Movement might be found in the extent to which the non-German chalutzo-Zionist youth movements mentioned above were influenced by its ideas and practice. In some cases one might argue that such an influence did not exist. So, for instance, Near indicates the rejection on the part of the Gordonia youth movement of the idea of youth culture (Near 1992, 122). In this case, however, one might say that though the movement rejected ideas connected with the German Youth Movement, Near's account suggests that aspects of its practice took similar form to Youth Movement practice (Near 1992, 122–25). A much less ambiguous example of an alternative approach is the Hechalutz movement, which differed very markedly in structure and ideology from the Youth Movement (Near 1992, 119–20).

However, Near noted that '[h]istorically, the spread of the Zionist youth movements among central and Western European Jewry is also a function of the influence of the German youth movements such as the Wandervogel and the Blau-Weiss' (Near 1992, 294). Perhaps the best example of this is the Hashomer Hatzair movement, one of the most important of all the chalutzo-Zionist youth movements. Kibbutz Artzi was formed by Hashomer Hatzair, and was organically linked to it throughout its existence; its full name was Hakibbutz Haartzi shel Hashomer Hatzair – the Territorial Kibbutz of the Young Guard (Hashomer Hatzair remains active in both Israel and the diaspora). Hashomer Hatzair was formed in Galicia from a merger of two earlier bodies in 1913 under the name Hashomer, with Hatzair being added in 1919 (Margalit 1969, 29).

A crucial period in the lives of the founders of the Hashomer Hatzair was spent, according to Margalit, in Vienna, as refugees during World War I. (Galicia was in the Hapsburg empire at the time of the war.) While in Vienna the Shomrim (as members were known) came into contact with a number of influences from the Jewish youth movement. They met Blau-Weiß members (Margalit 1969, 31). Interestingly, they also met Siegfried Bernfeld, and participated in activities organised by Bernfeld and his *Jerubaal* circle, including Jewish youth rallies in 1917 and 1918. (Hoffer 1965 gives some excellent background information on the ideas and activity of Siegfried Bernfeld. Philip Lee Utley is presently engaged in writing a biography of this fascinating figure, who became an important psychoanalyst.) In this milieu they came into contact with the ideas of Gustav Wyneken, then, as we have seen, a figure of some note in the German Youth Movement. Although Margalit was at pains to draw distinctions between the Hashomer Hatzair and the Wandervogel – and quite rightly, given the massive differences of background and experience – his overall account tended to suggest that the Shomrim did actually take on board a lot from their interactions with the Youth Movement. Indeed, we might suggest that a clearer periodisation of the Youth Movement might have led Margalit to a more nuanced approach. He notes that it was Wyneken's tendency that they were closest to (Margalit 1969, 31–37). Wyneken's influence was, as we saw, more with the Freideutsche Youth rather than with the Wandervogel. Seen in this light, perhaps we might suggest that the Shomrim need to be seen in terms of interactions with the Freideutsche phase of the Youth Movement. Hashomer Hatzair in fact became active in Germany in the period following 1928, when the first serious efforts were made to spread the movement's ideas there. That said, Reinharz showed that there had been abortive discussions in Danzig in 1923 between the Shomrim and the Blau-Weiß movement about the latter joining Hashomer Hatzair (Reinharz 1986, 175. Reinharz 1986 and Reinharz 1987 taken together form a detailed history of Hashomer Hatzair in Germany from 1928 into the period of the Holocaust.)

Hashomer Hatzair had a period of activity in Great Britain, lasting from its foundation in Britain by refugees from Europe during World War II until around the mid-1970s. It recruited indigenous Jewish youth and at its peak it had around 500 members, with branches in a number of areas including several parts of London, Manchester, Leeds and Liverpool. Shomrim from Britain made aliyah to four kibbutzim in Israel: Hama'Apil, Yasur, Zikim and Nahshonim. The movement in Britain followed the 'Youth for itself' format, and had a very strong scouting side, with a stress on camping and hiking activities embodying a 'Back to nature' ethos. There were connections with the Woodcraft Folk, a still-extant British leftist youth group that was part of a historical splinter from the Scout movement in the post-World War I period that also produced the Kindred of the Kibbo Kift. The Kindred's leader John Hargrave had some influence in the German Youth Movement, and the Folk had also had connections with the German Youth Movement before the Nazi seizure of power. (See Paul 1951 for both the Folk in its early days, and the Kindred. The Kindred left the Scouts in 1920, and the Folk seceded from the Kindred around 1925. A third organisation, the Order of Woodcraft Chivalry, which was part of the 'alternative scouting' world of the Folk and Kindred, started up in 1916, but had not been part of the Scouts. It also had contacts with the German Youth Movement. See Edgell 1992.) There appears to have been a considerable degree of practical communal life in the movement. For example, a group established a commune in Stalybridge, near Manchester, whose members worked in the mining industry. The Shomrim in Britain in the late 1940s and early 1950s also appear to have been fascinated by the Wandervögel. All this activity and thought took place in the context of a fierce commitment to the world movement's political outlook of radical leftism.[6]

The example of Hashomer Hatzair suggests that ideas and practice from the German Youth Movement leached into the non-German Zionist youth movements, often through the medium of the German Jewish youth movement. This even seems to be the case with the Hechalutz in Near's account (Near 1992, 295). So, to conclude, there is a good case for seeing the German Youth Movement as being a significant root of the Kibbutz, although it is clear that it is one root among several: Russian Populism, socialist thinking, ideas from specific types of Zionism being among other obvious intellectual tendencies.

At a practical level the role of all the youth movements, whether Youth Movement-influenced or not, was summed up cogently by Near: by the end of the 1930s 'each movement had become a major source of manpower for a particular kibbutz movement, with a defined political and social ideology' (Near 1992, 296). Interestingly, Near pointed out that '[a] considerable proportion of German immigrants went to the kibbutzim, the majority to the Kibbutz Me'uhad [a precursor of Takam] and the Kibbutz Dati, the religious kibbutz movement' (Near 1992, 230). Regarding Kibbutz Dati, Near has noted that 'the main source of religious pioneers was Germany' (Near 1992, 291). He showed that in 1941, 55 per cent of its members were of German origin, and noted the role of the Bachad movement in Dati's history (Near 1992, 291). This German influence makes Joseph Walk's account of religious pioneering groups in Germany especially interesting, and his account includes useful material on Bachad (Walk 1961).

These, then, are the three movements that will be examined in more detail in the subsequent chapters of this book. In the cases of the Bruderhof and the Integrierte Gemeinde claims about the relationship of the movement to the German Youth Movement (the Bruderhof's claim to a positive and continuing relationship to the spirit of the Youth Movement, the IG's claim to have moved on from the Youth Movement into a 'new thing') are made in the literature of the movements. In the case of the Kibbutz some of the connections between it and the Youth Movement will need to be teased out in a little more detail. However, in general terms, the material presented in this chapter should have served to show that the movements under examination represent to a greater or lesser extent one of the legacies of the German Youth Movement to contemporary society.

INTERCONNECTIONS

It is interesting to consider evidence of interconnection between the movements. The question of Bruderhof–Kibbutz relations has been examined by Professor Yaacov Oved, a kibbutznik and historian. His standard history of the Bruderhof, *The Witness of the Brothers* (Oved 1996), includes material on this question, although his earlier *Distant Brothers* (Oved 1993) brought much of this material together. The IG has a knowledge of the Kibbutz that dates back to a visit to Israel made by Traudl Wallbrecher in 1965, when kibbutzim were visited (Integrated Community 1996, 85). However, in the early 1980s connections between the IG and the Kibbutz on the one hand, and the IG and the Bruderhof on the other, started to blossom. In respect of the Kibbutz, the key figure has been Chaim Seeligmann, who first visited the IG in 1985. Since 1987 he has regularly lectured to the IG, and some of these lectures have been collected and published by the IG (Integrated Community 1996, 119). With regard to the Bruderhof, the first connection came in 1982 when two veteran members of the Bruderhof, Josef Ben Eliezer and Stan Ehrlich, made contact, a process that included a visit to the pump factory at Wangen which is one of the IG's economic enterprises. For some time the IG maintained a base in the USA near to the Woodcrest Bruderhof and a pattern of exchange between the communities followed (Urfelder Kreis 1996, 15).

In the mid-1990s a move towards formalisation of the three-way relationship started with the formation of the Urfeld Circle, named after the village in Bavaria where the IG has some facilities and which was where the first meeting was held in October 1995 (Urfelder Kreis 1996, 3). The Circle consisted of the Bruderhof, the IG and some kibbutznikim. While the two smaller movements appear to have been represented 'officially', the Kibbutz participants appear to have been a group of individuals representing themselves – although coming from quite a spectrum of kibbutzim. (The people mentioned on pp. 10–11 of Urfelder Kreis 1996 include members of the then three main federations – Takam, Dati and Artzi – including members of an urban kibbutz, affiliated to Takam.) By the time of the December 1996 meeting of the Circle, however, the Bruderhof were no longer involved. Indeed, this led to questions at that meeting (Catholic Integrated Community 1997, 3). In the published record of the December 1996 meeting, Arnold Stötzel of the IG did indeed broach the question of the Bruderhof's non-participation, but did so in the form of a biblical comparison with the Rechabites, and a suggestion that, rather like the Rechabites, the Bruderhof distances itself from the world (Catholic Integrated Community 1997, 25–26). This is a viewpoint that the Bruderhof might well dispute, and it does not really give us an indication of what actually occurred in the time between October 1995 and December 1996. Chaim Seeligmann in 1996 suggested that there were, at the time of a recent visit to Europe (20 August–25 September, presumably 1996), difficulties between the IG and the Bruderhof, not least due to strong objections on the part of the IG to the Bruderhof's contacts with the Nation of Islam (Seeligmann 1996).

The meeting with the Nation of Islam (NoI) was reported in the Bruderhof's journal, *The Plough*. To understand this development a sequence of reports in that journal can be considered. In summer 1995 a report appeared about meetings with the Integrierte Gemeinde, with a very positive tone (Arnold and Müller 1995). In November/December 1995, Ruben Ayala of the Bruderhof reported on the recent Million Man March, organised by the NoI, in which he had participated (Ayala 1995). Skipping to the issue of autumn 1996, we find a report of a meeting of the NoI's national organising committee for its 'Day of Atonement' in New York, October 1996 (J. C. Arnold 1996b). Three members of the Bruderhof, including the then Elder, J. C. Arnold, attended this meeting at Louis Farrakhan's request (Farrakhan is the head of the NoI). A result of this was that in the November/December 1996 edition of *The Plough*, a letter appeared from 'Joel D.' of Kibbutz Tsuba in Israel, expressing reservations about the meeting, and suggesting that the NoI and Farrakhan had an anti-Semitic record ('Joel D.' 1996, 4). Some defence of the Bruderhof's position was offered by Miriam Potts in a general letter to Susan Stephens in the same issue. Stephens was questioning a number of positions taken by the Bruderhof, including the meeting with Farrakhan. Of that, it was said that it was only after a lot of discussion that the decision to meet Farrakhan was taken. 'He was calling for a national "Day of Atonement," and as white Americans we felt we had to respond in some way. I personally would do most anything to show my black brothers and sisters that I want to repent for what my race has done and is doing to theirs' (Stephens and Potts 1996, 31). It went on to suggest that the Bruderhof would rather make a mistake in good faith than keep its hands clean and be isolated from what was happening in the world around it.

Whether this was the only factor in the non-appearance of the Bruderhof at later meetings of the Urfeld Circle or not, it might well have been predicted that kibbutznikim would have had concerns, given their perception of the NoI (as shown in Joel D.'s letter), and as will become clearer when the theology of the IG is examined in greater detail, the same is true of the IG. The brief period of three-way unity had ended, and the Urfeld Circle continues, uniting the IG with those in the Kibbutz movement who wish to be involved in an intensive programme of joint discussion and activity with them. (The Circle has acquired premises of its own in Jerusalem.)

NOTES

1   See http://perefound.org/KIT4-5_01.html
2   See http://www.bruderhof.com/news/news35.htm
3   Discussion between Mike Tyldesley, Sophie Loeber and Hugo Brinkmann, Darvell Bruderhof, 17 August 1999.
4   Avrahami's pamphlet was published by the Takam research institute, Yad Tabenkim. Aliya in this context means wave of immigration. The Second Aliya was between 1904 and 1914, the Third between 1918 and 1923.
5   Interview between Mike Tyldesley and David Merron, London, 4 April 2001.
6   Information on Hashomer Hatzair in Britain; Interview between Mike Tyldesley and David Merron, London, 4 April, 2001. Merron was a member of Hashomer Hatzair in Britain from 1948 to 1956 when he went to Kibbutz Zikim.

Chapter 3

'Of One Mind' – The Bruderhof

THE LIFE

In terms of size, a bruderhof is really a communal village rather than a 'communal house' type of commune. A contemporary bruderhof might have in excess of 300 adults and children living on it. Recently, Darvell Bruderhof in East Sussex, England, indicated that it had 303 persons living there, 157 over 18 and 146 under 18 (Bunker et al. 1999, 140). A bruderhof will, accordingly, have a substantial number of buildings, including a number of blocks for accommodation. There will be a large dining room, a central feature of community life; there will be a small factory, informally called the workshop, in which production of Community Playthings educational toys and Rifton products for the disabled will be undertaken; there may also be blocks in which offices connected to the movement's publishing activities will be located, and in which an archive might be maintained. The bruderhof will also have a sewing room and a laundry. A school for the children under 14 years old will also be a feature – at 14 they go to local state schools. A kindergarten and baby house will be another important part of the site, and a large room in which the brotherhood of adult members – male and female – can hold meetings, both practical and religious, the latter being called gemeindestunde, will also be a central focal point. This list does not exhaust the facilities on the site, which might also include libraries for adults and children and other buildings connected with the community's agricultural activities. These are no longer of a commercial nature and are called 'gardening'.

Both the sites in England have had previous occupiers, one being a TB sanatorium and the other a physical education college. The American sites include at least one former hotel. Having said this, the Bruderhof 'customises' its sites, even if only in terms of atmosphere: the buildings are given names drawing upon the movement's history. So, the dining room building at Darvell is the Rhön house, evocatively named in memory of a site that the movement occupied in Germany between 1927 and 1937. The sight of the members around the 'hof' will also make clear to the casual passer-by that something extraordinary is happening: the men tend to wear blue or check shirts with jeans, often black. Many also have beards and braces. The women wear long blue dresses with a white shirt underneath and a polka-dot kerchief on their heads. Pictures and decorations in a naïve artistic style, often depicting flowers and trees, will be evident. The bruderhof has a distinct 'feel' apparent to all.

The Bruderhof has stated that 'the family is the primary unit of our community'. This statement is printed in every issue of the Bruderhof's journal (see, e.g., *The Plough Reader*, winter 2002, 69). The accommodation blocks are divided up to provide homes for the families and the single brothers and sisters composing the community. A large family will have the number of rooms it needs. There is a high proportion of large families in the Bruderhof, not least because of the movement's disapproval of contraception. This is reflected in the figures given earlier for the relative numbers of over- and under-18s living at Darvell.

Despite the importance placed upon the family in the Bruderhof and in its ideology, families actually only eat together at breakfast and on certain days when family meals are scheduled. Most meals are held communally in the dining room. A meal commences with a song and a prayer, and ends with a brief prayer. While the meal is eaten, a brother reads to the community. Sometimes this takes the form of a digest of world affairs for the assembly. The community generally does not use television or video. Radios and newspapers are not entirely absent, but my impression is that the bulk of members could easily go through life without listening to the radio or reading a newspaper except on rare occasions. These summaries are interesting, lively and comprehensive. The system does mean, however, that there is one main source of news concerning the outside world for members. Mealtimes are often joyous occasions, and when something special is happening in the community, a 'love meal' might be held in which the joyful aspects will be highlighted, with more singing than usual. Bruderhof singing at mealtimes is generally of a very high standard with proper rounds and harmonies being sung with vigour. Although some songs are effectively hymns, the whole effect is about as far from a staid church service as can be imagined.

Cooking is done communally by the sisters, on a rota basis, although food is actually served by the brothers. In like fashion, the sisters undertake the cleaning of the bruderhof. This is true of both the cleaning of the buildings and the cleaning and mending of the community's clothing. The brothers mainly provide the workforce for the workshop. At Darvell this has the proportions of a small to medium-sized factory. A major occupation in the workshop is making high-quality educational toys and equipment from maple wood, under the Community Playthings brand name. It is fair to say that the brand has a quite high level of penetration into its market in Britain, which is largely primary and infant schools. However, if one is tempted to imagine a group of quaintly dressed men doing artisanal-style woodwork, one could not be much further from the truth. The workshop uses some extremely well-thought-out systems to make many of the tasks fairly straightforward and easily learned by guests. Visitors to the community are expected to work while at the site, men working in the workshop with the brothers and women with the sisters. The workshop also utilises Japanese-style 'Just in Time' organisational systems, and there is a degree of computerisation in the factory.

The workshop also produces the Rifton line of products for the disabled. These also appear to be a successful enterprise, and the community has developed a system for their use called MOVE in conjunction with professionals in the field from outside the community. Taken together, Community Playthings and Rifton are the major source of income for the community, although it does have some other money-making enterprises such as Rifton Aviation Services, a corporate aviation business that it owns. This is a substantial enterprise, with a major facility at Stewart International Airport in New York State.[1] If a large number of orders for Community Playthings or Rifton products come in at a specific time then a 'work push' will ensue, in which all the adult community (male and female) will work hard to ensure that orders are met on time. This can involve the members getting into the factory at around 5.00am if needed. The Kibbutz of the 1950s and 1960s had a similar system, called giyusim, or mobilisations (Merron 1999, 149).

The working day at the bruderhof is strongly structured. Work commences early – around 7.30am the brothers will be in the workshop, and the sisters leave domestic tasks at around 8.00am to go to their places of work. Mid-morning snacks form an important social feature of the day, especially for the brothers, because it is hard to talk in the workshop over the sound of the machinery; this is rather less a problem for the sisters. After the lunch break there is a period of time away from work, when parents can be with their children. This is a legacy of the time the community spent in Paraguay, when the heat of the mid-day sun dictated a siesta. The afternoon is spent at work, and after the evening meal various different activities are pursued: brotherhood meeting, play rehearsals, music practice, sport. Most members will be in bed early in order to be up and ready for work the next day. Weekends vary: brothers work on Saturday mornings but not afternoons. There are household religious meetings on Sundays.

Aside from the strong structure to the day and week, the year is also structured. Advent and Easter are particularly important in this respect, and are taken extremely seriously within the community. The family is the primary unit of the community, but the foregoing indicates that much of the life of the community is strongly focused on the community as a whole. Eating and working are communal activities. The children in effect form cohorts that grow up together, working their way through the kindergarten and school. For the young and unmarried people at the community there is a 'shalom' group in which they meet.

The Bruderhof as a whole is also, in principle, a church. It is founded on the notion that the accounts given of the early Christian Church in the New Testament – and especially the Acts of the Apostles – indicate that the normal form of a Christian church is communal. To be a member of the Bruderhof is to be a member of this church. Prospective members may, after hearing about the

Bruderhof, ask to visit a community. This presents no problem; visitors are welcome at all the sites. If a visitor comes to feel that this is the life that they are called to then a lengthy visit of perhaps a year or six months might ensue. If the prospective member is still convinced that this is the life to which they wish to dedicate themselves, they can ask to become a novice member. After a period in the novitiate, during which they start to participate in the more formal aspects of the life of the community, they may become part of a baptism preparation group. These groups are intensive study groups which go away from the community for a short period of perhaps a week or two to prepare for the step they are about to take. At the end of this process the prospective member may join the community, at this point surrendering all goods and monies to the community. As a member, she or he may participate in brotherhood meetings, both those that deal with the running of the community and the gemeindestunde worship meetings.

The church has a hierarchy. Most importantly at the level of the community there is a minister, indeed probably more than one in any given community, although one will be senior, called the Servant of the Word. The name derives from the Hutterite name for a minister, and seems to have been adopted at the time of the uniting with the Hutterites in the early 1930s. Above the Servants in the hierarchy is the Elder. There is one Elder for the whole Bruderhof. Before Johann Christoph Arnold's accession in 1983 his father, Heinrich (Heini) Arnold held the position. These are grandson and son, respectively, of the co-founder of the Bruderhof, Eberhard Arnold. (The other main co-founders were Arnold's wife Emmy, née Von Hollander, and her sister Else Von Hollander.) The Bruderhof would regard the characterisation of the Servants and Elder as a hierarchy as deeply problematic. For them, the Servants and the Elder are men who serve the community. They do lead it, but this is presented as a burden laid upon them rather than an accretion of power. Heini Arnold argued

> [a]ny true service done for the church – including the service of leadership – is done as by an organ of the body, and it must therefore be done lovingly, sincerely, honestly and in a childlike way. Someone who carries a responsibility is no higher than someone who does not: no one is higher, and no one is lower. We are all members of one body. (J. H. Arnold 1994, 106)

He also argued that a 'true Christian church cannot be a living organism unless there is clear leadership' (J. H. Arnold 1994, 106). It is certainly true that in the community's stormy history many Servants have lost their positions and may well have rued ever having been raised to the post.

The brotherhood does not operate democratically; rather, it operates on the basis of unanimity. For a decision to be taken unanimous agreement has to be secured at a brotherhood meeting. Unanimity has, for the Bruderhof, a spiritual significance that is also of importance. A member who has an unresolved issue with another member should not attend the gemeindestunde service. There, a united circle waits for the spirit to descend should it have the grace to do so. If the spirit descends, then the community may, for a time, be given the grace of actually being a spirit-led community. For this to happen, God alone can be responsible. True community is not the result of any human act. A united brotherhood is only a prerequisite of community, it is not community as such. One way in which unity can be approached is to adhere to the First Law in Sannerz, Sannerz being the first site of the community in Germany between 1920 and 1927. This law, written by Eberhard Arnold in August 1925, states:

> There is no law but that of *love*. Love is *joy* in others. What then is anger at them?
>
> If we have joy in our brothers and sisters, we will pass it on in words of love. *Words of anger* and worry about members of the Brotherhood are *out of the question*. In Sannerz there must *never* be talk, either open or hidden, against a brother or sister, against their peculiarities and *under no circumstances behind their back. Talking in one's own family is no exception.*
>
> Without the commandment of silence there is no faithfulness and thus no community. The only way is to do the straightforwardly brotherly service of *admonition* to the one whose weaknesses cause something in us to react. Open and *direct admonition* brings a deepening of friendship and will not be resented. Only when the two cannot find each other's hearts in this direct manner is it necessary to draw in a third person who can be trusted to lead to a solution that unites them in the highest and deepest things.
>
> Each household member should hang up a copy of this warning *at his place of work* where he can always see it. (E. Arnold 1976a, 48–49, all italics in original)

Should a member run into the sort of difficulties that are envisaged by the First Law, then ultimately they may end up outside the community. This is a difficult issue, because at baptism new members make vows that are considered as binding for life. To break the vows is an extremely serious step. The result is that persons may be asked (or indeed, told) to leave the community. It is perhaps worth examining two examples of this use of church discipline. Both can be found in the official Bruderhof history of the years from the mid-1950s to the mid-1970s, *Torches Rekindled* (Mow 1991). The first example is that of Hans Zumpe. Zumpe, Eberhard Arnold's son-in-law, had been a key figure in the Bruderhof following the death of Eberhard Arnold in 1935. In June 1960 it was discovered that Zumpe had been living in adultery for some time. This constituted a major problem in the Bruderhof's eyes. Mow continued by noting that 'it was impossible to come to church discipline and forgiveness because his attitude was not one of repentance but even one of resistance . . . In the following years there were many attempts to reach out to him by letter, by phone and by visits. He was asked to seek repentance in order to find reconciliation but he never did' (Mow 1991,

150–51). What Mow did not state but rather implied is that Zumpe was actually expelled from the community, although with the possibility of a return in certain circumstances. It should be said that aspects of Mow's account have been vigorously challenged by Zumpe's daughter (see Bohlken-Zumpe 1993).

A more dramatic example of church discipline is to be found in the 'Great Crisis' of 1961. At the start of the crisis there were 10 bruderhofs in the USA, England, Germany and Paraguay. By 1966 there were three bruderhofs left in the northeast USA. The crisis shows that church discipline may, in an extreme situation, result in many people being expelled from the community. Mow argued that a 'concern about people being sent away grew out of the terrible anguish of the hour' (Mow 1991, 169). One aspect of this concern may have been the numbers involved. Oved suggests that at the end of the 1950s around 1,700 people lived on the movement's 10 bruderhofs (Oved 1996, 207). As a result of the crisis Oved noted that 'there were some 600 people who were asked to "exclude" themselves or who chose to leave of their own volition' (Oved 1996, 231). This episode, regardless of the rights and wrongs surrounding it, serves to show that the Bruderhof is prepared to go to considerable lengths in the pursuit of church discipline when it is convinced that it is necessary.

The combination of the surrender of goods on joining the Bruderhof and the pursuit of church discipline, as detailed here, might be seen as being likely to result in a degree of social conformism within the movement. The example of 1961 shows that the consequences of not remaining in unity with the rest of the brotherhood can be very hard, and this is especially the case given that members no longer have any material resources to fall back upon.

HISTORY

The Bruderhof is a disciplined church-community in which all goods are held in common. No one owns anything and no one holds any money. If someone is leaving the site for any reason, then they have to obtain any cash they may require from the communal treasury. The life of the community reflects in its view the vision that Eberhard Arnold developed in the period around the end of World War I, when he moved from being a conventional, bourgeois Christian (secretary of the German Student Christians) to his new brand of radical Christian communism. The Bruderhof today is very much the product of its history. This is true even down to the details of its daily schedule and practice. Some of the older members who lived in Paraguay with the movement still drink Yerba Mate tea.

The Bruderhof emerged from conferences and debates that were going on in the nascent Neuwerk Christian socialist youth group and also from discussion meetings that had been held by the Arnolds at their house in Berlin (Emmy Arnold, 1999, Ch. 3). The Bruderhof's own view is that in certain respects it really started in 1907, the year that Eberhard Arnold first met Emmy Von Hollander.

Hence, Heini Arnold: 'I ask myself constantly: How was it possible for this community, founded in Christ, as represented as early as 1907 by Opa, Oma, and Tata, to develop that way and to be so thoroughly twisted into the opposite?' (Mow 1991, 309. Opa, Oma and Tata are Eberhard Arnold, Emmy Arnold and Else Von Hollander respectively.) The actual beginning of the community came in summer 1920, when a start was made in Sannerz, a village in Hesse. This was close to other activities of a like tendency, such as the group around Georg Flemmig in Schlüctern, and the Habertshof Neuwerk community at Elm. It could, however, be suggested that 1920 was a false start, because by the summer of 1922 the majority of full members no longer wished to continue and Eberhard Arnold's group of those who wished to carry on was a rump of seven out of the 23 full members (see Baum 1998, Ch. 9 for the story of this first crisis). Of the seven who restarted the community in October 1922, four were from the Arnold family circle: Eberhard and Emmy, along with Emmy's sisters Else and Monika Von Hollander (Baum 1998, 140).

The renewed Bruderhof continued its witness for a Christian communism, with publishing activities continuing despite the split with Neuwerk. In the place of *Das Neue Werk* the community had access to the pages of *Die Wegwarte*, and in the place of the Neuwerk publishing house the community had the Eberhard Arnold publishing house. In 1924 the community was involved in a struggle with what it regarded as the demonic possession of a 16-year-old female living in the community, Lotte Henze. As Baum noted, this was the only occasion that Arnold spoke of demonic possession (Baum 1998, 165). Baum's account indicated a degree of success in this struggle. However, Emmy Arnold noted that although the problems did not recur while Lotte was at the Bruderhof, she actually left the community after a year or so. She subsequently visited the community and was later imprisoned by the Nazis in a concentration camp because of her communist activities (Emmy Arnold 1999, 82). Both Baum and Emmy Arnold pointed to the similarities of the Henze case with that of the 1842 Gottliebin Dittus case, in which Johann Christoph Blumhardt faced a similar struggle with demonic possession. Both showed that the Blumhardt example was in Eberhard Arnold's mind at this time, quoting reports by Eberhard Arnold in which the Blumhardts are named (Baum 1998, 165; Emmy Arnold 1999, 80).

At this point it is worth considering the Blumhardt connection. When Eberhard Arnold wrote his last letter to the community he mentioned the Youth Movement, the Hutterites and the attitude of faith of the two Blumhardts in connection with the movement's future. The two Blumhardts were father, Johann Christoph (1805–1880), and son, Christoph Friedrich (1842–1919). The elder was pastor of Möttlingen in the Black Forest area of Germany until 1852, when he moved to Bad Boll in Baden Würrtemburg. Christoph Friedrich followed his father as pastor at Bad Boll, until he was forced out of the state church after becoming a Social Democratic Party representative in the Baden Würrtemburg state parliament in 1900. At this time the Social Democratic Party was a Marxist party, and it was extremely unusual for a pastor even to be a party member. The younger Blumhardt was seen as an inspiration by the Swiss Religious Socialist Leonhard Ragaz, who produced a book of selections from the Blumhardts. A number of books on Blumhardt themes came from followers of Ragaz, including Robert Lejeune's *Christoph Blumhardt und seine Botschaft*, translated into English and published by the Bruderhof (Lejeune 1963). The Blumhardts were also an inspiration for the twentieth-century giant of Protestant theology, Karl Barth (Gorringe 1999, esp. 28–30). Hermann Hesse, an important figure for many in the Youth Movement, was taken to Bad Boll when a child to be helped by Christoph Blumhardt (Freedman 1979, 46–47). The Bruderhof has attempted to ensure that the works of the Blumhardts are available to English-speaking readers, most recently with the publication of *Action in Waiting* (Blumhardt 1998), a substantial new collection of translated sermons by Christoph Blumhardt. In the following year an extract from Friedrich Zuendel's biography of the elder Blumhardt was published, *The Awakening* (Zuendel 1999), which deals specifically with the Gottliebin Dittus affair.

In 1927 the Sannerz period ended with a move to the Rhön Bruderhof in Fulda, a few miles to the northeast. The Bruderhof had been aware of the continued existence of the Hutterian Brethren communal movement of North America from early 1921 (Baum 1998, 134), and the next crucial step in the life of the Bruderhof was the decision to seek contact with them. Baum shows that a letter starting this process was sent in 1928 (Baum 1998, p. 189). Following some exchanges, Eberhard Arnold set out to visit the Hutterian Brethren in late May 1930. The story of this visit (which also took in some contacts with the Doukhobours, who did not impress Arnold) has been told in the histories of the movement (Baum 1998; Emmy Arnold 1999). There is also a book, *Brothers Unite* (Hutterian Brethren 1988), which includes documents such as letters exchanged between the Bruderhof and the Hutterians, and Arnold's diary of the time in North America, along with letters and telegrams between Arnold and the Bruderhof in Germany. Arnold visited Hutterian bruderhofs (the word bruderhof is originally Hutterian) in South Dakota, Manitoba and Alberta. By the end of the journey Arnold had achieved one of his goals: he was ordained by the Hutterian Brethren and the Bruderhof was accepted as part of the Hutterian Brethren. Another goal was not achieved: there had been a hope that the uniting with the Hutterians would be accompanied by financial donations from them. However, as Baum put it, '[o]nly a fraction of the hoped-for twenty-five thousand dollars – the sum needed to pay off debts and further build up the Rhön Bruderhof – had been collected' (Baum 1998, 203).

Regardless of the financial issue, the important fact was that the Bruderhof became part of the Hutterian Brethren. This has been a relationship that has marked the movement's history ever since. The unity lasted until 1955, breaking under the impact of a damaging dispute involving the Forest River (Hutterian) Bruderhof, after a shaky period of about six years. It was revived in 1974, then lapsed again in a rather messy process lasting from 1990 (when two of the three Hutterian conferences, the Darius- and Lehrer-leuts, revoked the unity) to 1995, when the Bruderhof itself published a strongly worded statement about the Hutterians that effectively ended their link with the divided third conference, the Schmiede-leut (see Hofer 1998, 131–40, for an account of this that takes a pro-Hutterian viewpoint. For the Bruderhof's statement see J. C. Arnold 1995. Hofer's book is an interesting, non-academic introduction to the Hutterian Brethren.)

The next major challenge in the Bruderhof's history was the Nazi seizure of power in 1933. The Bruderhof's Christian principles resulted in conflict with the new regime, and in time it left Germany. The new site for the Bruderhof was England, where it settled close to Ashton Keynes, near Swindon, at the Cotswold Bruderhof established in 1937. The period of emigration (which included a spell during which the movement had a site in Lichtenstein as well as the Rhön Bruderhof) occurred immediately after the death of the leader of the community, Eberhard Arnold, in 1935 during a leg operation. The Bruderhof had two years, between 1937 and 1939, in England before the outbreak of World War II. At this time, and indeed into the period of the war, the movement's absolute pacifism caused it to become a 'magnet' for members of the large English pacifist movement of the time, the Peace Pledge Union (PPU). The PPU had seen an upsurge in interest in the idea of life in community, and some elements of this upsurge translated into an increased English membership (there had been English members in the Rhön period).

World War II presented problems for the Bruderhof. These can be summed up as pacifism and German nationality. English male members could potentially be called up to the forces. They would thus have had to obtain conscientious objector status. This was a difficulty, although far from insuperable. A large proportion of the Bruderhof's membership was German. In the conditions of the time the Bruderhof decided that, as its German members were in imminent danger of internment as enemy aliens, it would leave Britain (Durnbaugh 1991, 71). Cutting a long and complicated story short, between November 1940 and May 1941 the community successfully relocated to Paraguay. Not quite all left, however. Three members were left behind to complete the winding-up process. Pacifists and seekers after Christian community continued to arrive at Ashton Keynes, and the result was that in March 1942 a bruderhof was started in Shropshire, the Wheathill Bruderhof, which, as Durnbaugh points out, by 1952 had 200 members (Durnbaugh 1991, 75).

The period following 1941, however, saw the bulk of the movement living in Paraguay, in the Chaco area. Durnbaugh usefully summarises the situation. In effect three colonies made up the overall settlement, known as Primavera ('Springtime'). These were Isla Margarita, the first of the colonies, then Loma Hoby, started in 1942, and finally Ibate, opened in 1946. By 1953 there were 700 people living in the Primavera settlement. There was a hospital, which was used by neighbouring Indians, and agricultural enterprises, including timber and farming (Durnbaugh 1991, 74–75). At this stage the Primavera settlement was the centre of the movement.

This situation was not to last very long. In 1954 a bruderhof was started in New York state. This was the Woodcrest Bruderhof, at Rifton. This is now the longest established bruderhof, and is the 'spiritual home' of the movement. By 1956 Woodcrest had 150 members and by 1958 two more communities had been formed in the northeast USA: New Meadow Run in Pennsylvania (still inhabited today, but initially called Oak Lake) and a site in Connecticut called Evergreen and later Deer Spring, now closed (Durnbaugh 1991, 75–76). In addition, a second English site, Bulstrode, was started in 1958; an attempt to revive the movement in Germany was made at the Sinnthalhof in 1956; and between 1952 and 1960 there was a site in Uraguay, El Arado ('The Plough').

It could be suggested that the movement had weathered the undoubted dislocation forced upon it in 1941 with the move to Paraguay. By the late 1950s, at the height of its expansion, it was a substantial movement spread over three continents with ten bruderhofs. It was at just this point that the movement went into its most profound crisis. As already indicated, the crisis of 1961 resulted, at least in Oved's estimation, in the loss of 600 of the Bruderhof's then population of 1,700. It also resulted a little later in a brief period in which the movement retrenched on three sites fairly close to one another in the northeast USA.

THE CRISIS

It is extremely difficult to state adequately what the crisis in the Bruderhof was actually about. It might be suggested that the crisis has been perceived by the 'winners' and 'losers' as actually being about different things, so varied are their accounts on questions of fact, motivation and even outcome. Probably the best guide to the complexities of the crisis is to be found in Yaacov Oved's account of it in his history of the movement, *The Witness of the Brothers* (Oved 1996, Ch. 8). Oved provides a guide to the swirling currents of the crisis that draws upon both contemporary Bruderhof sources and sources that represent the viewpoint of some of those who left the community. His account suggests that there were a number of factors causing complications in the movement at the time. Finance was one issue. Whereas the Paraguayan bruderhofs had never really been financially viable, and the movement had depended upon donations and assistance for their upkeep, the North American communities were doing well economically, especially after the Woodcrest community acquired the Community Playthings brand. Oved suggests that there may have been elements of ethnic tensions in the communities. This is a complex issue: broadly there seems to have been a division between 'warm-hearted' Germans and Americans and 'cold-hearted' English. However, this may not have been mainly a question of national background so much as a question of ideology. The Americans were under the influence of Heini

Arnold, Servant of the Word at Woodcrest from February 1955, and it is perhaps as a result of that rather than national questions that the problems with the English arose. The English members who did get into this conflict (and it is by no means all of them, just as all the Germans did not line up behind Heini Arnold) came to be perceived by their opponents as insufficiently Christocentric, and still mired in the liberal and humanistic ideas they held in the pre-World War II period when they had been pacifists.

Oved also suggests that there were conflicts among the leading figures in the Bruderhof that became evident in the late 1950s. Oved points to the roles of the sons of Eberhard Arnold – Hans-Hermann, Hardy and Heini – on the one hand, along with that of his sons-in-law – Hans Zumpe and Balz Trümpi – on the other. Oved also indicates that there were a series of disputes going back to the period following Eberhard Arnold's death and extending into the early Paraguayan years, in which questions of the legacy of Eberhard Arnold to the movement and the role of his sons in it played their part. It is clear from his account that not everyone in the movement regarded Eberhard Arnold and his sons in a positive light. His sons had suffered exclusion from the community in the 1940s, Heini for two years (Oved 1996, 136). Issues such as these seem also to have played a part.

The Bruderhof today regards the 1961 split as an unfortunate but necessary process. The community had departed from the path of Christian community and moved towards liberal humanism. Heini Arnold, along with others including his wife and his mother, helped to overcome this direction. As Mow put it, 'from 1935 onward . . . a direction contrary to Eberhard Arnold's was brought into the communities, and . . . Heini and Annemarie and Emmy and a number of others kept in their hearts and also fought for a restoration of the vision and love to Jesus that Eberhard had represented and had been given by God' (Mow 1991, 161). Mow's account also includes the following statement, which presents the current Bruderhof viewpoint very clearly:

> [o]n this earth there is always a spiritual struggle going on; *the two atmospheres are always in conflict.* It is essentially the atmosphere that matters, not individuals, even where it has been necessary to use names to avoid confusion. There is a spirit in this world that wants to destroy the brotherly life based on love to Jesus, and that spirit wants to destroy it right now, right here among us. Every one of us has the responsibility to seek that love through which we may live the first commandment 'to love God' and the second commandment 'to love the brothers.' Then the brotherly life can be lived, and this is what we seek together. (Mow 1991, 124–25, italics in original)

In this context, the crisis was an inevitable, necessary and ultimately positive thing, although Mow's account indicates that the Bruderhof now acknowledges that some things may have happened that should not have happened.

How is the crisis viewed by some of those who are no longer in the Bruderhof? A clear view was given by Robert Peck, an American who joined the movement in its Paraguayan phase, which he sees in a very positive light. He states that

> [m]y thesis . . . is that during its healthy period the Bruderhof united many people of different persuasions into one warm-hearted, broad-minded community of a broad Christian faith, and that because of narrow-minded overzealousness and a power struggle the emphasis turned to a particular expression of a particular kind of religious experience and faith, resulting in a closed-minded, fear-dominated community. (Peck 1987, 112)

Peck argues that the Paraguayan communities responded to some questions from the American communities by looking for the roots of a problem.

> The community indulged in a several-year-long orgy of navel gazing. During the confusion one of the founder's sons was raised to virtual sainthood status in the resuscitation of a decades old leadership struggle. He was backed by a number of recent American converts, who with the overzealousness of the newly converted represented a narrow-minded evangelical strain sometimes found in American Protestantism. (Peck 1987, 121)

Peck suggests that in Christian communities it is difficult to resist the accusations of one claiming to wield a sword in the name of Jesus, and that it was equally difficult to resist the claim that the community had retreated from its origins and must return to them. It is quite clear that the son that Peck refers to is Heini Arnold. Peck presents the crisis as a combination of Heini Arnold switching the direction of the movement from, in Peck's terms, broad-minded Christianity to narrow-minded Christianity, and also taking the chance to settle some old scores in a power play. Perhaps there is a little common ground shared by Mow and Peck, inasmuch as both indicate that the crisis represented a shift in viewpoint. What for Mow was a shift away from a non-Christocentric approach represented a shift to a narrow-minded approach for Peck.

The crisis has shaped the Bruderhof ever since, for fairly obvious reasons. After the initial retrenchment, the movement gradually expanded again. A site was opened in England in 1971, the Darvell Bruderhof. This was followed by the formation of further American sites in the 1980s and early 1990s. There was an abortive effort in Germany between 1989 and 1995, the Michaelshof. Around the time the Michaelshof shut, a second English bruderhof, Beech Grove, opened. Finally, we should note a brief venture in Africa, at Palm Grove in Nigeria between 1992 and 1994, when unity was sought with an indigenous Christian group, and the current efforts in Australia. The Bruderhof has now apparently expanded its membership beyond the numbers it had in the late 1950s.

In the current phase of its activities, the charge levelled at it by the Integrierte Gemeinde, namely 'Rechabitism' or withdrawal from the world, seems to be wide of the mark. The movement's journal, *The Plough Reader* (formerly *The Plough*), contains articles about issues that the movement has been concerned with in recent years, generally called 'Peace and Justice' issues in Christian circles. The radical leftist tenor of much that is in the journal attracts some unfavourable readers' letters. However, the contents reflect an increased willingness on the part of the movement to get involved in campaigning around social issues, notably war and peace and also the death penalty in the USA. This is even more true, perhaps, of the youth magazine that was connected with the Bruderhof movement, *blu*. This was started in 1998, closing in mid-2001, apparently for financial reasons.[2] It was notable for featuring a large amount of material on Third World issues, along with stories about struggles involving African-Americans, Hispanic Americans and First Nation Americans. Each issue came with a CD. These tended to feature hip-hop bands, including some with interesting affiliations. The CD for number six includes a track from the Poor Righteous Teachers, a band having connections with the Five Percent Nation, a splinter from the Nation of Islam (Neal 1999, 170). The Bruderhof has also been prominent in the campaign to free Mumia Abu Jamal, a Philadelphia activist currently under sentence of death. Jamal is connected to the Move group in Philadelphia, which espouses a distinctly non-Christian religious viewpoint. Indeed, it is notable that in recent years the Bruderhof's journals have published material indicating connections with non-Christian groups. Christopher Zimmerman wrote a report of a visit to the French Plum Village Buddhist community which presented that community in a very positive light (Zimmerman 1998). Subsequently, the community put a book by the founder of that Buddhist community on sale in its magazine-catalogue (*Love in Action*, by Thich Nhat Hanh. See *The Plough Reader*, fall 1999, 11). This does, perhaps, suggest that some caution is required in assessing the arguments put forward by Peck. It seems unlikely that a straightforwardly fundamentalist or 'narrow-minded' Christian movement would take these kinds of steps.

PATTERNS IN BRUDERHOF HISTORY

The Bruderhof's history has been a stormy and interesting one. With Mow's perspective on the sources of struggle within the movement still appearing to represent the thinking of the Bruderhof, it must continue to expect storms and stress in the years to come. To pull this discussion together, it is worth considering efforts to 'periodise' this history. Does it exhibit any sort of pattern, and if so how can the pattern be characterised? Both Mow and at least one external commentator have seen a pattern.

There is an implicit periodisation in Mow's account. It can be extrapolated as follows: the spirit inspired the founding generation of the Bruderhof, but after the death of Eberhard Arnold a counter-tendency (of an evil, spiritual nature) set in and gradually took hold. The spirit inspired, in its turn, a movement against this distortion. The 'atmospheres' came into conflict and – due ultimately to grace, not human action – the original spirit of the movement won out in the great crisis. This presents a three-stage history: roughly, 1920–1935, 1935–1961, and 1961 to the present day. A text distributed by the Bruderhof, but written by a non-member, gives a useful characterisation of the 'middle period' as seen by the Bruderhof today.

> Jesus Christ as the center point, decision-making through consultation with the Bible, and the leading of the community through the Holy Spirit, all fell more and more into the background. Instead, the community became an ideal for its own sake. Less and less did spiritual unity and consensus determine the course. A democratic majority began to take control. (Eggers 1988, 153)

In his account Mow makes comments such as this: 'every one of us has to decide whether he is on the side of Jesus and of love and compassion that give clarity to discern and find the way, or whether he is on the side of power, efficiency, gifts, or anything that misleads us into a crisis situation' (Mow 1991, 169). It is evident from what has been seen of, for instance, Robert Peck's account that some among the 600 who left the movement in 1961 felt that they were in the former, rather than the latter camp. The subtitle of Mow's book, 'The Bruderhof's Struggle for Renewal' indicates the implicit periodisation that Mow imposes on the movement's history.

By contrast, Benjamin Zablocki's book, *The Joyful Community* (Zablocki 1980), is the best-known academic study of the Bruderhof. Zablocki, in his second chapter, offers a periodisation which, rather than referring to spiritual issues in the way that Mow's does, refers instead to sociological categories. In particular, his approach is informed by the thinking of Ferdinand Tönnies, and more strongly, that of Herman Schmalenbach, whose concept of 'communion' (Bund in the original German) is especially important to his account. Zablocki offers a seven-stage periodisation in which there is a movement from 'communion' to 'church community'.

Zablocki suggests that the first stage, communion, lasted from 1920 to 1926. These were the Sannerz years, which Zablocki suggests were characterised by spontaneity rather than structure, and in which life had 'a certain funky quality' (Zablocki 1980, 73). The next stage Zablocki calls Charismatic community, and he dates it from 1926 to 1935. These were mainly the Rhön years, although the cut-off point is the death of Eberhard Arnold. In this stage structurally things got tighter; distinctions between members and guests became more marked, meetings were restricted to full members and so forth. Also, the movement grew beyond the immediate circle of the Arnold family, and this period, according to Zablocki, saw the introduction of elements of a division of labour. The quality of life changed too: 'Life at Rhön was quieter, more serious, more subdued than it had been at Sannerz' (Zablocki 1980, 74). This was not because people were ageing; rather it was because the movement was growing out of the communion phase. This was the period in which the Hutterian link was made, and the adoption of Hutterian forms is seen by Zablocki as a counterpoise to the spontaneity of the Youth Movement traditions, and of help in preserving the community in the years after Eberhard Arnold's death.

The next period according to Zablocki was one of 'Transitional Community', between 1935 and 1941. This was the period in which the Bruderhof relocated from Germany to England, and which followed hard on the heels of the death of Eberhard Arnold. It was, accordingly, a period in which the major task for the community was to hold together and survive, despite any differences within the movement and its leadership. Zablocki suggests that the Hutterian forms (such as the designation of Servants of the Word) ensured that there were executive roles of a formal nature and that this was crucial to enabling a collective leadership to grow up. The next phase was that of 'Isolated Sect', the first part of the Paraguayan years, 1941 to 1950. Zablocki argues that this period saw the forging of a 'people' out of a disparate group of folk – rather like the forty years in the wilderness for the Israelites. He noted an increase from 350 to 600 inhabitants of the Primavera colonies between 1941 and 1950, almost entirely accounted for by new babies. This shows the sheer isolation of the movement at this time. Zablocki argues that it was in this stage that English emerged as the language of the community (Zablocki 1980, 85). Zablocki also notes that the daily routine of the Bruderhof evolved early in the Paraguayan years, and had changed little by the time he was writing, in the early 1970s (Zablocki 1980, 88. The first edition of Zablocki's book appeared in 1971.)

Between 1950 and 1958, following a dispute with the Hutterians on some points of church order, Zablocki suggests that the Bruderhof was a 'Communitarian Social Movement'. For Zablocki, this was a period of liberalisation and expansion. This was the period in which the movement expanded into North America for the first time. Although Zablocki points to much that was achieved in the way of outreach – the holding of youth conferences, the sheer numbers of people visiting Woodcrest – he also suggests that there was a growth in tensions, especially after the relaxation of some of the Hutterian forms. Zablocki's sixth phase was the 'Years of Crisis and Schism' between 1959 and 1962. Other than points already considered, it is worth noting two comments made by Zablocki. First, he argues that there was no real leadership left in Primavera at the time of the crisis. Competent leaders had tended to drift to assignments in the Northern Hemisphere. Second, he suggests that the younger generation at Primavera tended to support Woodcrest (for both points, Zablocki 1980, 107).

Zablocki's final phase is 1962 onwards – the same as Mow's. In this phase, which Zablocki designates as 'Church-Community', he suggests that the

Bruderhof thought of itself as a church among churches, rather than an intentional community (albeit Christian) among intentional communities (Zablocki 1980, 110). The periods of isolated sect and social movement were repudiated, according to Zablocki. Rather, the movement believed itself to be returning to the path of Eberhard Arnold. The problem it faced as a community was now the possibility of smugness and apathy. In this it might be suggested that Zablocki proved incorrect. The path of the Bruderhof proved to be just as full of struggle, as we have seen. In the most recent years we can mention the split with the Hutterians, the failure of the Nigerian and German experiments, the problems with the IG and finally the rise of an organised group of dissident ex-members called Keep in Touch that appears to have caused the community a certain amount of anxiety. Additionally, while there has been some continuity of leadership in the community since 1962, with the smooth replacement (at least apparently) of Heini Arnold as Elder by his son Christoph following Heini's death in 1982, one might wonder if Zablocki would feel that the recent social concerns and their expression by the Bruderhof still allow us to see it in the 'Church-Community' phase.

Zablocki and Mow gave very different overviews of Bruderhof history. Mow saw the history in spiritual terms. Zablocki presented an alternative view based on sociological thinking. Mow and Zablocki would be united, it may be suggested, in seeing the other's account as woefully inadequate. For Mow, Zablocki's account could be construed as missing the role of the opposing spirits that are in conflict, and which play their conflict out where humans try to live the Christian life. The type of account offered by Mow might be seen by Zablocki as an apologetic that left questions of power and the unconscious out of account, and represented an 'official line' to be served up to members and would-be converts as a way of socialising them into the world-view of the leadership.

IDEOLOGY

We can now turn to the ideology of the movement. The best way to do this is to look at the thinking of Eberhard Arnold as presented in material either directly published by the Bruderhof, or presented in a couple of books of selected texts produced with their active collaboration. As the community ostensibly went through the upheaval of 1961 to return to the way he tried to follow, this examination will provide a useful insight into the Bruderhof's own view of its ideology.

Considering Arnold's rationale for a life in community, we find him arguing starkly in 1925 that '[l]ife in community is no less than a necessity for us – it is an inescapable "must" that determines everything we do and think . . . We must live in community because all life created by God exists in a communal order and works towards community' (E. Arnold 1995, 1). This argument that community is a 'must' for Christians was buttressed by references on Arnold's part to the way in which the early church in Jerusalem was organised: '[w]e oppose outright the present order of society. We represent a different order, that of the communal Church as it was in Jerusalem after the Holy Spirit was poured out' (Hutterian Society of Brothers and Yoder 1984, 52, quoting Arnold in 1933). The Jerusalem Church illustrated a general point. 'Christ's love makes us want to give up possessions and live in community of goods' (Hutterian Society of Brothers and Yoder 1984, 65). We thus find Arnold pointing to the way in which the communal life has broken out among followers of Christ time after time down the centuries, mentioning the Montanists, the monastics, the Waldensians, the Franciscans, the Anabaptists, the Quakers, the Moravians and others in one list of such outbreaks (E. Arnold 1995, 8–9). A communal life follows from, and is demanded by, the experience of the love of Christ. Arnold illustrates this point with his historical examples, the most significant of which is the early church in Jerusalem.

This life in community is not an easy path to be taken. Indeed, for Arnold, it is not possible on the basis of human potential alone. He argued in 1933,

> the basis of our communal life is God and God alone. But we cannot say we have acquired this basis and now we own religion as one's own property. What we have must be given to us new each day. It is a dreadful thought, but we have to face it: We can lose it any day. All we can say is that we are placed on this foundation by God's grace. (Hutterian Society of Brothers and Yoder 1984, 67)

Arnold put it in rather more striking terms in 1934: '[o]ur Bruderhof is not Church through being composed of believing and living people or through the sum of the believers. The Bruderhof *becomes* Church whenever the Holy Spirit, the Jerusalem above, comes down upon us; whenever the Church above unites us in the Holy Spirit' (E. Arnold 1965, 38).

If community can only be given by God's grace, what is required of the individual Christians who go to make it up? The first thing is decision. Individuals have to take a personal and voluntary decision that they are called by Christ to a life of community. Arnold started his religious masterwork, *Innerland*, by pointing out that '[i]t is an appeal for decision in the area of faith and beliefs, directed to the hearts of all those who do not want to forget or lose God and his ultimate Kingdom' (E. Arnold 1976b, 1). This means that the communism of the Bruderhof is completely voluntary. Writing about the Jerusalem Church in 1933, Arnold argued that on 'the economic level it meant that they gave up all private property and lived in complete community of goods, free from any compulsion ... We cannot put this burden [life in community] on anybody unless he or she prizes the greatness of God's Kingdom above everything else and feels inwardly certain that there is no other way to go' (Hutterian Society of Brothers and Yoder 1984, 52).

Having made the decision, what is next required of the Christian? Crucially, it is the abnegation of the self. In his 1925 work on *Why We Live in Community*, Arnold suggested that '[c]ommunity life is like martyrdom by fire: it means the daily sacrifice of all our strength and all our rights, all the claims we commonly make on life and assume to be justified. In the symbol of fire the individual logs burn away so that, united, its glowing flames send out warmth and light again and again into the land' (E. Arnold 1995, 14). Arnold could be very caustic on this point. He argued in 1933,

> [p]eople who live with themselves in the center – who think about themselves all day long, who see everything in relation to themselves and from their own point of view – are seriously ill. They are mentally disturbed. They are far from becoming true brothers and sisters. They are lost, even in the midst of a com-munal household. (J. C. Arnold 2000, 96)

The last two sentences here seem to suggest that Arnold's comments are meant generally, but are aimed at persons already living in the Bruderhof, or commu-nities like it. In some ways Arnold's stance here followed from his insistence that community is only feasible due to God, and not as a result of human activities. In the same talk from 1933 he further suggested that 'God's cause is a cause for which we are not needed. We are not indispensable. We are not just unimportant; we are an obstacle. We are adversaries of the cause. Redemption cannot begin until we recognize this and see ourselves, and our piety, as adversaries' (J. C. Arnold 2000, 92). In a speech at the Tolstoy Club in Vienna in 1929, Arnold made it clear that this renunciation should be seen as not simply an act of renunciation for its own sake, but, rather, as an affirmation of life, a liberation from illusion for the sake of a new birth (J. C. Arnold 2000, 102). This act of self-abnegation is presented using different images throughout the various works of Arnold, and in those of subse-quent followers. An image that became favoured was from the works of the old Hutterians, and focused on the way a grain of wheat had to cease to be such to become part of the loaf of bread. This image is alluded to in a fascinating corre-spondence between Eberhard Arnold's son, Eberhard ('Hardy') Arnold and the Swiss communitarian Henri Lasserre. Lasserre clearly differed with the Bruderhof on this issue, but more generally regarded the movement favourably. In a corre-spondence from 1939 he attempted in a friendly way to work out these differences. In a response to one of Lasserre's letters, Hardy Arnold noted,

> [w]e do not by any means want to be totalitarian in the political or cultural sense of the word. But in its fullest sense of being something whole, or com-plete, or all embracing, we are 'totalitarian'. In other words, we believe *God* is 'totalitarian' because he demands the *whole* man. You stumble in this respect over the parable of the loaf, in which the grains have been ground to flour. (Thomson 1949, 78, italics in original)

The self was seen (and is still seen by the Bruderhof) as the crucial barrier to com-munity. For the Bruderhof, the spirit that fights against efforts to live the

Christian life will target the weaknesses of self among the movement's members. The degree of seriousness with which the Bruderhof takes the abnegation of self can be seen in an article published in an issue of *The Plough*. The article by a Bruderhof member examines a tricky situation that had occurred in her work-place at a bruderhof. The article includes a self-examination in which the author analyses things with reference to her own actions, coming to the conclusion that it was her sin that had been a factor in the problem. 'Silence – my sin! . . . Passivity – my sin!' (Manke 1994, 17).

So, community is only possible thanks to God's grace. It has to be entered into voluntarily by Christians impelled to get rid of their possessions by Christ's love. This requires a firm, voluntary decision, and then the renunciation of the self in an act of liberatory re-birth. The individual serious about taking this difficult path will exhibit something Arnold called the 'Childlike Spirit'. Arnold indicated in 1933 that '[t]he kingdom of God belongs to children. For this reason we can be led to the divine truth only if we have the childlike spirit' (J. C. Arnold 2000, 67). Arnold gave some pointers about the content of the childlike spirit. In a talk in 1935 he suggested that what he called 'genuine' children are open and honest. They tell adults what they feel. They do not keep quiet in front of someone and then talk about that person behind their back. The same, he suggested, was true of childlike souls in the church. Later in the same talk he argued that when the church received a tiny child, it also received Jesus. Here, he noted, the word child included all with a childlike heart. He listed some of the characteristics of the person with a childlike heart. They would be chaste, have pure hearts, would not wish to be great, and would be unable to show any great accomplishments (J. C. Arnold 2000, 68–69).

Sufficient has been shown, hopefully, to make it clear that Arnold was far from optimistic about the human condition when considered apart from the grace of God. Christian community of life, work and goods was far from being a straight-forward and easy path. Assuming it is to be attempted, what then can be said about the community as a whole? First, that the community should be spirit-led, not ruled by legalistic codes. As Arnold put it in 1925, the 'early Christians lived in the Spirit. The Spirit blows like the wind – it is never rigid like iron or stone. The Spirit is infinitely more sensitive and delicate than the inflexible designs of the intellect or the cold, hard frameworks of governmental or societal structures' (E. Arnold 1995, 12). This argument develops from Arnold's view of the meaning of the Sermon on the Mount. (This is a key text for Arnold, and the Bruderhof has collected a number of his writings on it in the collection *Salt and Light*; E. Arnold 1986). He stated, 'Jesus brings us a new ethic in the Sermon on the Mount. Whereas the morality of the scribes and Pharisees is an outward right-eousness – the product of legalism and the coercion of society, church, and state – the new righteousness shows its nature as inner freedom' (quotation in J. C. Arnold 2000, 60, though undated and unsourced). Arnold put this in another way in his *Innerland*: '[c]ircumscribed self-love and heartless legalism are the enemies of the Gospel of unity and freedom. The true freedom of a heart ruled by God does away with superficial legalism' (Arnold 1976b, 61–62).

The desire to do away with 'legalism' does not mean that the Bruderhof is an anarchistic commune where 'anything goes'. 'Uncompromising discipline is needed to keep the Church community united and pure . . . The weapons used in this discipline are brotherly correction and the clear judgement of the Church' (Eberhard Arnold in 1928, cited in Hutterian Society of Brothers and Yoder 1984, 128). This discipline could include exclusion from the community. On this point Arnold was clear, stating in 1933 that the 'Church has authority from God to forgive sins on the one hand or to exclude on the other' (Hutterian Society of Brothers and Yoder 1984, 128). The Bruderhof is a disciplined church, as shown in the account of the Great Crisis. There is, however, a reason why such discipline is needed. Arnold took up in 1935 the image of the City on the Hill, from the Sermon on the Mount. Light would shine over the land from its windows, so that the rest of us outside would look up and realise '[t]here is a united city, a united Church!' (Hutterian Society of Brothers and Yoder 1984, 56). The key word here is unity. Arnold did not mean this in any weak sense. For him unity was to be total. In 1929 he suggested that unimpaired

> unanimity is indispensable for anything the community undertakes . . . This unanimity is only possible because of our faith that God uses His Spirit to say the same to each individual . . . This Spirit not only assures us of our salvation – that he has accepted us – but His speaking to us also makes us certain even in the so-called 'trifles' or small matters . . . Unanimity is the first sign. (Hutterian Society of Brothers and Yoder 1984, 56–57)

Heini Arnold, in a letter for his son Christoph appended to Mow's history, suggests – as one of a number of ways in which the community moved in a direction opposite to that taken in Halle (pre-Bruderhof) and Sannerz – that the Bruderhof introduced, at some unspecified point, the practice of majority voting (Mow 1991, 312). Heini Arnold does not even bother to condemn this; it is evidently unacceptable as a move from unanimity. The spirit-led church will be communal, disciplined and unanimous, providing it is listening sufficiently closely to the voice of the spirit, telling all members the same thing, even in the smallest matter. The main obstacle to the church hearing the voice of the spirit is the human 'self', which needs constantly to go through the process of abnegation.

We can conclude this examination of the ideology of the Bruderhof by considering the relationship of the Bruderhof to the outside world. Two possible lines can be found in Bruderhof material. The first direction could be called 'activism'. Eberhard Arnold stated in 1932 that

> [o]ur community life first came into being because of the widespread need around us. The reason we left the big cities was not to withdraw from the world.

> And in moving to this place on a mountain (so very isolated at first sight) we
> had no intention of evading our responsibility to society. Rather we felt that by
> concentrating our forces we might best be able to influence society at large. And
> still today our first and foremost concern is that our communal life may have
> an effect on the world around us. (Hutterian Society of Brothers and Yoder
> 1984, 70)

This was a clear statement indicating that Arnold, at a late stage in his career,
retained a belief that Christian community was a social witness, and also that the
movement was to be involved in world-changing activities. Arnold's son Heini,
however, articulated a more withdrawn attitude to the world. 'It is a paradox: we
must separate ourselves from our corrupt generation – and we cannot do that
sharply enough – but we must also unite with Christ, who died for every individual of this same generation' (J. H. Arnold 1994, 93, quotation not dated). In
Bruderhof literature it is probably true to suggest that there is – certainly at the
present time – a stronger emphasis on world engagement rather than world withdrawal. Heini Arnold's comment should be seen, perhaps, as a corrective, a viewpoint that can be called upon if the movement comes to feel that it has perhaps
taken, or is proposing to take, a step too far towards the corrupt generation.

THE ROOTS OF EBERHARD ARNOLD'S THOUGHT

A good approach to finding the roots of Eberhard Arnold's thinking is to take
his 'last testament' and examine the three groupings mentioned there – the Youth
Movement, the Blumhardts and the Hutterians. These will be considered, and to
them can be added what could be called Jewish Communitarian Socialist
thought, meaning the thinking of Gustav Landauer and Martin Buber. However,
before considering these distinct intellectual tendencies, it should be noted that
prior to the turn towards life in Christian community, Arnold had been an
Evangelical Christian. Baum's biography of Arnold is useful in detailing the pre-
Bruderhof phase of Arnold's life, outlining his thinking at that time. Baum shows
that Arnold broke with the state Church in Germany in 1908, a decision which
meant that he was not able to complete his theological studies. Arnold ended up
becoming a Doctor of Philosophy. His successful thesis, submitted to the
University of Erlangen in late 1909, was on 'Early Christian and Anti-Christian
Elements in the Development of Friedrich Nietzsche' (Baum 1998, 53).
Interestingly, Baum also points to the importance of the issue of believers' (as
opposed to infant) baptism in Arnold's break with the state Church (Baum 1998,
37). This perhaps prefigured his connection with the Hutterians, who were and
are Anabaptists. Their earlier break with 'official' Christianity had also involved
this issue, although, as with Arnold, there were many other issues involved.

   We can now turn to the Blumhardts, and their significance for the ideology of
Eberhard Arnold and the Bruderhof. This is an issue made perhaps even sharper

than was previously the case with the publication of Julius Rubin's *The Other Side of Joy*, an extremely critical account of the Bruderhof using sociological and psychological analyses. Rubin states that 'Eberhard Arnold consciously adopted the Innerland devotional piety and the idea of *Gemeinde* from Christoph Blumhardt' (Rubin 2000, 61). Rubin thus suggests that at least one of the Blumhardts was centrally important to the thinking of Eberhard Arnold and therefore the Bruderhof, which Rubin sees as, in Ralph Waldo Emerson's terms, the 'lengthened shadow' of Arnold.

There are certain obvious ways in which the Blumhardt legacy remains important to the Bruderhof. The community retains a belief in the literal importance of spiritual forces in human affairs. Mow's terminology about the conflict of spiritual atmospheres shows this. The possibility of this resulting in demonic possession is still accepted. Just as the elder Blumhardt had the Gottliebin Dittus case, and Eberhard Arnold had the Lotte Henze case, so in 1959 Heini Arnold dealt with the 'Miriam Way' case which Mow states clearly was a case of possession (Mow 1991, 127. 'Miriam Way' is a pseudonym. There was no completely successful outcome in this case.)

Paradoxically, however, one of the most interesting themes in the thought of Christoph Blumhardt appears to have had little impact on Eberhard Arnold. This is his critique of religion. For Christoph Blumhardt religion was a major obstacle to the spread of the real meaning of Christ's message, and this critique included Christianity. 'Nothing is more dangerous to the advancement of God's kingdom than religion: for it is what makes us heathens. But this is what Christianity has become. Do you not know that it is possible to kill Christ with such Christianity?' (Blumhardt 1998, 74). This line of argument had an impact upon the Swiss Religious Socialist Leonhard Ragaz (see notably the section in Bock's reader of Ragaz writings entitled 'Not religion but the Kingdom of God', Bock 1984, 27–38). Gorringe shows the same is true of Karl Barth (Gorringe 1999, 41–43). '"The unhappy word 'religion' was not heard at Möttlingen and Bad Boll" he wrote in his article on the younger Blumhardt' (Gorringe 1999, 42). This argument seems to be of little significance for Arnold, despite the importance placed upon it by Ragaz and Barth, both of whom he had contact with. That said, it does appear to be an argument that the Bruderhof is taking on board, as is shown by Charles Moore's introduction to the recent Bruderhof-published anthology, *Action in Waiting* (Blumhardt 1998, especially xxv).

In his last testament Arnold referred to the Blumhardts' 'attitude of faith'. This does actually sum up the tenor of the debt of Arnold to the Blumhardts, and it does not conflict with the arguments offered by Rubin. A chapter in the collection of texts by Eberhard and Emmy Arnold, *Seeking for the Kingdom of God*, on 'The Significance of the Blumhardts' tends to bear this out. Broadly this attitude of faith includes a clear belief in the conflict of spiritual atmospheres, a belief in the effectiveness of the Holy Spirit rather than human action, and, with the younger Blumhardt, an understanding that this effectiveness would also be apparent in the world and in questions of justice (E. and E. Arnold 1974, 257–67). The Blumhardts accordingly represented a sort of combination of spiritual-mindedness and practical social concern that went beyond simple concern for salvation of individual souls on the one hand, and straightforward identification of Christianity with the socialist programme on the other hand. These would be the mistakes – from Arnold's point of view – of pietism on the one hand and of religious socialism on the other hand.

Let us now consider the Hutterian impact on Arnold. The Bruderhof did not get the idea of living a communal life from the Hutterians. Indeed, despite his clear admiration for aspects of Hutterian practice, which fuelled his desire for unity with the Hutterians, Eberhard Arnold in fact voiced criticisms of the Hutterian Brothers at the time of his visit to them. Baum points out a few of these issues in his account: the lack of economic unity among Hutterian colonies, each colony being independent, a very different practice to the Bruderhof, and one which leads to disparities that clearly concerned Arnold; a failure to have a common Elder for the whole of the three leute; and a failure to get involved in mission activities (Baum 1998, 199–200). Arnold suggested that the model for the Bruderhof was the Hutterianism of 1529 to 1589, whereas the Hutterians themselves tended to model their faith on the Hutterianism of the years 1650 to 1700 (Baum 1998, 207). This perhaps accounts for the phrase 'genuine, old Hutterianism' in the testamentary letter. So, there were always at least potential areas of conflict in the relationship between the Bruderhof and the Hutterians. Nonetheless, Arnold and the Bruderhof did get certain things from the relationship. We can point to three such acquisitions.

The first is that they acquired a historical treasury of witness to Christian community. There was an enormous amount of Hutterian written material that argued the case for life in community, non-resistance, and many of the other values that the community had arrived at by themselves. Baum pointed out that as a result of Arnold's visit to the colonies, the 'Rhön Bruderhof suddenly found itself housing the most comprehensive library of Anabaptist writings in Europe' (Baum 1998, 203). The community translated many of these and made them available in English for the first time. Some outstanding examples of this work include the Plough edition of the *Chronicle of the Hutterian Brethren*, the Hutterians' history book, and (perhaps most importantly) the translation of Peter Rideman's *Confession of Faith* (Rideman 1974), the key ideological text of Hutterianism, originally published in 1545. Interestingly, the original English edition of this translation appeared in 1950, at a time when the Bruderhof had poor relations with the Hutterians and, in today's Bruderhof view, had strayed from the correct path.

From this treasury Arnold secondly acquired a 'framework' for viewing the contemporary world and the tasks of Christians in it. This was true in both 'theoretical' terms and also more practically. At the theoretical level we can see it in the final chapter of *Innerland*, on 'The Living Word', in which Arnold powerfully draws upon Anabaptist sources (including Thomas Münzer) in his spiritual guidance (E. Arnold 1976b, 441–525). At a more practical level, in *The World Situation and our Task*, Arnold read the situation facing the Bruderhof in the fateful days of late 1934 in terms of the era of the Peasants' War and the early days of the Hutterians (E. Arnold 1992).

Finally, as suggested by Zablocki, the Bruderhof acquired structural order from the Hutterians. At the uniting in 1930 the Bruderhof became bound by the regulations of the Hutterian Church. Although, as Baum makes clear, this was never to mean an attempt by the Bruderhof to become completely like a Hutterian colony – and he suggested that Arnold never supported this notion – it did have implications (Baum 1998, 207). So, while the Bruderhof never gave up singing accompanied by instruments, it did mean, for instance an attempt to wear Hutterian dress. It perhaps also meant a willingness to make some ideological shifts. It may be that Eberhard Arnold's talk 'On Woman's Calling' from 1934 represents an attempt to nudge the community towards a deeper acceptance of the Hutterian view in respect of the different divinely allotted roles of men and women. 'I believe that our modern attitude has mistaken the calling of woman. What we find in the Hutterian movement over the centuries must certainly not be confused with the subjection of women; they have really discovered the true expression of her nature' (E. Arnold 1965, 28). While in large measure the community has taken the line Arnold propounded in this talk to heart, it is interesting to observe that even when in unity with the Hutterians the Bruderhof allowed women to participate in brotherhood meetings and speak in them, an anathema to the Hutterians. Even if the Hutterian orders were never completely adopted, they did provide a lasting structural form for the movement that Arnold took on and bequeathed to the Bruderhof.

The third source mentioned in the 'last testament' letter was, of course, the Youth Movement itself. The connections between the movement and the Bruderhof have been considered, but it is worth asking whether there were any intellectual debts to that movement. In an account of the early years of the Youth Movement, Arnold, in 1933, stressed its impact on the development of his understanding of community. He specifically mentioned the hiking groups. 'This was not an experience of individuals hiking in twos or threes in the woods or on the heath, but something given to small groups, who went out into nature and sensed a mysterious bond with God the Creator behind nature and behind the communal experience of their group, which could only be explained as something of God' (E. and E. Arnold 1974, 241). This suggests that the impulse towards community in the minds of the circle around Eberhard Arnold was significantly affected by the Youth Movement experience, and indeed that their experiences in the movement were something of a 'school' for community. It also shows Arnold's tendency to see a religious significance to the Youth Movement.

Arnold's reflections on the Youth Movement are borne out in two respects by Fritz Borinksi and Werner Milch's (insider) account. First, in writing about the years 1919 to 1923, years that saw the birth of the Bruderhof, they note of the movement and its vision at that stage: '[t]his faith was in the last resort religious' (Borinski and Milch 1982, 20). Indeed, considering the movement as a whole, between 1896 and 1933, they suggest that there was 'a distinct religious colouring' (Borinski and Milch 1982, 34) to its activities. Borinski was involved from 1930 in the publication *Neue Blätter für den Sozialismus* (*New Papers for Socialism*) with religious socialists such as Paul Tillich and Eduard Heimann (Borinski and Milch 1982, 137, German text), and so may have shared the attitudes of Arnold on this point. Second, at a more practical level, Borinski and Milch support Arnold's arguments about the Youth Movement as a sort of 'school' for community in the following: '[t]heir financial arrangements whilst on their wanderings were "primitive communistic"; each person handed in his money to the communal fund and nobody had the right to use any sum for himself' (Borinski and Milch 1982, 7). Interestingly, a similar system of pooling money is still in use in the chalutzo-Zionist and socialist youth movement of the Jewish diaspora, Habonim-Dror.[3]

Arnold also mentioned the Evangelical Christian revival movement in this text, suggesting that Sannerz and the Bruderhof community came into being as a result of the impact of the youth and revival movements. The text pointed to a collision between the individualism of the revival movement and the communal aspects of the Youth Movement. So, when Arnold wrote of the life-attitude of the Youth Movement in his 'last testament' we can read this as at least including a significant element of a drive to community. The love of nature and other such aspects of the life-attitude of the Youth Movement are also attested to in the text. This does suggest that the Youth Movement's intellectual impact on Arnold was significant in important ways.

We have already shown that the Youth Movement affected the way in which Arnold dressed and other aspects of his behaviour. In discussion with veteran members of the Bruderhof with memories of the Youth Movement, a stress was laid on the extent to which the Youth Movement encouraged a separation from bourgeois lifestyles.[4] Given Eberhard Arnold's social origins – his father was a university professor – and the fact that his wife and her sister also came from a similar social background, this aspect of the Youth Movement should be seen as significant in his thought and practice and that of the Bruderhof. The way of life adopted by the Bruderhof had, and has, a distinctly 'no-frills' aspect to it. While the bruderhofs are cleaned scrupulously, and the food is plentiful and wholesome, there are no material luxuries and definitely no 'airs and graces'; they are certainly not bourgeois. In this context the word 'bourgeois' does not perhaps have the significance it has in Marxist discourse. Borinski and Milch pointed out that the German Youth Movement was a bourgeois movement. Accordingly the word 'bourgeois' acquired a deeply pejorative sense, because to be 'bourgeois' was to live according to the requirements of parents and teachers (Borinski and Milch 1982, 6). The anti-bourgeois lifestyle of the Bruderhof can be seen in this context as reflecting the decision of the young Eberhard and Emmy Arnold to strike out on a very different path through life than was expected by their families. This decision – which goes back well before their encounter with the Youth Movement – might be one reason they were able to relate to that movement when they encountered it.

Finally, we can briefly consider Arnold's intellectual links with the tradition of Jewish Communitarian Socialist thinking that is represented by the thought of Gustav Landauer and Martin Buber. This is important in the overall context of this book because Landauer and Buber were of significance to the Kibbutz movement, and Buber was, and indeed is, of great importance for the Integrierte Gemeinde. If we commence by examining Landauer, we should be aware that, despite Baum's speculation (Baum 1998, 120) that Arnold and Landauer might have met, there is no evidence that they did. Given the regard Arnold had for Landauer it seems likely that had they met, posterity would have been informed. So what we have here is a case of intellectual affinity. Arnold had read and admired the work of Landauer. It is easily possible to find parallels between the thought of Landauer and that of Arnold (see Tyldesley 1996 on this and the general question of Arnold, the Bruderhof and Landauer). It may be asked, however, whether Landauer had any impact upon Arnold and the Bruderhof other than at a rather general level. In answer, it could be suggested that Landauer affected one aspect of continuing Bruderhof practice in an important way.

In his magnum opus, the *Aufruf zum Sozialismus* (the English translation is called *For Socialism* – Landauer 1978 – although a more adequate translation would be 'Call to Socialism') and elsewhere Landauer called for socialists to leave the cities and move to the countryside in order to found settlements or communities. This call was based upon Landauer's historical understanding, and belief that there were traces of unificatory spirit in the countryside. The Bruderhof has always sited its communities in the countryside. On at least one occasion Arnold showed some awareness of this aspect of Landauer's thought. In *The World Situation* he said of the Hutterian bruderhofs of the post-Peasants' War period, '[w]hat Gustav Landauer demanded – that land and spirit must meet – was fulfilled here' (E. Arnold 1992, 6). Perhaps the siting of bruderhofs in the countryside, allowing land and spirit to meet, is a concrete legacy of Landauer's thought in the practice of the Bruderhof. In the history of the Reba Place Fellowship, an inner-city Chicago Mennonite community, some intriguing comments are recorded. The Fellowship – or the people who went on to form it – had discussions with the Bruderhof in 1957. They remembered being warned against a city-based community effort by the Bruderhof, but a letter in their archives suggested a rather more favourable response by the bruderhofers (Jackson and Jackson 1987, 37, 47).

If we turn to Martin Buber, there were a number of instances of direct contact between Buber and Arnold and the Bruderhof. It has been shown that there are at least two instances in the 1920s and early 1930s when Buber actually visited the Bruderhof (Tyldesley 1994). Furthermore, other examples of direct contact between Buber and members of the Bruderhof have been established, and it has also been shown that there were a number of instances of correspondence between Arnold and Buber (Tyldesley 1994). Two of these letters are of some interest. A letter from Arnold to Buber in 1921 indicated that Arnold was working on a biography of Landauer in the form of a collection of his letters. This never appeared under the aegis of the Neuwerk Verlag, although a little later in the 1920s Buber did actually produce something very similar. The other piece of correspondence is from 1927 and shows that Arnold and Buber were working in the same circles in Frankfurt, involved in the organising of a conference. There were also later efforts to re-initiate contact in the 1960s, although little seems to have come of them (Tyldesley 1994).

Even though Arnold had written favourably about Buber in *Die Furche*, a student Christian journal, for November 1917 (for the nub of the argument see Tyldesley 1994, 265–67), it is not really clear that Buber had a major theoretical impact upon Arnold. Put rather differently, it is hard to point to any particular argument in Arnold's writings that would appear to depend crucially on Buber. Buber was read by the Bruderhof, and indeed remains important for them. However, it seems to be at a fairly general level, and as one whose arguments flow along similar lines. Perhaps Arnold found some of his own ideas in some of Buber's writings, as Aaron David Gordon did with Landauer. Of the two thinkers, it might be suggested that Landauer's more direct and less academic writings have had a more profound long-term impact upon the Bruderhof. While it is clear that Arnold was an intellectual who could handle abstract ideas in theology and philosophy with aplomb, and indeed it is also the case that other people so gifted have been part of the movement, there has been a tendency for the movement as a whole to recoil from presenting its ideas in the way that Buber did in, say, *I and Thou*. Addressing a fellow theologian, Arnold suggested that 'we must become free from theological introspection; we must be won for the holy cause by a glowing, inner fire. You must become free first from your pronounced tendency to theologize, and second from your own markedly cramped will. Accept your fate: you are a theologian. But now you must become a child!' (J. C. Arnold 2000, 67). The demands of the childlike spirit mean that the Bruderhof will always be on guard against over-intellectualisation.

CONCLUSION

The Bruderhof and its 'Hosts'
To conclude this consideration of the Bruderhof, let us summarise our findings on the two issues that underlie the book as a whole. These are, first, to consider the impact of the movements on their host societies and their interactions with those societies, and second, to examine the ways in which the movements have attempted to create 'alternative societies' and economies.

On the first point, we have seen that the Bruderhof has an ambiguous approach to its host societies. (This is, of course, to be expected in the context of

Oved's comments about the relationship between communities and the societies they have separated themselves from.) On the one hand, there is a definite social concern. The Bruderhof sees the world as it stands today as unjust, and wishes to see change that will result in a betterment of the conditions of the poor, ultimately by the creation of a society embodying the Kingdom of God, an act that can only result from the grace of God and not from human action. This does not mean that the Bruderhof will not engage in social action at all. Currently it is very active on some issues, notably, for instance, the movement against the death penalty in the USA. However, it also has a viewpoint that will tend to make it wary of too close an involvement in external organisations. The church must separate itself from the corrupt generation. (Need it be stated that every generation is the corrupt generation?) This tension plays out in a social activism that is aware of boundaries; the boundaries of the Bruderhof are always well maintained.

This means that the social impact of the movement might well be seen as being limited. At the present time the Bruderhof does tend to make the newspapers and media in general with some of its social justice activities, especially those involving its children. So, it has an impact on society, albeit a very limited one. Arguably in slightly earlier periods – perhaps from the crisis until around the mid-1990s – Zablocki's 'Church among Churches' notion has some validity, and its impact might have been focused more in the direction of other churches. Indeed, for some time after the crisis, it may well have made very little impact on society, and not really attempted to. This is the burden of Whitworth's characterisation of the post-1961 Bruderhof (Whitworth 1975, 205). Whitworth's portrait of the Bruderhof remains useful, with the clear exception of this point. Whitworth predicted that a return to a more involved stance was unlikely (Whitworth 1975, 205). All this is, of course, relative. In any given country the Bruderhof has only ever been a tiny minority. Its impact on society can only ever have been marginal, except perhaps in the immediate vicinity of the communities, and among interested and sympathetic outsiders.

This ambiguous policy will hold true for all aspects of its interactions with the host society. The values of the movement, as eloquently expressed in, say, J. C. Arnold's *A Plea for Purity* (1996a), are so different from values prevailing in contemporary secular society that Heini Arnold's warning must come into play regardless of the depth of its desire to change the society around it. Its views on a whole range of sexual issues must lead it to find certain aspects of modern life deeply disturbing when it comes into contact with them. Broadly, its views on homosexuality, the roles of women and men, sex education and many other like issues, as expressed by Arnold in his *Plea for Purity*, are out of keeping with Western post-1960s liberal notions.

The Bruderhof as Alternative Society
As to the alternative society and economy that the Bruderhof has created, we can venture some comments. Its alternative economy sees it function, in effect, as one

'company' among many in society. It produces items for sale on the open market. The money it makes from this activity supports the community. We saw that since the late 1950s the activities associated with Community Playthings have alleviated its previous dependence on the charity of outsiders. That said, within the community the profitable activities are simply one of a number of work activities that are organised by the community. Cooking, cleaning and general management of the needs and requirements of the community are also part of this task of organisation. The movement does do a lot of things 'in house'. It calls upon the abilities of its members in fields such as medicine and agriculture. Given the size of the community this means that it can cut down its dependence on the outside world to an extent that is way beyond the capacity of many smaller communities, let alone ordinary families.

This is not done because the movement has a specific aim of being self-sufficient. Some of its activities preclude this. The community runs various vehicles – cars, mini-buses, coaches and even aircraft. Short of acquiring an oil well and refinery it will have to buy fuel from outside the community. One could multiply such examples. However, if it does have a tendency to self-sufficiency, this may be because it ultimately believes that persecution might be around the corner. As J. C. Arnold puts it, '[t]wo thousand years have not made our present world any more tolerant of Jesus' message than the world of his time. Those who are unwilling to accept his way will always be resentful and even vindictive to those who witness to it, and a clash is inevitable' (J. C. Arnold 1996a, 146). The Bruderhof has learnt this lesson in its own history down the years and it would be strange if it has not put some aspects of this experience into the design of its economic functioning.

The Bruderhof's alternative society is intentionally a total experience. Its ideology means that the notion of a private sphere is absent from its thinking, indeed, an anathema to it. It is an integrated community based upon a number of different sites. Members do not join the Darvell Bruderhof (for instance); they join the Bruderhof as a church, and will live where the church decides. This is not to say that members are pushed around willy-nilly. There is a degree of inter-movement between sites, however. Of course, the chance to live in the USA for a part of one's life might actually be a bonus for a British member. As has been indicated, there is always a great deal of activity on the hof, and so within the alternative society of the Bruderhof social needs are met. One might not leave the hof very often, but possibly because one is simply too busy to rather than because of any putative 'ban' or the like. From observation, people seem to be able to come and go as they need to, and the Bruderhof seems reasonably relaxed about members from Darvell wandering into Robertsbridge – although Robertsbridge, the village in rural East Sussex where Darvell is situated, is a rather different prospect than London.

Above all, the alternative society of the Bruderhof is one in which members are well aware that they are at the storm centre of the conflict of the atmospheres of the Spirits of Jesus and of Evil. This is far from saying that they feel they have achieved something like a miniature version of the Kingdom of God in their communities. What has been said above should have disabused the reader of any thought that they take that kind of view. Rather, it is to suggest, as Mow did, that the Bruderhof sees itself as being involved in the struggle between those atmospheres, and in a sense that dramatises the life in the communities. The Bruderhof has had a very stormy history. Prior to the Great Crisis it might be said that many of the storms lashed the community from the outside. With the minimal exception of the *Keep in Touch* group, this is no longer the case. But there have been plenty of storms and stresses from within the Bruderhof and its world. As well as keeping busy in a physical sense, the alternative society of the Bruderhof allows its members to keep busy on the psychic level.

NOTES

1 See Rifton Aviation Services website http://riftonav.com for details of the nature of this undertaking.
2 See http://blumagazine.net/closing.htm
3 See the article 'Strength and Courage' by Jonathan Freedland. This appeared in the *Jewish Chronicle*, 20 August 1999, and is on the website of Kvutzat Yovel http://207.21.194.249/kvutsatyovel/netscape/strength.htm
4 Discussion between Sophie Löber and Hugo Brinkmann with Mike Tyldesley, at Darvell Bruderhof, 17 August 1999.

Chapter 4

'Exodus' – The Integrierte Gemeinde

LIVING TOGETHER IN THE INTEGRIERTE GEMEINDE

Unlike the Bruderhof, the IG is not structured in the classical 'commune' mode. It does not consist of a group of people who have voluntarily agreed to pool their goods and money. That said, the IG's members do share their lives, and do form a community. Traudl Wallbrecher, key figure and 'founder' of the IG, pointed out that '[e]ach member is responsible for his finances, but in agreement with the Community he makes everything available for the common tasks' (Integrated Community 1996, 59). How, then, does the IG operate? The cellular unit of the IG could be called the 'table community'. This is a group of people who eat and talk together fairly frequently. There does not appear to be a regulation as to how many times per week the table community should eat together, but it is likely that they meet daily, though perhaps with some minor exceptions. The table community is perhaps best seen in the context of the IG's stress on the notion of the 'new family'. For the IG, Jews and Christians together should form a 'People of God'. The People of God is the believer's new family, and the table community is a concrete manifestation of this new family. In a sense one moves from the old, blood family into a new family composed of believers. The table communities may well be composed of groups of IG members who live in the same houses, called 'integration houses'. These appear to be a less important feature of the IG than was the case, with more members living outside. The diminution in importance of the integration house does not in any way lessen the role of the table communities.

A number of table communities in an area will together form a geographical community of the IG. There are, for example, six such geographical communities of the IG in Munich. These communities are not large: on average each community will have around 100 members. This is not an accident but relates to the theology of the movement. One of the leading theologians of the IG has indicated the biblical reasons why communities should have no more than 120 members. Gerhard Lohfink stated in his book *Does God Need the Church?* that 'a community should not contain more than 120 people. Only at that size can it remain a concrete assembly in which no one is invisible, in which each member can be aware of the sorrow and happiness, the cares and joys of the others' (Lohfink 1999, 221–22, an exegesis of Acts 1:15–26). So we find communities of a surveyable size, in which everyone knows one another. These communities meet regularly, often in a set room that may be in a building connected with an IG enterprise, for 'assemblies'.

The IG also assembles on a regular basis during the year to celebrate the feasts of the Roman Catholic Church. As well as feasts for specific IG communities, these feasts can be more general events, involving participants drawn from some or all the geographical communities. In some cases parts of the feast are relayed using radio to those not present. The feast may appear to be simply the community getting together to celebrate a meal, and at one level it is. However, it is also much more. The feasts are meticulously organised, often with live (classical) music. The preparations are lengthy and the arrangements are made down to the finest detail. The feast is actually a significant aspect of the IG's religious life, and this has deep roots in the IG's theology.

The IG has a collective leadership. The IG communities as a whole have a co-ordinating team, but each geographical community also has a leadership, a 'Figure of Twelve' elected on Maundy Thursday every year. These are seen as the centre of each community, and the concept has an obvious connection to the Twelve Apostles who sat at the table with Christ at his last supper. Again, the stress is on eating together, a table community. As with the Bruderhof, the IG operates on the basis of unanimity: 'In those years the Community found unanimity to be the greatest force of God amongst men' (Traudl Wallbrecher in Integrated Community 1996, 58). As well as the formal position, it should be stressed that there is what could be called a hierarchy of esteem in the IG. Certain people in the movement figure prominently in the literature produced by it, and can be seen as voicing the movement's message. The original founder figure, Traudl Wallbrecher, is still alive and prominent in the movement's literature, although IG literature tends to play down the whole notion of 'founding' and suggests instead that the process was one of rediscovering a path that had been open for people to take since the time of Christ. Her daughter Mechthild Wallbrecher also figures strongly. Herbert Wallbrecher, Mrs Wallbrecher's husband, died in 1997. He played an important role in the development of the IG's economic activities. Other than the Wallbrecher family, there are a number of members who appear to an outside observer to have a prominence within the movement. Perhaps most prominent, because of their literary activities, are the team of theologians connected to the movement. Some key names here include Gerhard Lohfink, Rudolf Pesch, Ludwig Weimer and Arnold Stözel. This is not an exhaustive list, and younger theologians are also gaining in prominence.

Theology has an immensely important role in the IG; a member described it in an aside as an 'empirical science' for the IG. Much of the IG's published material is theological in nature. The meetings of the geographical communities often have theological discussions as their focus. The IG seems to pick up a stream of new members from among theology students. Some are former pupils of Lohfink and Pesch, who, prior to their joining the IG, were professors of theology, and both remain significant figures in German Catholic theology. As a result, the theologians in the IG – who do other things as their jobs of work, several being priests and Pesch now being a journalist for the Catholic daily *Tagespost* – are central to its activities. Their theology reflects their experience in the IG, and so this is not a community with a benevolent dictatorship of Platonic theologian-kings. The point is rather that these figures articulate the IG's under-standing in the public sphere, and quite often also in the forums that the IG is involved in creating. The volumes of the proceedings of the Urfeld Circle feature articles from these theologians, sitting alongside rather different contributions from kibbutznikim.

Apart from weekly assemblies, feasts and the table communities in the integra-tion houses, the IG's activities can be summed up under four headings, which are in the movement's statutes. 'The members of the Catholic Integrated Community connect their lives in all fields in many different ways. They take up common initiatives in the fields of manual crafts and artistic design, economy, medicine and education' (Catholic Integrated Community 1998, 10).

We can start by considering the economic aspect of the community. There are a number of economic enterprises connected with the IG: examples include the Integra Co-operative Bank in Munich, the Wangen Pump Factory at Wangen in the Allgäu, and Klösterl-Apotheke in Munich. The Wangen Pump Factory sup-plied some of the pumping machinery used by Joseph Beuys in his 'Honeypump' art exhibit of 1977. The 'Honeypump' is recorded in the book *'Honey is Flowing in All Directions'*. Towards the end of this unpaginated book the factory's four-page bill to Beuys is reproduced complete (Beuys 1997). The community has described aspects of the organisational structure of the pump factory in its news-paper (Peter 2001). As indicated when previously discussing the bank, these enterprises (although described as 'Common Enterprises' – Integrated Community 1996, 228) are not owned by the community as a whole but by indi-viduals or groups of individuals within the IG. This arrangement should be seen, however, within the context of the quotation from Traudl Wallbrecher cited earlier; members are responsible for their finances, but in agreement with the community make everything available for the common tasks. This means that the legal position of ownership is perhaps best seen as secondary. The status of someone as a property-owner is not as significant as their status as community member.

The second area of activity of the IG is education. The community is involved with the operation of a number of schools operated by the Schulverein Integrierte Gemeinde eV. (Schools Association Integrated Community). The schools range from a kindergarten through to a grammar school (gymnasium), taking in primary schools and a middle school. These are situated in the Walchensee area of south Bavaria and in Munich. The schools are private schools, obviously with a Catholic ethos. They do attract a certain amount of state subvention, as do all private schools meeting certain standards in Germany. Unlike the Bruderhof's school system, they are not designed for the children of IG members alone but are open to the public. The IG says that the schools are not run as a money-making enterprise. Perhaps more correctly, it should be said that they are not intended primarily to make money, and this distinguishes them from the economic enterprises. That said, they do fulfil one economic function, and this is that they are a source of employment for IG members who are teachers and who wish to move into an area such as Munich, where participation in the community is possible in a more meaningful manner than elsewhere in Germany. This may especially be the case for people who are interested in the community and who live in one of the many towns in Germany where there is no community. Someone from, say, Berlin who wished to join the community would have to move over to somewhere such as Munich (see Anon 2000b, an article in the IG's bulletin which considers a family from the Karlsruhe area who moved to Munich. One of the adults in the family got a teaching post at an IG school there.)

The schools are not based on a specific pedagogic principle; in this respect they are not like the Steiner-Waldorf Schools, for instance, which have a very specific syllabus and set of teaching methods based upon Rudolf Steiner's indications. They are 'normal' schools, although certainly the grammar school is smaller than many such schools, and accordingly has smaller numbers in each class than might be expected in other gymnasia. The schools did, however, evolve from the experience of the community. In the period of the late 1960s, when the IG actually started the practice of 'integration' (living a common life by integrating members' life activities) and thus acquired its present name, members started to learn skills appropriate to education through the practice of sharing childcare in the afternoons. This practice has informed the schools run by the community. Finally, the IG's most recent educational initiative is the setting up of a college of domestic science in the south of Bavaria. This is at a fairly early stage of development at the time of writing.

The final two aspects of the community's activities are manual crafts and artistic design, and medicine. Taking design and craft first, within the community there are architects and quite a proportion of building or rebuilding work on community buildings is designed and effected 'in house'. (Some visual examples of this can be found in *Today*: Integrated Community 1996, 233, showing property in the Waltherstrasse area of Munich.) In respect of medicine, there are a significant number of medical practitioners in the IG, and a number of them practise in IG property such as the integration houses in the Waltherstrasse. In addition, the community runs a small private infirmary in Munich, under the aegis of the St Cosmas Association.

From this brief resume it can be seen that there is a thriving economic and vocational aspect to the community, and members might well find themselves able to work in workplaces that are – remembering the way in which property is owned within the IG – effectively part of the community in a wider sense. In addition to the undertakings described in the four areas above, there are also other IG-connected workplaces. Two parishes are 'run' by the IG for their dioceses, and this includes staffing by IG priests. Although this is a fairly small-scale development, it has immense significance for the IG. Guido Horst wrote an article for the *Tagespost* of 21 October 1999 about the IG. This article is subtitled 'The long way from the youth movement to the renewed Parish-Community' and Horst refers to the 'operative goal' of the IG as being the Church consisting of renewed parish-communities.[1] At Bad Tölz there is also a certain amount of central administration for the IG as a whole. This involves activities such as archives, and printing and publishing. Thus, as well as the sharing of life in the geographical communities and the table communities, the IG does see a degree of community in the working life.

If someone comes into contact with the IG – perhaps by personal acquaintance with a member, or perhaps through reading Gerhard Lohfink's *Braucht Gott die Kirche?* (Lohfink 1998) – and decides that they wish to follow this up by exploring the possibility that the IG is for them, how do they proceed? Initially they may be invited to lectures and discussions on theology at a local community, if there is one in their area. Assuming that they do this, and that they wish to proceed into the life of the community, they will then have to go into a lengthy programme. There is a three-year information period and a three-year catechumenate. This introduces the prospective member to the ideas of the community and allows them to absorb these ideas. However, this is not all that would be happening at this stage. The community also ensures that all its young would-be members (male and female) undergo a period of apprenticeship in either a manual craft, or in a household or commercial skill. This is required even if they are going to go to university. (The preference is for this to be done prior to university; Integrated Community 1996, 80.) This stipulation, which means that even the priests who are members of the IG have another practical 'trade', relates very strongly to the underlying value that the IG places on freedom. The IG questions whether one can be a freely committed member of a community if one depends upon that community for one's livelihood (this issue can be seen as having relevance for the Kibbutz and the Bruderhof). The IG's system means that everyone in the community has got an economic option: at least in theory (and more than likely in practice) the apprenticeship means that they will be able to make a living should they decide to leave the community. Thus, the membership is not bound into the community by economic dependency but by a freely made commitment.

Becoming a member of the IG is, accordingly, a process that, while different from joining the Bruderhof, is every bit as protracted and demanding. While some of the demands are of a different type, ultimately membership requires a willingness to join a community which operates through unanimity and which makes very serious demands upon a person and their life. Committing one's life to the Bruderhof means joining a community that, as we have seen, has a history of stress and conflict. The IG does seem to be a rather different type of community in this respect, though there have been splinters. However, we will see when we examine the history of the IG in some detail that while its history has nothing comparable to the Great Crisis of the Bruderhof, it is a community that has been shaped by two tragic events.

THE IG IN THE ROMAN CATHOLIC CHURCH

The precise status of the IG within the Roman Catholic Church is that of Apostolic Association. The community is granted such status within the dioceses it operates in by the local bishop, to whom it considers itself in service. It first received such status in 1978, it being granted by Archbishop Degenhardt of Paderborn and Cardinal Ratzinger, Archbishop of Munich, on an experimental basis for five years. Final approval was given in 1985. Cardinal Ratzinger's letter of episcopal approval shows that this approval was granted under canon law statute 686 of the ecclesiastical law code of the Church, and that the sense of the term Apostolic Association is given in the decree *Apostolicam actuositatem* issued at Vatican II (for Ratzinger's letter and the other information about this issue, see Integrated Community 1996, 108). Degenhardt had been a long-standing friend of the IG, having personal connections with the Wallbrechers over many years. For instance, Degenhardt had belonged to the Neudeutschland Bund in Hagen, as had Herbert Wallbrecher (for this point, and other aspects of the connections between the IG and Degenhardt, see Stötzel 2001).

Cardinal Ratzinger has developed a close relationship with the IG. He first visited the community in October 1976. At least one book of the cardinal's has been published by the community's publishing house (Ratzinger 1999 is an English translation of this book), and we find his work quoted frequently in, for example, Lohfink's *Does God Need the Church?*, dedicated to Ratzinger. This connection is important in helping us to situate the IG in the present-day Roman Catholic Church. Ratzinger is a very controversial figure, being the prefect of the Congregation for the Doctrine of the Faith, the keeper of the Church's theological orthodoxy. Often seen as the 'second in command' of the Vatican, Ratzinger has been in a key position under Pope John Paul II to enforce what can be seen as a 'conservative' theological agenda on the Church. Ratzinger has argued that his present line is one that sees Vatican II as a reformist process and not the revolution that theological 'liberals' have painted it (Stourton 1998, 203). Allen has, in his recent biography of Ratzinger, presented a substantial account of Ratzinger's career from a broadly 'liberal' (and hence rather critical, if personally friendly) Catholic view. His account suggests that Ratzinger was immensely influential on the Vatican II process, and in a 'liberal' direction. One of his chapters is entitled 'An Erstwhile Liberal' (Allen 2000. This book does not mention the IG.) In this respect the final, autobiographical chapter of Lohfink's book is interesting. Called 'The Church and I' it describes a drift into a liberal, oppositional Catholicism, which is gradually rejected for the different approach taken by the IG. This should signal to us the following: the IG is not an insurrectionary group within the Church. At least this is not the position any longer; we shall see shortly that it did have its troubles with the institutions of the Church in the past.

It also needs to be stressed that the IG is far from being the only such Apostolic Association within the Roman Catholic Church. The rubric of Apostolic Association seems to be the 'legal' way in which the Roman Catholic Church has been able to incorporate the activity of the 'New Ecclesial Movements and Communities' into its structures. Like the IG, these are lay movements (though, as with the IG, some have priests in membership) of Catholics that are active in various ways. A feature of recent Catholic life is a series of meetings at which the movements have come together for seminars and the like. The current phase of this started at Pentecost 1998, when there was a vigil and a meeting with 250,000 present in St Peter's Square, with the Pope attending. There have been subsequent meetings, notably in Rome in June 1999.[2] This latter seminar was organised by the Pontifical Council for the Laity in co-operation with the Congregation for Bishops and the Congregation for the Doctrine of the Faith. The involvement of the latter, and its prefect, Cardinal Ratzinger, can be taken as an indication of the importance that the very highest reaches of the Catholic Church place upon the 'movements'.

In the context of these movements the IG appears to be one of the smaller fry. Some of them are large, international bodies that have carved out an important niche for themselves within contemporary Catholicism. Organisations such as Communione e Liberazione, the Neo-Catechumenal Way, the Focolare Movement and the Catholic Charismatic Renewal movement all count their membership in many thousands. Even the Communita di Sant'Egidio (Saint Giles Community), one of the smaller and more interesting of these movements, claims 40,000 members.[3] Although some of these movements are quite long-standing, in many ways they are only now developing a role in the Church. They could be seen as a conservative lay bulwark against the depredations of liberalism and liberation theology. This is the view expressed by Gordon Urquhart in his book *The Pope's Armada*, which is an extremely critical account of three of the most important movements, the Focolare, the Neo-Catechumenal Way and Communione e Liberazione (Urquhart 1996. Urquhart is an ex-member of Focolare.) An alternative view might be that in the emphasis some (for instance Focolare) place on spirituality they may represent a putative Catholic alternative to the Pentecostal movement within Christianity, and perhaps to the 'New Age' scene. Moreover, community is a key feature of these movements. IG is far from the only movement that stresses community. The L'Arche movement works largely through communities, and the Focolare movement has a core of members who live in community.

Although the IG participates in the meetings of the movements, it does appear to be rather on the fringes of this whole scene. There are some possibilities as to why this is the case. The first is that the IG is not one of the leading movements in terms of size. However, against this we should note the prominent position in the 'world' of the movements of Andrea Riccardi, whose Sant'Egidio is much smaller than some of the other groupings. The second might be a certain distancing by the IG itself. The flamboyant demeanour of some of the movements – again Focolare is a good example, as it has what the British tabloid press would no doubt call a 'happy clappy', rather folksy style with lots of guitars and singing – is a long way from the sober outlook of the IG. More importantly, although groups such as Focolare do have members who take their theology very seriously, their accessible approach does perhaps run rather counter to the very earnest stress on theology that one finds in the IG.

HISTORY

The Junger Bund had been founded largely on the initiative of Traudl Wallbrecher in 1948. In the run-up to this move Traudl Wallbrecher (then Traudl Weiß) made a speech to a national meeting of Heliand in which she said in part that '[w]e do not want simply to take up either the romantic or the bourgeois forms again. We must be careful not to create a misleading image. We want to fulfill all things with their meaning. It is not aestheticism that matters it's theology' (Integrated Community 1996, 65). This comment prefigured the focus on theology that has been a feature of the IG and its thinking. The comment on Romanticism is surely a judgement on the Youth Movement.

Wallbrecher developed these views at least in part as a result of considering the experience of the Nazi years. She had made connections with the Weiße Rose resistance movement during the war years, so her position on Nazism could be nothing other than unremitting hostility. (On the Weiße Rose see Scholl 1983; Siefken 1994a; 1994b.) However, she also started to consider the question '[h]ow could this have happened in the midst of this baptized, so-called Christian Occident?' (Integrated Community 1996, 63). Wallbrecher came to the conclusion that the Holocaust had destroyed the earlier, traditional form of Christianity, which envisaged a unity of Church and world, and especially of Christianity and the Western cultural tradition (Integrated Community 1996, 63). We should, perhaps, read this argument as implying an intellectual destruction of the rationale for the earlier form of Christianity. In this context a return to the forms of life that had prevailed before the Nazis was out of the question; how could hiking and camping and singing resume as if nothing had happened in the interim?

In retrospect, the IG has commented on just what it was that the community was doing in the late 1940s.

> There were quite a few attempts at new beginnings also during those postwar
> years among Christians, yet they tended to lead rather towards a conformity

with the 'Zeitgeist', the spirit of the age, than to a turning around, and to a real new beginning. The 'Junger Bund' asked itself, what is it that Christianity has lost? Can one find this again, or has it outlived itself altogether? At the beginning of the Modern Age the religious orders of Dominicus and Francis had written a new theology, and had looked for and found a new way of following Jesus. The task is similar today: A 'theology after the Enlightenment' is needed, and a new form of life is needed for people who want to live as followers of Jesus, i.e. belonging to his discipleship. (Integrated Community 1996, 71)

All this is a retrospective assessment of a process that was happening through the actions of, initially, a group of young Catholic women, 50 to 60 strong, with the help of a small number of sympathetic clergy and university lecturers. Photographs from this period (Integrated Community 1996, 67) show that while there were some fairly immediate changes in style – for instance the getting rid of banners and the like – the Junger Bund was only gradually emerging from the Youth Movement. Camping and open-air meetings were a feature of activity, as the IG's own history shows. Aside from this, the Bund also got involved in producing plays, and going together to the theatre. This is also something that is continued to this day, with trips to the cinema together. (It is also hardly a break with the German Youth Movement, where such activities were also commonplace, certainly in its later, Bündische phase. See Borinski and Milch 1982, 30–31.)

Three events of lasting importance for the IG occurred in 1953. The first was the purchase by the group of the Marlene Kirchner Haus (not given this name until after Kirchner's death in 1966). This was originally a log cabin in the woods above the Walchensee, near the village of Urfeld. In the time since the purchase there has been a gradual process of extension of the cabin. The cabin was bought as a place for the community to celebrate the feasts that are such an important part of its life. Its essential function remains the same, and in many ways it can be seen as the spiritual centre of the movement, as well as a place, in itself, of great beauty. Second, in the same week that the log cabin at Urfeld was bought, the Wallbrechers bought the house at 18 Herzog Heinrich Straße in Munich that has been the movement's centre in Munich ever since. This gave the movement a base of its own in the city. Finally, in 1953 the community met Walter Cohen (Integrated Community 1996, 75–76). Cohen was the son of a Quaker mother and a Jewish father. He joined the group in 1954. 'He is a survivor of the Holocaust. His first contribution is to point out that "Jesus was a Jew and not a Christian"' (Catholic Integrated Community 1998, 2). The IG's own history stated that '[h]is impetus has carried the Community until this day' (Integrated Community 1996, 76).

Two points might be suggested as providing a key to that statement. The history itself noted that Cohen was concerned with the congruence between talking about theology and putting it into practice – in other words, are the things we say we believe actually the things we do? In retrospect the community feels that a solution to this question was only found with the growth of 'integration' in the community's practice after 1968. The other point is that Cohen made 'committed contributions to the understanding of Judaism as the root of Christianity' (Integrated Community 1996, 76). This is very important for an understanding of the IG's theological world-view. The IG stresses the Jewish roots of Christianity, referring to what it calls 'Jewish-Christian thinking' (Integrated Community 1996, 77). Paradoxically, Cohen left the community in 1957, after only three years of membership. The history of the IG suggests that this was due to arguments with Dr Goergen, the priest connected with the community at that time. Cohen died in 1959, two years later, at the age of 31. This was the first of two tragic events that have marked the IG's history.

At this stage the IG was in a transitional phase. It was no longer anything like the Junger Bund, but had yet to develop into something resembling the community of the present day. For a period in the 1950s the Wallbrecher family lived and worked in Hagen, Westphalia. While they attempted to build a group there, and had some successes, it did not cohere into a full section of the Munich-based community (although a community did start in Hagen in 1971). The Wallbrechers spent a lot of time on the road between Hagen, Munich and the log cabin at Urfeld. The Munich group developed a degree of intellectual incoherence in the late 1950s, and so the Wallbrechers returned there in 1960, moving into 18 Herzog Heinrich Straße. A move towards a more committed lifestyle ensued, with attendance at Urfeld feasts becoming conditional upon attendance at seminars, and a perhaps predictable result: 'More people left than stayed' (Integrated Community 1996, 84). However, theological work continued and the group started to understand that 'community' was central to their theological project. In 1965 Traudl Wallbrecher (along with Dr Goergen) visited Israel, and in particular went to see some kibbutzim. 'Traudl Wallbrecher, however, also knew that the form of life of the Kibbutz could not be a possibility for us in Germany and for our task of reform within the Church. And she searched for similar new ways for the Community. A secular institute? A house sharing fellowship? A commune? The New could not be any of these . . .' (Integrated Community 1996, 85).

If the 'New' was not to be any of the options listed above, then its form started to become clearer in the minds of the community as a result of the second tragedy that they faced. This was the death aged 33 of Marlene Kirchner. Kirchner had, as a girl, been a member of the Heliand Bund, and subsequently the Junger Bund. She had drifted away, returning to the community in 1964 with her husband and two children. She died at Easter 1966 (at the time of a community feast) from pneumonia leading to a coronary inflammation. The doctors suggested that her death resulted from overwork (Integrated Community 1996, 89). This obviously caused tremendous soul searching in the community. Some members drew the conclusion that the type of life that the community had chosen to follow was too demanding for people in the ordinary run of life, and left the community. Some reacted by attempting to work out how they could have pre-vented the situation which resulted in Kirchner's death from arising.

> These others stayed. They tried to find the answer. In the years to come, by interweaving their possibilities and talents, they built up a life-fellowship of married and unmarried people together with their priests; a community of people who supplement and support each other and as a whole try to follow the mission of Jesus . . . Out of this grew a new form of the 'Familia Dei' in the midst of the secular world. (Integrated Community 1996, 89)

The integration process began from the depths of the second tragedy that the community had faced. The community's history notes that the process arising from Kirchner's death took two and a half years to play out, so there was not an immediate change in the way of life as might be implied in the foregoing.

The next important event in the IG's history was the secession of Aloys Goergen and a number of people who supported him, in October 1968. For the IG this represented a break by Goergen with the vision of Guardini. Whether this was the case or not is, in a sense, unimportant. The statement suggested a desire on the part of the IG to present itself as holding to that vision, a theme which shall be considered in more depth when we look at the world-view of the IG. It is, on the basis of the material presented by the IG, hard to discern why Goergen left. They suggest that he was committed to an 'aesthetics of faith' (Integrated Community 1996, 96). This is not elaborated. Elsewhere they have suggested that he was interested in a project of reforming art, liturgy and the Church, and was opposed to the notion of integration (Catholic Integrated Community 1998, 3). The practical consequences were twofold. First, as he was the only priest connected with the IG, a request was made to the then Archbishop of Munich, Cardinal Doepfner, for a priest to oversee the community. This was granted, and the community was entrusted to the Munich student chaplain, at the community's request (Integrated Community 1996, 95). This suggests that the membership of the community in and around 1968 was mainly composed of stu-dents, and this is borne out in its history (Integrated Community 1996, 92). This is noteworthy, as 1968 was a time of considerable unrest in the German student body. It may well be that today a number of experienced IG members have back-grounds in the generation and social milieu that set western Europe alight with their revolt in the late 1960s. Some support for this argument can be found in the article of M. Winter and A. Stötzel, 'Die 68er: Ein Minister denkt nach – wir auch' (The 68ers: A Minister thinks back – we too). This is about a couple who were participants in the 1968 movements and who found their way to the IG in the mid-1970s (Winter and Stötzel 2001).

The second consequence has been of significance to the IG over the years. The IG claimed that Goergen described the community as a sect following his depar-ture (Integrated Community 1996, 95). This is a charge that has been levelled at the community on a number of occasions since, and in meeting members of the community one forms the impression that it remains a view taken of the IG by certain sections of Catholicism in Germany, and that this has affected aspects of the IG's view of its own position. It seems to regard itself as embattled within German Catholicism.

In 1969 the community started up a periodical that had the German title *Die Integrierte Gemeinde*. As the community's history laconically noted, '[a] few months later the readers of the periodical transferred this title to the Community herself and gave her this name' (Integrated Community 1996, 95). This is how and when the IG became known as the Integrated Community. The name reflects the ideas connected with the word and concept 'integration' that had developed in the community in the years after the death of Marlene Kirchner.

The new phase of the community's history was not plain sailing, however. In the years 1972 to 1974 the community received a number of letters from the office of the vicar general of the archbishopric of Munich indicating theological concerns about the community, and expressly forbidding it to use a form of words in its title that mentioned the archdiocese. This was part of a process that led to action on the part of the community in July 1976, when members went into the cathedrals of the four dioceses in which communities then existed and indicated that they would not leave until the leaders of the community were granted an audience with Cardinal Doepfner. The meeting (which the IG had been asking for since 1969) was granted. Doepfner conducted the interview and issued a statement. In its history the IG stresses the fact that Doepfner declared that they were not a sect. Small sections of newspaper stories are reproduced in the part of the history dealing with this event (Integrated Community 1996, 104). It is difficult to make much out from these extracts but it is clear that the 'sect' label was a major concern, and that the name of Dr Goergen figures quite prominently. This phase of the IG's history started to be resolved with its recognition as an Apostolic Association in 1978 on a trial basis, and more fully in 1985. However, in discussion with IG members it is clear that although the IG does have a standing within the Church – and given the close ties to Cardinal Ratzinger one might speculate that for at least the foreseeable future this standing will be protected – it is still, as indicated above, the focus of some degree of suspicion and opposition. In part this may be because of the fractured nature of contemporary German Catholicism. In the debate in mid-2000 between the Vatican and the German bishops on the issue of the involvement of Church agencies in the abortion process, the IG was clearly on the side of the Vatican, as was the paper that the IG has connections with, *Tagespost*. To have taken this position inevitably meant annoying other sections of the Church, and hence, perhaps, conflict. In this respect it is interesting to note that the arrangement whereby the IG provides priests for the Urfeld parish in southern Bavaria takes place under the auspices of the bishopric of Augsburg, and not that of Munich. No such arrangement has been agreed in the community's 'home town', an indication, perhaps, of tensions.

In the next phase of the community's life a number of meetings took place that have proved, in two cases at least, to have had important long-term implications for the movement. The first of these was the visit of Bishop Christopher Mwoleka, bishop of Rulenge in Tanzania, to the community in November 1977. This led to a long-term relationship, which eventually blossomed into the start of a Tanzanian community in 1988. In 1992 this was formally inaugurated, and now the community is present in a number of locations including Morogoro/Melala in rural Tanzania and also in Dar-es-Salaam, the capital of the country. The second meeting was in 1982, when the IG and the Bruderhof commenced what ultimately proved to be an abortive relationship that ended in the mid-1990s. In 1985 the third meeting was with Chaim Seeligmann of the Kibbutz movement. This led into the chain of events that resulted in the Urfeld Circle. This continues to meet, despite the withdrawal of the Bruderhof, and it continues to be a very significant factor in the IG's life.

This phase is, perhaps, the one in which the community still remains. It has been marked by the development of the concept of integration, an expansion of horizons with the work in Tanzania, and the deeper development of the connection to Jewish thought that commenced with Walter Cohen's involvement and has taken a practical shape in the relationship with the Kibbutz movement. The Junger Bund, as we saw, started with 50 to 60 members in the late 1940s. By the late 1960s, the IG had around 80 members (Integrated Community 1996, 92). In the twenty years between 1948 and 1968, the membership thus hardly changed numerically. In the following thirty years, however, the movement advanced to the position today, with a membership of more than a thousand. This path has not always been straightforward. The community's own history shows that in the years 1988 and 1989 it was a target of a press campaign, notably in the Munich daily *Süddeutsche Zeitung*. This saw the old accusations of the IG being a sect resurrected, along with allegations of financial chicanery. The IG saw these off, with the assistance of the bishop of Augsburg.

IDEOLOGY

The obvious starting point in considering the ideology of the IG is that it is Roman Catholic. Indeed, with its identification with the person and approach of Cardinal Ratzinger it can be seen as lying clearly within the current leading (if not uncontested) viewpoint within contemporary Catholicism. Questioning members of the IG about just what sort of organisation the IG is, one might hear the argument that the IG is not really a movement within the Church, but basically a group of Catholics who don't want their Catholicism to be confined to going to church on a Sunday. We have seen that the origins of the IG lie very firmly within the Catholic youth movement of the immediate post-war period, however much the IG may have distanced itself from that point of origin. We have also seen the stress that the IG places upon its official recognition by the Church with all that that recognition implies for the charge that it is a 'sect'.

All that said, it is important to note that the IG does stand out from 'run of the mill' Catholicism in a number of ways, and perhaps the most important is its stress on the Jewish root of Christianity. The argument that they advance on this point is not unique. In recent years there has been a serious effort to say something rather similar from within the Jewish community, notably in the work of Geza Vermes around the theme 'Jesus the Jew'. However, Vermes' argument is that 'Christianity' is a construction bearing little relationship to the real meaning of what Jesus of Nazareth had to say. Vermes reclaims, as it were, Jesus for Judaism. 'By the end of the first century Christianity had lost sight of the real Jesus and of the original meaning of his message. Paul, John and their churches replaced him by the otherworldly Christ of faith, and his insistence on personal effort, concentration and trust in God by a reliance in the saving merits of an eternal, divine redeemer' (Vermes 2000, 263). From within the Christian tradition attempts have been made to reclaim the essentially Jewish nature of the message of Jesus, although without the emphasis that Vermes gave to the argument that, in effect, Paul and John 'created' a Christianity unrecognisable to Jesus himself. An important, if now rather dated, effort can be found in the work of John Macmurray, where this theme can be seen to run from the 1930s to the 1960s. Perhaps his most interesting book expressing this view is *The Clue to History* (Macmurray 1938). Macmurray wrote this book when not a member of any church. In old age he became a Quaker, but his work is today a focus of interest for a small but devoted audience of North American Catholics. Another example of an attempt to stress the Jewish root of Christianity is to be found in one of the key works of the important African-American theologian, Howard Thurman, *Jesus and the Disinherited*, first published in 1949. In developing his argument Thurman suggested, '[h]ow different might have been the story of the last two thousand years on this planet grown old from suffering if the link between Jesus and Israel had never been severed!' (Thurman 1997, 124).

One of the theologians of the IG, Gerhard Lohfink, has expressed the view it puts forward on this question.

> In Jesus and the Church founded on him Israel's history again takes one of those turns that no-one expects, that overturns everything. It is usually forgotten that what happened then in Galilee and afterward in Jerusalem was not something strange and alien to Israel; it was Jewish history. The actors were, after all, without exception, Jews. Jesus was a Jew, Mary was a Jew, all the Apostles were Jews. It is banal to say it, of course, but unfortunately there is still good reason to say it to Christians. The *ekklesia* came into existence in Israel, understanding itself as the eschatological Israel gathered by God, and it is therefore inextricably and forever bound to the whole of Israel. (Lohfink 1999, 240–41)

Moreover, the IG contends that Judaism and Christianity are not 'religions', an argument that has some similarities with those of Barth and the Blumhardts. Gerhard Lohfink argued that '[w]e are here face to face with the difference between faith and religion. Religion does not require faith. It imposes itself on people and is in some sense evident. It is the thing that is clear to everyone' (Lohfink 1999, 95). He pointed out the 'interchangeability' of the gods of antiquity, with, for instance, the Greek Zeus being equatable to the Roman Jupiter.

> From this point of view Israel brought the world something new. Its God was not interchangeable with others, but instead demanded an allegiance that excluded all other Gods. We can also describe the difference between religion and faith, which is at the same time the difference between religion and revelation, as follows: religion asks about the great mysteries of existence. (Lohfink 1999, 95)

Ludwig Weimer, in a speech to the Urfeld Circle, 'On the distinction between religion and revelation', stated that it 'took me almost 20 years to understand why religion actually exists, why it was both as great a misfortune as it was a fortune; how one can cleanse this religion and why Judaism and Christianity, looked at closely, are no religions' (Weimer in Catholic Integrated Community 1997, 94).

For the IG, it is clear, there is an intimate and unbreakable connection at the deepest level between Judaism and Christianity. In practical terms the meaning of this connection can be examined by looking at the argument that the IG has developed about the 'People of God'. Weimer in another lecture to the Urfeld Circle ('Wherefore a People of God?') put this argument succinctly.

> The central concept of the Judeo-Christian faith is neither 'God' nor 'state', also not 'state-god' nor 'God-state', but 'People of God' – where the two basic questions [finding meaning in life and living happily together] are answered in conjunction with one another in a correct mutual enlightenment and purification through a new life form: Community – the compound network of life fellowships. The history of Israel was and is a striving for the right form, for the redeeming and liberating form of this People, and the history of the Church is a striving for the realization of the solution found by the Jew Jesus from Nazareth. (Weimer in Catholic Integrated Community 1997, 53)

The notion of the People of God is the centrepiece of Lohfink's book, perhaps the most comprehensive introduction in English to the thought of the IG; indeed, its subtitle is 'Toward a Theology of the People of God'. In a document produced by the community the weight of this notion for the IG was revealed: 'God's forgotten solution is the international People of God, consisting of Christians and Jews. It grows in freedom and is gathered in free will from all the nations of the earth' (Integrated Community 1996, 38).

However, the People of God is not the only crucial concept for the IG. Another central theme in their theology is the 'new family'. Discussing the contemporary Church, they noted that '[t]he celebration of the Eucharist is seen not so much as the sign and centre of a shared life, but as a mystic symbol for the strengthening of the individual, even though this symbol remains tied into the rite of the daily liturgy of the Church. An organically grown fellowship of life and table of the "New Family" can be perceived nowhere' (Integrated Community 1996, 33). Lohfink indicated where, for the IG, the possibility of this 'new family' exists and indeed just what it involves.

> Jesus is founding a new family, that is, the basis on which people who have nothing at all to do with one another can join together in unconditional solidarity. It is the place where true reconciliation with God and one another becomes possible. But people cannot create this new possibility for themselves. It must come from the cross. It had to be grounded in the death of Jesus. (Lohfink 1999, 200)

As Lohfink makes clear a little earlier in his text, the final part of this important quotation indicates the dependence of the 'new family' upon Agape. Agape is the Greek word for 'brotherly love' according to the 1975 *Pocket Oxford Dictionary*. In this context it is often contrasted with Eros, or sexual love, indicating the nature of divine love, which is held to go beyond and be more inclusive than Eros. However, the *Pocket Oxford* also notes that Agape was the name of a Christian feast held in connection with the Lord's Supper, and in the context of the IG this meaning should also be borne in mind. Traudl Wallbrecher contextualised the 'new family' in a summary of what the community had learned in its experiences.

> She [the IG] discovered the 'assembly', the 'ecclesia', anew in its advisory and guiding strength, and tried out the 'vita communis', the 'New Family' of married people, children, and singles, men and women, lay-persons and priests. In the gathering of the New Family of those whom He has called for this mission – a gathering always newly enabled by God – the Community again found the 'Figure of the Twelve', who sit at the table with Jesus. (Integrated Community 1996, 58)

Wallbrecher spelt out the theme of Agape and enablement by God in the same text. 'What ultimately holds the Integrated Community together is alone the Agape given to her by God, which is neither her own work nor her own merit' (Integrated Community 1996, 59). In the argument about the new family advanced by the IG we accordingly find a view that community is dependent upon God's grace similar to that advanced by Eberhard Arnold in the context of the Bruderhof.

The ideas of 'People of God' and the 'new family' are the central focal points of the theology of the IG, and, moreover, they fit together. This can be seen in a text by the leading IG theologians Gerhard Lohfink and Rudolf Pesch, unfortunately not available in English, called *Volk Gottes als 'Neue Familie'* (*People of God as 'New Family'*). A section of the text does amplify the title usefully. After a discussion of the description in St John's Gospel of the washing of the disciples' feet by Jesus at the Last Supper, Lohfink and Pesch argued '[d]amit sind wir beim Tun Jesu selbst angelegt. Es ist ganz in der Tradition Israels verwurzelt. Aber durch seine Botschaft und Praxis tritt nun endgültig in Erscheinung, daß das Gottesvolk Neue Familie sein soll.' ('With this we have reached close to the act of Jesus himself. It is entirely rooted in the tradition of Israel. But through his message and activity finally it becomes apparent that the People of God shall be a New Family.') (Lohfink and Pesch 1995, 237). The possibility opened up by the Crucifixion is that the People of God shall be composed of people from all nations, living as a new family, a family that goes beyond the old family of blood ties, and allows the previously unconnected to live in unconditional solidarity. The two concepts, accordingly, fit together so closely that they could be seen as two sides of the same coin.

Before moving on from the People of God and the new family, we should note that in stressing these terms the IG is not in any way going outside of the boundaries of Catholic thinking. In particular the concept of the People of God is a central motif of post-Vatican II Roman Catholic self-understanding. In an introductory book on *The Catholic Faith*, Fr Roderick Strange discusses the Catholic Church's view of itself with reference to the Vatican II document *Lumen Gentium* ('The Light of the Nations'). He states categorically in this discussion that '[t]he Church is the people of God' (Strange 1996, 42). This discussion of the IG's understanding of the terms People of God and new family should be seen as a very brief introduction to a topic about which the theologians of the IG have written extensively. As will have been gathered, much of this material focuses on the connection between Judaism and Christianity, perhaps the distinguishing mark of much IG theology. We can now move on to a consideration of the way in which the IG theologically presents its community form as a way of living its theology, in the way demanded of it by Walter Cohen in the 1950s.

LIVING THE THEOLOGY

In this respect a text by Rudolf Pesch and Traudl Wallbrecher is useful. It is a transcript of a presentation by Pesch on the structures of the IG given at a meeting of the Urfeld Circle. Wallbrecher also made some points in this discussion, which included questions from kibbutznikim. (The text is called 'Contributions, questions and answers concerning the structure and the history of the Integrated Community and on unanimity' in Urfelder Kreis 1996.) Pesch started with a discussion of the 'communion of the table'. He asserted that the table communion with God and one another is central to Israel's history of revelation. Pesch drew a parallel between the story of the law-giving to Moses on

Sinai and stories concerning Jesus on the Mountain. In these latter, Pesch pointed out, Jesus had his new family around him. In the case of Moses with his three confidants and the Elders, Pesch suggested that the Bible indicates that they ate and drank before God. He also noted that Isaiah's promise for the end of days is a festive meal of all nations on Mount Zion. Pesch argued that in the stories of Jesus on the Mountain, a message is clear. 'Jesus wants nothing more than what had already been underway in Israel for centuries since the days of Sinai. On all possible occasions he emphasizes inexplicitly and explicitly that the Torah and the prophets suffice' (Urfelder Kreis 1996, 69). In this tradition, Pesch argued, Jesus made the communion of the table the centre of his mission, and he argues that the IG has re-experienced that everything that could be called co-ordination, governance, responsibility and gathering originates from the communion of the table.

This takes us naturally on to the feast. Pesch was speaking in Urfeld, and suggested that the IG was born from the celebration of the feasts at the place where he was speaking, especially the feast of Easter. The IG grew from the place of the feast into Munich, Rome, Tanzania and so forth, spreading organically like a plant. Hence, the communion of the table and the feast were reiterated by Pesch in this text. In our earlier consideration of the reality of the IG we saw the way in which the structure of the community focuses around the table communities which can be seen as its building blocks, and the way in which the year is structured by the community around the feasts. Pesch's text starts us on the way to understanding the theological underpinning of this, especially by showing a biblical basis for the table communities. Returning to Lohfink's book we can extend this understanding.

The extent to which the IG's notion of community is bound up with the image of the common meal can be seen from the fact that Lohfink entitled a chapter 'Table Manners in the Reign of God'. There is an extremely serious theological point underlying all this. Lohfink discusses in his book the story of the feeding of the five thousand as presented in the Gospel of Mark. He suggests that the text is about the formation of the crowds into what he calls the end-time people of God by Jesus.

> It is apparently necessary for that end-time people of God to be organized in a clearly visible manner into dining communities. Only when the scattered people of God allows itself to be gathered and comes together in a visible way around Jesus, its eschatological shepherd, can the miracle take place. Only then can the festive banquet of the reign of God happen. Only then can the glory of the meal shine forth. (Lohfink 1999, 147)

Lohfink argues that that the Church can sometimes merely preach and send people away hungry. It can sometimes engage in campaigns against hunger but it does not, indeed cannot, change society in this way. Rather, as at the feeding of the five thousand, it can and should become the People of God gathered by Jesus into the new society in which the abundance of the reign of God shines forth. This happened in the early Church after Easter. 'After Easter the Church would gather with eschatological rejoicing for festive meals (Acts 2:46) at which all shared with one another – not only bread, but their whole existence' (Lohfink 1999, 148). Lohfink draws a fascinating conclusion from this: '[e]xcess, wealth, and profligate luxury are thus the signs of the time of salvation – not economy, meagerness, wretchedness, and neediness' (Lohfink 1999, 149). This conclusion is interesting inasmuch as it chimes with a throwaway comment made by a community member, to the effect that the IG is not a mendicant order. Its members certainly do not live in the kind of rough and ready surroundings of the Bruderhof. The flats and homes of its members are well appointed, and the members dress well by conventional standards.

Lohfink considers the political implications of Jesus's message. He argues that Jesus was not interested in damning all forms of human rule. He didn't question the need for the state, but was not concerned to provide assurances for it either. 'His interest is solely in God's new society, which in the midst of the old world is beginning the unheard-of new thing' (Lohfink 1999, 181). He suggested that we can sum this new thing up in a simple phrase – no longer desiring to rule, but rather to serve the cause of God and thereby to serve other people. However, serving in this context must not be understood in a bland way. Originally it meant serving at table, a task left, in the ancient world, to slaves, servants or women.

> It was precisely at table that the contrast between the superiors who recline and the slaves or women who must serve is especially palpable . . . Thus it is no accident that Jesus shapes the new society he begins with his disciples by starting at the common table. Here the true revolution commences; here is the beginning of the classless society. (Lohfink 1999, 182)

Lohfink gives a description of the table manners in the reign of God that summarises this part of his book:

> [p]art of the table manners of the reign of God is that there are no more classes: all sit at the same table. Another part of those table manners is that each first looks to see that the others have everything they need; only then do they think of their own plates. It is also part of these table manners that the greatest is the servant of all; this alone shows that such a one is able to exercise an office. Finally, it is part of these manners that one does not seek the best place but the worst. (Lohfink 1999, 183)

From this it can be seen that the stress on the table community and the feasts in the practice of the IG is no eccentricity. Rather it is founded upon a theological underpinning that takes its rationale from an exegesis of the gospel. Lohfink tied the practice of the IG in to events in the New Testament such as the Last Supper and the feeding of the five thousand in an interpretation that saw those events as being part of the Bible narrative for deep reasons, rather than chance. The feeding of the five thousand is not 'just another' miracle; rather it points to the way in which Christians can and should live in the here and now of the twenty-first century.

Returning now to Pesch's account of the community, we can note what he said about the 'assembly'. The 'assembly' of the local communities meets weekly, and is one of the basic forms taken by the community. Pesch argued that the assembly 'of those called into it' (Urfelder Kreis 1996, 71) is the decision-making body of the community. At this point Traudl Wallbrecher pointed out that the rather strange form of words – being called into the assembly – meant that it was those who of their own accord, over a period of time, wished to participate who were involved. This illustrates two points: first, the voluntary nature of the community, and second, the fact that entry into the community can take a longish period of time – she suggested that it is six to ten years, although immediately stated that with some people it is quite a fast process and that it is hard to tie the process down in statutes. Wallbrecher noted that women belong in the assembly, as does the priest. The responsibility for the community is carried by the assembly, and not just by the priest. But the priest always belongs to the 'Figure of Twelve' in the community (Urfelder Kreis 1996, 72).

Pesch gave a rationale for the Figure of Twelve structure, pointing out that in the New Testament Jesus chose 12 apostles from out of his 70 disciples. The Twelve refers back to the 12 tribes of Israel, and is a symbol of refoundation. The Twelve themselves were the ones who Jesus knew he could place responsibility upon. Pesch suggested that the main responsibility of the Twelve was to ensure unanimity in the People of God. He indicated some of the roots of the Figure of Twelve – the system of leadership in the IG. However, he indicated that the community only started to think in terms of the Figure of Twelve following a speech by Cardinal Ratzinger in 1991.

The discussion indicated the difficulty that those kibbutznikim present had in agreeing with the IG's notion of unanimity. Traudl Wallbrecher noted that this was perhaps the greatest difference between the IG and the Kibbutz (Urfelder Kreis 1996, 73). However, both she and Pesch made clear that the Figure of Twelve were responsible for unanimity in the community. This is another aspect of IG structure that is, in fact, very closely connected to a theological argument. Again, if we turn to Lohfink, we will find that this notion of the Twelve as being responsible for unanimity in the assembly of the community is derived from New Testament exegesis. He considered an incident of disagreement in the early Church depicted in the Acts of the Apostles (Acts 6:1–7). The precise incident is, as Lohfink notes, not important. The point is the way in which a situation of 'grumbling' in the early Church gets resolved. The mechanism for resolution was set out by Lohfink. 'To resolve the conflict the Twelve take the initiative, for they are especially responsible for the unanimity of the community' (Lohfink 1999, 227). This incident results in a clearer structuring of the Church community. With the choice of seven deacons the issue is resolved and the community's structures clarified. However the crucial point is this: '[t]he suggestion made by the Twelve receives the assent of the whole assembly. No vote is taken; the community must make its decision by consensus. If there were no unanimity the decision would have to be postponed' (Lohfink 1999, 227). This should not be taken to imply that there is no voting in the IG at all. The IG's Twelve are chosen in a fairly complex balloting system, described by Pesch in his text (Urfelder Kreis 1996, 73–74).

The purpose of this discussion has been to show some of the ways in which the IG attempts to live its theology. It was noted earlier that the IG today points to Walter Cohen's question about the congruence of theological talk and everyday practice. The IG feels that it did not reach a solution to this issue until 1968, with the actual formation of the Integrated Community under that name. This section has shown that the IG's practice in the areas of the table communities, the feast and in aspects of its structures such as the assembly, unanimity and the Figure of Twelve are represented as efforts to translate its theological understanding into everyday practice. In discussing the Figure of Twelve, Traudl Wallbrecher made clear the extent to which the Twelve are involved in everyday issues, mentioning the role of the Twelve in areas of community life such as the upbringing of children, sick members, the pump factory at Wangen and the like (Urfelder Kreis 1996, 73). From this, incidentally, we can infer, although it is not explicitly stated, that as well as a Figure of Twelve for the individual communities, the IG's overall co-ordinating leadership probably takes this form.

This has been a consideration of just a few issues in community life, and no claim as to comprehensiveness is made. Other aspects of community structure could no doubt be similarly analysed. A fascinating example here is the comments made by Lohfink about the existence of prophetic voices in the present-day church. These comments have major implications for the practice of leadership in the community. After asserting that there are contemporary prophets, and that prophecy involves primarily discernment and is not just about seeing the future – more formally, prophecy is primarily diagnostic, not prognostic – he says the following:

> [i]t continually happens that those with the gift of discernment see the true situation of the Church and world. They uncover false images that individuals and the community have of themselves. They see the world in the laser beam of the gospel. They see what concrete actions are to be taken. In taking such people and their prophetic charism seriously a community formed by the New Testament is different from all the assemblies in our society, in which endless opinions collide because one's own position or that of one's own group is

unconditionally defended. (Lohfink 1999, 229. Lohfink gave the names of four persons he considered to be such prophets. Lohfink 1999, 325.)

HISTORICAL SENSIBILITIES

To conclude our consideration of the ideology of the IG, we should examine the socio-political vision that it espouses. This vision is embedded in a view of history and the point in history that we can see contemporary society as occupying. The IG does not have very much to say about socio-political issues directly, unlike the Kibbutz, which has, as we saw, been rooted in the socialist and Zionist movements, or the Bruderhof, which has always had a socio-political edge to its witness, something especially true today. What it does have to say, however, links very closely to its historical sensibility, so we will start by looking at that.

The IG sees this point in time as being crucially when the notion of a state Church, or as it is sometimes put, a 'Christian Empire', is definitely at an end. In a talk to the Urfeld Circle, IG theologian Arnold Stötzel recalled the time when the German kings went down to Rome to collect the crown of the Holy Roman Empire from the Pope. This represented, for Stötzel, the fact that they wished to found an Empire in which there would be no separation between the religious and secular spheres. 'This notion of Christian Empire, accompanied since the 19th century by the new myths of Nationalism and Socialism, underwent its life-threatening climax and perversion in the Nazi Empire' ('Concerning the vision of the Urfeld Circle', in Catholic Integrated Community 1997, 28). Lohfink argues that there had, in fact, been a long period, starting with the recognition of Christianity as the state religion of the Roman Empire, that he designates as the 'experiment with statehood' (Lohfink 1999, 118). He argues that this was a detour for the church. However, we now live after the Enlightenment, and this perhaps gives us another clue as to where we stand in history. As Stötzel put it, '[i]n the form of the original community we have seen a completely new chance arising since the Age of the European Enlightenment. It was the Age of Enlightenment, on the one hand, which brought about the secular state and made the freedom of the individual possible' (Catholic Integrated Community 1997, 28). Ludwig Weimer and Arnold Stötzel, in a piece called 'Notes on the messianic question', suggest that within the Empire in the Middle Ages the Church became the most embittered warrior against the idea of the Holy Empire. 'She [the Church] forced a wedge between the Emperor's realm and the Kingdom of God' (Integrated Community 1996, 196). This set in train the movement that led to the separation of Church and state, opening up a sphere of personal freedom, the most cherished achievement of Occidental history. Thus, the Enlightenment itself might be seen as a result of the battle between the Church and the Empire.

For the IG there is a new chance for the Church today. To some extent it is in a situation of danger, a point expressed by Weimer and Stötzel. 'Today's Church grew up in the framework of the Holy Roman Empire. With its end she lost her protective cover' (Integrated Community 1996, 199). However, Lohfink points to 'God's concern for the transformation of human society. This transformation can only occur in freedom' (Lohfink 1999, 119). For the IG, Christianity cannot be forced upon anyone. It has to be chosen freely by them. This is, of course, why they view the 'state Church' as a detour; it tried to eliminate freedom of conscience. Hence, the point in history that we find ourselves at is this: the old model has been discredited by its outcomes. There can be no new Holy Roman Empire of any sort, nor should there be. The Enlightenment has spread scepticism towards Christianity, but it has also allowed for freedom of individual conscience. This is an opportunity for the Church to become involved in the genuine conversion of people to Christianity through their free choice. So Weimer and Stötzel write about '[t]he radical change of modern awareness and self-understanding, namely that the individual can decide for himself freely whether he wants to believe or not, wants to belong to the Church or not' (Integrated Community 1996, 199). This is what the Church is confronted by today, and in a sense it should be no other way.

At this point we can note that this vision, though not identical, is similar to that presented by Romano Guardini. Krieg presents Guardini's vision as expressed in books such as *The End of the Modern Age* and *Freedom, Grace and Destiny* in a straightforward and accessible way. He noted that for Guardini there are three epochs of Western civilisation. The first lasted from 500BCE to 800CE. The second lasted from 800CE to 1300CE and the third, the modern age, started in the fourteenth century. This period reached its zenith in the nineteenth century, and it was moving to its conclusion in the twentieth century, to be replaced by a new epoch (Krieg 1997, 171–72). The modern age is marked for Guardini by two particular intellectual traits. The first is that it sees the universe as a limitless reality of time and space, with the concept of infinity no longer being about a transcendent reality. The second is a stress on the human as a knowing subject – an autonomous and rational being. Although some Christian ideas of an ethical nature have remained important in the twentieth century, Christian doctrine has been discarded (Krieg 1997, 172–73). In late modernity, even this has been gone beyond for Guardini. 'One thing that is refreshing about late modernity, Guardini points out, is that there is a new consistency and honesty in the rejection of the Judeo-Christian tradition' (Krieg 1997, 174). In other words, for Guardini we live in a post-Christian world. This situation, at the end of modernity, in fact offers up immense potential for hope as well as for ill. A merit of the post-Christian epoch for Guardini is that people can choose their values and live them out. As Guardini himself put it, '[t]he world to come will be filled with animosity and danger, but it will be a world open and clean. This danger within the new world will also have its cleansing effect upon the new Christian attitude, which in a special way must possess both truth and courage' (Guardini 1998, 105). Krieg also shows how Guardini adopted a nuanced approach to the Enlightenment, seeing merits as well as losses in the process. He suggests that, over a period of time, Guardini came to overcome the Romantic view held by some Catholics that a return to medieval political structures such as the Holy Roman Empire would be a good thing. In these views Guardini was not expressing identical stances to those of the IG. However, there is a degree of similarity. Guardini represented, for Krieg, an attempted overcoming of the Romantic strain in German Catholic thinking. We have already seen that the IG in its early days stated that it intended to do the same in the Catholic youth movement.

For the IG, freedom is an absolutely central concept. As we saw earlier, the international People of God, consisting of Jews and Christians, grows in freedom and is gathered in free will. A free choice must be made to join this people. This clearly implies a rejection of the 'Christian Empire' model, and instead leads to an altogether different approach. Stötzel painted a picture of Traudl Wallbrecher and the group around her, reflecting on the Holocaust. They asked the question: if not a 'Holy Roman Empire', then what might be the way forward in this situation? They considered the Old Testament as opened up to them by Jews such as Buber and Rosenzweig, and found that a new way was open. They found 'a form for today, which set out from the strict separation of Church and state, which set out from the profane and the religious, from faith and democracy not being blended and confused; the form of the Community' (Catholic Integrated Community 1997, 28). For the IG, then, the way in which the notion of freedom starts to play out is in the separation of its activities from the state. Indeed, the IG goes further; all its own activities are self-financed. 'For the Community the credibility and the survival of its new way depended upon financing its work free from and independent of state and Church monies' (Catholic Integrated Community 1998, 17). This position is controversial in German Catholic circles. It implies a need to end the arrangement whereby the Church receives monies via the state tax system. This would not necessarily be popular with all sections of the Church hierarchy. However, in conversation with IG members it became clear that there is a feeling that this system has to some extent compromised the Church, even if it has made it rich.

At the political level, the IG demands pluralism.

> Pluralism is the political solution for the protection of the freedom of the individual opinions and world views; it is the result of an enlightenment process: namely the insight that different views exist alongside each other and must tolerate each other. Pluralism – together with tolerance – is one of the most precious fruits of the European history of freedom. (Integrated Community 1996, 32)

This plays itself out in a number of ways. Members of the IG are involved in a number of political parties in Germany. A member suggested that all the democratic parties included members who were IG participants. One can surmise from conversations that this would mean the CDU/CSU parties, the SPD and the

FDP, but exclude, for instance, the PDS and the NPD. The interesting 'test case' would be the Greens, especially in the light of Green patronage of the IG's bank due to its ethical investment policy. At a policy level the pluralist stance may also have implications of a fairly general sort. A member explaining the IG's economic structures noted that they implied a liberal economic policy on the part of the authorities. The member concerned was a long-standing SPD member, and was at the time sitting next to an IG member who had been a CSU councillor in Munich. This is clearly a long way from the activist anti-capitalism of the present-day Bruderhof. That said, the IG does recognise serious problems in the structure of the contemporary economy. In an article presenting the Wangen pump factory for the IG's magazine, Kurt Peter expressed the view that socialisation of capital as practised in the former East Germany 'led to ruin because personal responsibility for capital and wealth production was forbidden' (Peter 2001, 4, trans. R. Crump). That said, however, understanding was shown of the position taken by anti-globalisation campaigners concerned with the high mobility of capital. The system of profit sharing (though not a workers' co-operative) adopted at the pump factory was presented as an answer to some of the problems discussed in the article.

These discussions have implications for the position of the IG vis-à-vis other members of society. Stötzel suggested that the form of the community 'made possible again the search for connection between the Law from Sinai and the Sermon on the Mount on the one hand and the secular world on the other. A form brought about voluntarily with one's own life. In freedom, separate from the heathens, but living under the same conditions of the secular world as they do' (Catholic Integrated Community 1997, 28). Accordingly, the IG does not demand that the whole of society adopts its form of life; far from it. It only wants those who freely wish to join to come to it. It is prepared to live under the same conditions as everyone else, and wishes to be allowed the freedom to live its life as a community in the way it sees fit. Freedom is taken so seriously by the IG that it provides its new members with an alternative way of making their livings should they decide to leave the community. Accordingly, the socio-political demands of the community take the form of a desire for a pluralistic political structure with a liberal economic order, and above all tolerance of diverse opinions. Within this framework they can live out their community lifestyle, and seek to proclaim the gospel.

Gerhard Lohfink clarified some aspects of the IG's argument in a piece in the IG's magazine *Heute in Kirche und Welt*. This considered the dispute between the majority of the German bishops on the one hand and the Pope and Cardinal Ratzinger on the other regarding the provision of assistance to women seeking abortion. Lohfink was concerned in this piece to argue for the clear separation of the Church and state, arguing that the Pope's line represented just this: 'a clear delineation between Church and State – for the well being of the Church and for the benefit of the State' (Lohfink 2000, 2, trans. R. Crump). Lohfink suggests that in contemporary society, though no one wants a state Church any longer, there is a tendency to see the Church as a 'sector' within society. 'The Church would have the role of a religious service provider within the wider context of contemporary society. . . . Beyond that the Church would definitely be welcomed in the arena of social affairs: that is in the many areas which the state is unable to deal with, at least not yet' (Lohfink 2000, 1). Lohfink argues that there is no question of opposing any or all co-operation between Church and state. Rather, if such co-operation takes place it should do so on the basis of the independence of the Church from the state. Moreover, '[i]f the Church sees itself as a branch of wider society then it will already have betrayed its independent position and its very own being. The Church is a society in itself – and indeed a society with its own form' (Lohfink 2000, 1). Where did Christianity derive this model from? 'One of the roots of the Christian *agape* came from the care for the poor evident in the Jewish synagogue communities' (Lohfink 2000, 2). Lohfink suggests that Christianity could have developed as a mystical religion, or been organised like an ancient cult association. But instead it developed in a form derived from the Jewish association of synagogue communities. This in turn developed from the Jewish people's painful experiment with state forms.

> They thought more deeply about the more fundamental reasons for the failure [of the state form] and recognised that the rule of the Lord brought people together in a different way from state rule, in unburdened solidarity and binding, emancipating unity. They formulated the Torah as a social code of a people who lived in a different way from those around them. (Lohfink 2000, 2)

The association of synagogue communities that came about was not a state – although it recognised the need for a judicial state. This was a basis for the early Church. 'Through them it became clear what God's people were: a network of places of peace spanning the world yet present in the very centre of pagan society so that everyone could choose whether to be a Christian or not; true communal existence, true society and yet not a state' (Lohfink 2000, 2). This important piece gives us further insight into the political pluralism demanded by the IG, with its presupposition of total Church independence, and its further implicit rejection of arguments for the abolition of the state.

CONCLUSION

The IG and its Hosts
We can now return to the two issues that underlie the book as a whole. It is clear that the IG is not a world-shunning organisation. Its main strength lies in urban communities, primarily, though not exclusively, in Munich. In Munich its members live and work in the city. They attend Roman Catholic churches alongside other people. We have even seen that some of its members have been city

councillors. Just as the IG is not a mendicant order, it is not a movement that goes to great lengths to cut itself off from society. An interesting point of comparison here is that whereas newspapers are not in great evidence at the Bruderhof, copies of the *Frankfurter Allgemeine Zeitung* are to be found on the premises of the IG, often along with the local Munich papers.

The IG interacts with society in Germany to a degree that is apparently greater than the interaction of the Bruderhof with its host societies. However, some caution needs to be exercised here. While members are aware of what is happening around them in the city, and in some cases are working with non-members and living in flats outside the integration houses, this does not guarantee that they will be actively interacting with society around them. For many IG members there is the possibility of living a fairly sheltered life centring around the community. Many IG members work in the community's enterprises. Some live in the integration houses. The IG holds frequent meetings at which members' attendance will be expected. The high demands of the community could result in a fairly isolated existence, even in the city, and even if this is not the intention of the IG.

The IG is accordingly in a position to make an impact upon society in Germany. However, its impact will be differential. One is considerably more likely to encounter the IG and its outlook by chance if one is a Catholic. For instance, a Catholic living in the parishes (admittedly very few in number) stewarded by the IG will become aware of the IG automatically. A reader of the *Tagespost* will come across the theologians of the IG through reading their pieces in that newspaper. Against that, one should note that the community enterprises are often not obviously 'different'. The Klösterl-Apotheke in the Waltherstraße in Munich is just another chemist's shop – a customer would not know that it was in any way different from the one around the corner in terms of the ownership and involvement of the people working in it. Clearly, the IG has had an impact in Catholic circles that is greater than its more general impact upon German society. However, its intended influence is great and general. Its statutes state that it 'tries in a world estranged from the Church to make the Gospel present in such a form that also those who have no contact with the Church can find access to the Catholic Church again' (Integrated Community 1996, 108). This is obviously, in an increasingly secularised Germany, an aim that demands an attempt at a large impact on its host society.

Despite this aim, we should note a comment by Stötzel. When talking about pluralism he argued that the IG would live in the same conditions of the secular world as the heathen, but would be separate from them. The IG thus aims to have an impact on the society it lives in, but also wishes to ensure a degree of separateness. One can see the tension here that we noted with the Bruderhof. The aim is to change the world, as is the Bruderhof's. However, the world is understood in terms that stress its fallen nature, and this demands a certain distance. This is perhaps an inevitable product of an 'orthodox' Christian approach, with its understanding of the condition of original sin. The communities are not necessarily suggesting that they are in any way 'better' than people outside them. However, there does seem to be a need felt in Christian communities for some distance from society, in which the desire to overcome the sinful condition of humanity is not generally acknowledged. In the case of the IG the problem may be compounded by those Catholics who take the 'wrong' line, for instance the bishops in the abortion dispute. If not all sections of the universal Church are pulling in the right direction, then this may have effects upon the community's work. Having said this, Oved's comments about ambiguity suggest that this is a phenomenon not unique to Christian communities, but one which might also be expected to figure in other communities, though perhaps in different forms.

IG as Alternative Society
If we consider the notion of the alternative society, we might suggest that this account of the IG has given a clear indication of the extent to which the IG acts as an alternative society for its members. In economic terms, this is embodied in a rather interesting way. The IG has its network of economic enterprises, owned by members as individuals or groups of individuals. To the eye of the outsider these will appear as simply a series of economic concerns which have no necessary connection to any overarching aim or ideology, with the possible exception of the bank. If one wants a certain type of pump, or to buy something from a chemist, one may come into contact with the community's enterprises. However, one would not necessarily know that one had been in contact with the IG. Indeed, Peter's account of the pump factory suggests that not all workers in that enterprise are necessarily IG members (Peter 2001, esp. 4).

The alternative society of the IG focuses around the table communities and the local assemblies. These are the setting of structured interaction for all IG members. As we have noted, in them there is a tremendous emphasis on theology. Assembly meetings may focus on theology, and discussions with IG members frequently turn in that direction. The IG seems to have evolved a style of 'doing' theology which is participative while also based on high intellectual standards. Pesch, Lohfink and the others are clearly not amateurs in this field, and within the community there is a degree of pride in the quality of the community's theology. There is a very specific pedagogic technique used by the IG theologians, focusing on the use of illustrated chalkboards which can be seen in some of the Urfeld Circle reports. This links to the way in which the meaning to the community of Walter Cohen is presented. He is seen as having challenged them to live their theology, not just to talk about it. Hence, while the practicalities are important, this also means that attention needs to be paid to the content of the theology. We might suggest that someone not really interested in theology would be unlikely to find the IG an attractive proposition.

If the Bruderhof's alternative society is capable of sharp delineation simply by virtue of the fact that one can point to a physical boundary and say that the life goes on in large measure within that boundary, the situation is less straightforward with the IG. What is perhaps a major difference between the Bruderhof and the IG is that now the alternative society of the IG 'overlaps' quite significantly with the Kibbutz. (The Bruderhof's relationship with the Hutterians arguably functioned in a similar way for it prior to the mid-1990s.) Through the mechanism of the Urfeld Circle the IG attempts to cement ties with the kibbutzim. They are successful in this aim; the circle meets and continues to function, and has acquired its own premises in Israel. Through the circle the IG is in relationship with only a segment of the Kibbutz as a whole. One might suggest that the relationship will not register as a very significant one for the Kibbutz movement. However, for the segment of the Kibbutz that is involved, there is clearly an intense process of meeting and discussing, and indeed exchanges, that goes on through the circle. The circle has seen participation by all segments (or former segments) of the Kibbutz movement; Dati, the religious Kibbutz, Artzi, the 'Marxist' section of the Kibbutz, as well as Takam, the mainstream social-democratic Kibbutz. In addition, there has been participation by members of the urban kibbutzim, the newest section of the Kibbutz, which crossed the old 'movement' boundary lines.

Given the strength of this relationship, which does seem to follow fairly logically from the IG's theological outlook with its stress on the Jewish roots of Christianity, we should clarify just how the IG sees the Kibbutz movement. In some 'Notes on the Messianic Question' Ludwig Weimer and Arnold Stötzel said of the kibbutznikim,

> [t]hey are, even though non-believers in the understanding of orthodoxy, the sons of the prophets all the same and maybe they are the 'true sons' of Karl Marx. The kibbutzim, which they built up as a life-form, constitute a singular, creative combination of Jewish Old Testament tradition and modernity, based on the ideals of voluntariness and equality of the individual and geared towards the common realization of a humane, free society. (Integrated Community 1996, 194)

This is how the IG sees the Kibbutz, and it is on this basis that the co-operation and interaction between the IG and that section of the Kibbutz that is involved in the Urfeld Circle proceeds.

The alternative society and economy of the IG provide a framework for its members' lives in a number of ways. This framework starts with the table communities and the local assemblies. It encompasses the possibility, at least, of work in the economic enterprises associated with the IG. There is also educational and medical provision. There is a linkage with another communal movement that realises some of the most cherished theological teachings of the community. Perhaps above all, there is the feast and the preparation for it that give the lives of the members a structure through the year. Although living in the city, by and large, and although not a mendicant order that goes out of its way to shun the rest of the world, the IG presents a powerful alternative society, which can be seen to give members the possibility of living a life outside the parameters of the rest of the German population.

NOTES

1   See German text of this article: http://www.schulte-schulenberg.de/logkecic.htm
2   See http://www.legionofchrist.org/eng/articles/en99100802.htm
3   See http://www.santegidio.org/contatto/cosa_e.html for these figures. A useful book on Sant'Egidio is *Sant'Egidio, Rome and the World,* a series of interviews with Andrea Riccardi, the movement's founder; Riccardi 1999.

Chapter 5

Kehilatenyu –
Our Community – The Kibbutz

WHAT IS 'KIBBUTZ'?

The Kibbutz is far larger than either of the other movements examined in this book, being home to 115,000 inhabitants, as against 2,500 members of the Bruderhof, and slightly more than 1,000 members of the Integrierte Gemeinde. Clearly, the Kibbutz is in a different league of social phenomena to the other movements. However, the Kibbutz is also a much more varied movement than the others. It is pluralistic in both thought and origins in ways that significantly mark it off from the Bruderhof and the Integrierte Gemeinde. That said, both the IG through the Urfeld Circle and the Bruderhof through its acknowledgement of the work of Yaacov Oved on links between the movements have seen themselves as having a bond with the Kibbutz. (For Bruderhof–Kibbutz connections, see Oved 1993, a book which was distributed by the Bruderhof's publishing business.)

The Kibbutz, like the Bruderhof but unlike the IG, takes the form of a commune. However, unlike the Bruderhof, there is now a great deal of independence for the individual commune within the overall movement. Today, and this may be a change from the past, the situation is such that Eli Avrahami, in his introductory pamphlet on the Kibbutz, suggests that it is difficult 'to present a "model" of Kibbutz that holds true for and includes all the kibbutzim' (Avrahami 1998, 20). Indeed, Moshe Kerem went so far as to suggest that perhaps there was such a level of difference between kibbutzim – especially between the rich and poor kibbutzim – that really there was no longer a single organisational framework that can meaningfully comprehend all kibbutzim (in Leichman and Paz 1994, 242).

Such arguments might be better assessed when we have given some attention to the kibbutzim as they stand today. Initially, however, we can briefly consider just what the Kibbutz is, considered as all the 267 kibbutzim along with the ancillary structures that they have created. It is held together by a number of bonds, both formal and informal. At the formal level, we can note the national kibbutz movements in Israel – Dati, Takam, Artzi having been the main ones, with Takam and Artzi having merged in 2000. As will be shown when the history of the Kibbutz is considered, these movements were previously important in the lives of the kibbutzim. However, Avrahami notes that '[h]istorical processes brought about a blurring of the differences between kibbutzim of the different Kibbutz movements' (Avrahami 1998, 19), and he also mentions 'the slackening of the connection with the nation-wide Movement center and the weakening of its authority regarding individual kibbutzim' (Avrahami 1998, 20). The individual kibbutz movements are especially significant for this book because of the extent to which they were involved with Youth Movement groups. Another formal bond, and one that connects to the Zionist aspect of the movement, is that technically the land occupied by the kibbutzim is owned by the Jewish National Fund, and leased to the kibbutzim on long-term leases at nominal rent levels (Warhurst 1999, 67).

At a less formal level, we might consider the consensus within the Kibbutz about what constitutes a kibbutz. Avrahami noted a few general principles: common ownership of the means of production and consumption; mutual responsibility and help; democratic self-management; connection of individual kibbutzim with a national movement and connection to the Histadrut (a trade union movement, but also something of an 'alternative society' in the pre-state period, which maintained important welfare functions well into the 1990s) and the Zionist-socialist parties; and finally the principle of self-labour and not employing hired labour (Avrahami 1998, 13). While these are helpful for getting a grasp of the Kibbutz, Avrahami also points out that the crisis of the 1980s resulted in the thorough examination of all these principles, a process that continued into the 1990s, and that this re-examination is resulting in changes being made to the social values and economic principles of the Kibbutz (Avrahami 1998, 20). That this reconsideration has been a difficult process can be seen by the problems at Kibbutz Ein Zivan, which in 1992 decided to move away from pooled incomes to a system of paying members according to the market value of their work and got into trouble with its movement (Leichman and Paz 1994, 256–63).

Given the size of the Kibbutz as against the other movements we are considering, it is perhaps understandable that there are no easy answers to some of these definitional questions. The lesson from the Ein Zivan example is that rather than worrying too much about formal definitions, we should pay attention to the kibbutzim and what they are actually doing and how they are living their lives. Before we move on, however, it is perhaps worth asking just why people decided to live in the kibbutzim in the first place. What did the originators of the Kibbutz think they were doing?

Henry Near has argued that the two ideological trends that most influenced the nascent Kibbutz were Zionism and socialism. Although it can be shown, using the case of Aaron David Gordon, that there might be some scope for argument and that we accordingly need to remember that the Kibbutz is not ideologically monolithic, Near certainly has a case. Avrahami supports this, with his principles including a number that are identifiably socialist. This is followed up by his section dealing with the practical activities of the Kibbutz in the 'nation-building' phase of Israeli life (including activities prior to Israeli independence in 1948) which is headed 'In service of Zionist fulfilment' (Avrahami 1998, 16). This includes a sub-heading of 'political-security' activities. By this he meant that the Kibbutz created settlements in areas where there was no prior Jewish settlement, in order to establish a foothold and to secure borders; these include the so-called 'Wall and Tower' settlements, mountain settlements and Negev outposts (Avrahami 1998, 16). The Kibbutz could be seen as intended to realise socialism and assist the process of establishing and securing a Jewish state or home in Palestine. These are the views of two writers who are also kibbutznikim. There is, however, another view. It can be summed up very succinctly in the words of Zeev Steernhell: 'the kibbutzim and moshavim (this is an embarrassing truth for all those for whom the kibbutz was a raison d'etre for an entire existence) were not a means to a social revolution but tools in forging national sovereignty' (Steernhell 1998, 325). Steernhell's book is a fierce attack upon the entire tradition of labour Zionism, and focuses on what he saw as its pretension to socialism, a pretension that acted as a fig leaf for its essentially nationalistic aims. The Kibbutz, as can be gathered from the above, comes off no more lightly than any other institution of labour Zionism. In this book my tendency will be to quote from Kibbutz sources for the history and ideology of the movement, often because these sources are also witness statements from participants in activities of interest to the study. Steernhell's book offers an important alternative reading of the historical events and ideological viewpoints to those readings that originate from within the Kibbutz. His perspective would agree that the Kibbutz could be seen as a Zionist institution, but suggest that its claims to socialist legitimacy must be treated with some suspicion.

Having given some thought to the Kibbutz as an institution, we can now focus on the elements of that institution, the kibbutzim themselves. Noting Avrahami's point about growing diversity we can make some points of a general nature before moving on to think about the individual communities. Considering, first, the geographical location of the kibbutzim, Near included a map in the second volume of his history of the movement (Near 1997, 374–75) showing the locations of kibbutzim in 1995. This showed that the heartland of the Kibbutz was still the Galilee area (the first kibbutz, Degania, was located close to Lake Galilee). The pattern over the rest of the country was of a spread of kibbutzim down the coastal strip, with a band joining that strip to Jerusalem, and a small scattering of kibbutzim in the Negev, with a 'cluster' to the south of Be'er Sheva and another cluster to the north of Eilat. The Galilean heartland included the Upper Galilee, between Syria and Lebanon, and also included the Golan Heights, where there were a number of kibbutzim. There were kibbutzim in the vicinity of the towns and cities of Israel (aside from the urban kibbutzim that will be treated separately). However, Near's map indicated that the bulk of kibbutzim remained rural.

It also showed that there were few kibbutzim in the West Bank. In general Near's map suggested that with the exception of Golan the Kibbutz was largely confined to the pre-1967 borders of Israel. (As a matter of fact, some kibbutzim started up in the area conquered in 1967 in the Sinai were simply left when that area was ceded back to Egypt as part of the peace process.) Figures issued in 2000 by the Central Bureau of Statistics, a government body, along with the Takam research institute Yad Tabenkim, broke down the locations by district: 130 in the north, 65 in the south, 31 in the centre, 23 in the Haifa district, eight in the Jerusalem district, one in the Tel Aviv district, leaving nine in Judea, Samaria (i.e. the West Bank) and Gaza (Central Bureau of Statistics and Yad Tabenkin 2000).

We can now consider the look and 'feel' of the kibbutzim. This is a difficult issue to examine due to the movement's diversity. A traditional (i.e. non-urban) kibbutz might have a number of notable features. Historically the dining room has been of importance, something that may be changing. However, the communal meal is still significant in at least some kibbutzim, although its importance is perhaps less overt than in the Bruderhof or the IG. Anecdotally, two points of difference stand out: first, there can be an element of choice of food (by and large this is not a feature at the Bruderhof); second, the meal does not have the 'superstructure' of significance that it does in the Bruderhof – there was no one person reading out a story or report, and there were certainly no prayers or songs that united the room at Kibbutz meals attended by this author. The comparison with the table communities of the IG is also significant. Kibbutzim are significantly larger bodies than the communities of the IG. They average 430 or so inhabitants and this could be larger given temporary foreign 'guest' workers who may be passing through. We saw that the IG's local communities never exceed 120 members on principle. The table communities number much fewer than that – from impression they appear to be 10 to 15 at maximum. So, with the exception of feasts, the IG dines in significantly smaller numbers, thus allowing a meaningful interaction between diners. The IG and Bruderhof accordingly make their communal meals important events within the communities, though in different ways. A fascinating piece by kibbutznik author Neil Harris started with a 'journey' across a kibbutz dining room, in which a series of tables were passed, at each of which a different discussion was taking place.

> Your journey continues, and despite the hushed tones you still manage to take in 'I'm telling you, she's using private money.' All four heads move conspiratorially a little closer so as not to be heard, but despite their efforts you discover that word has it that that is how 'she' purchased the washing machine and that 'she' owns an apartment in town that 'she' is secretly renting out to maintain her private income. (Leichman and Paz 1994, 159. This was written in 1993.)

Harris gives us a picture of a dining room in which a number of coteries discuss their own interests, which in the case quoted simply came down to gossiping about a fellow member. Perhaps things were different in the past. This is a very different picture to that of the IG's table communities and feasts, and the Bruderhof's communal meals.

The dining room, which for Avrahami was the heart of the kibbutz despite the growth of family dining, is a large room and is also used for the kibbutz general meeting along with special festive meals that the community may convene. The general assembly is sometimes broadcast on closed-circuit television to members who do not actually go to it. As Near noted, 'One interesting development was the introduction of closed-circuit television in a great many kibbutzim: matters of local interest such as key committee meetings, general assemblies and cultural events were broadcast, and it was reported that this was a successful means of stimulating attention and participation' (Near 1997, 349). This last clause is significant, as it suggests that there was (and probably is) a certain degree of apathy towards kibbutz affairs among the kibbutznikim. This is not the case in the IG and in the Bruderhof, where there appears to be an expectation that members in good standing will participate in brotherhood or assembly meetings. (Recall the decision on the part of the IG at a certain point in its history that only participants in seminars in Munich could participate in the feasts.) Having said this, Warhurst stressed the role in the governance of the kibbutzim of the committees that supplement the general assembly, suggesting that on a typical kibbutz there may have been as many as 30 such committees, with between 30 and 50 per cent of members annually participating in them (Warhurst 1999, 68).

Another large room in the central building of the kibbutz is the clubroom. This is for more informal events, such as social evenings. Regarding living accommodation, whatever may have been the case in the past, members now have reasonably well-appointed apartments. In one case seen by the author, these apartments were actually substantial sub-divisions of bungalows scattered throughout the grounds of the kibbutz. In many cases the bungalows had trees close by, an important factor as they provided shade from the fierce heat that was noticeable, certainly in June, between around 10.00am and 6.00pm. Children now sleep at night in the members' apartments, and not together and away from their parents in the Children's Houses. This old practice was a renowned and distinctive feature of the Kibbutz (it led to significant interest in the Kibbutz on the part of sociologists and psychologists). In fact, though very widely practised from the 1920s onwards, it was never universal, as Near shows (Near 1997, 302–03). By the early 1990s it was only continued in the Kibbutz Artzi, and Near indicates that the practice ended when, at the close of the Gulf War, parents – who had been advised at the start of the war to bring their children into their own accommodation by the civil defence authorities – simply kept their children with them in defiance of the movement's official 'line' (Near 1997, 350).

The work departments of the kibbutz are now varied. The kibbutzim are no longer exclusively agrarian communes. Indeed, from the late 1980s onwards industry surpassed agriculture as the largest branch of employment on the

Kibbutz, with education the third largest branch. Warhurst's recent book is perhaps the most useful and accessible account of Kibbutz industrialisation, both in general and in terms of the specific kibbutz he examined (Warhurst 1999). Including non-kibbutz residents, by 1998 12,000 people were employed in Kibbutz agriculture, as against 30,000 in Kibbutz industry, only 38 per cent of whom were kibbutz members. Branches of industry mentioned in the statistical summary produced by the government and the Kibbutz include three main areas of work: plastics, rubber and chemicals; foods and beverages; and metal, metal products and machinery. These three branches account for around 75 per cent of employment and 80 per cent of income. The kibbutzim are also increasingly getting into the hotel and tourism industry. In 1995, 5,900 people worked in tourism and restaurants, with 6,500 in finance and business services, 7,000 in health and welfare, and 10,200 in education (Avrahami 1998, 28). Avrahami noted a constant decline in agriculture as against industry, a decline that will surely see it overtaken by education in terms of numbers employed. The figures discussed point to the importance of 'welfare' functions within the Kibbutz, and also to the general breach of Avrahami's principle of self-labour and avoidance of the hiring of non-members. (Near showed that this has been an issue since the early 1950s. Near 1997, 245.)

COMMITMENT

Turning to the process of joining a kibbutz, a typical procedure involves a period of a year of being a candidate member, after which the members' committee deals with the case, giving the entire membership the chance to raise objections. Then there is a vote, and a would-be member must receive at least 75 per cent of the votes.[1] In the newer urban kibbutzim the process is similar. Kibbutz Tamuz has a page on its website devoted to the issue of 'How to join Kibbutz Tamuz'. It specifies a procedure that involves moving in as a candidate after a number of meetings. Candidacy usually lasts about one year. However, as the kibbutz notes, its style of life is very different to more traditional kibbutzim, and perhaps its process is designed to ensure that would-be members appreciate this.[2] In the 'mainstream' Kibbutz the process of joining was also previously a very serious affair, according to the memoirs of David Merron, a British Hashomer Hatzair veteran who lived on a Kibbutz Artzi kibbutz in the 1950s and 1960s. He structured his memoirs as a sequence of stories, and one concerned a non-Jewish couple who applied to join the kibbutz. This caused a great deal of soul searching and dispute in the community. 'Becoming a member was a deep commitment – accepting our rules and standard of living, handing in all private money, taking full part in the after hours work rotas and accepting our system of collective education for their child. But first they had to be accepted as candidates for six months' (Merron 1999, 54).

Once accepted into the kibbutz, the depth of commitment required would seem to vary considerably, and to be generally considerably less than used to be the case (though not perhaps at Tamuz; its website suggests that their lifestyle 'can be demanding'). Consider the following comment from Moshe Kerem:

> I was reminded of my own case when my wife and I watched a dozen people suddenly find money and leave the country after we had contributed our life savings to the fund that paid their fare to Israel. Every kibbutznik has similar stories. But we refused to learn from this experience. The ideal and its realization were worth paying such piddling prices. (Leichman and Paz 1994, 243)

Would this level of commitment be required today? Perhaps not. In his account of the years between 1977 and 1995, Near noted that '[t]he acceptance of the principle of private means was by now widespread, and found expression in matters such as permission for members to travel abroad at their own expense' (Near 1997, 349).

A recent novel indicated the degree of commitment that was previously required by Kibbutz members. It concerned a successful politician who had been a member of a Kibbutz Artzi kibbutz, but who had left. A press report had suggested that he had studied at the expense of the kibbutz.

> The truth of the matter was that he had left because he wanted to study law, but the higher-education committee had recommended that he wait his turn and in the meantime study 'something we need on the kibbutz,' such as economics or agriculture. And at the *sicha* [i.e. general meeting] too the members had told him to wait his turn, and 'then we'll see'. (Gur 1995, 12. This novel was originally published in Israel.)

This raises the issue of the extent to which kibbutznikim can be said to have 'private lives'. Here we find a clear contrast with the other two movements that we have studied. Both the IG and the Bruderhof have monolithic ideologies that in some respects would challenge conventional notions of a sphere of private life. J. C. Arnold for the Bruderhof suggested that '[c]ontrary to the widely held belief that the healthiest relationship is the most private one, we feel that engagement and marriage are concerns of the whole church, not just of the individuals involved' (J. C. Arnold 1996, 91). This appears to have been the case with the early Kibbutz too, although perhaps not in such a clear-cut manner. (For evidence of this, see the remarkable article by Muki Tsur in Leichman and Paz 1994, 'The Intimate Kibbutz', 13–17.) Walter Laqueur's autobiographical account of his days on Kibbutz Hazorea, founded by the Werkleute youth movement, showed that this was still an important issue in the early 1940s. 'Clothing in those faraway days was communal; there were no "private" shirts, and often no shoes either. Every Friday afternoon one went to the communal laundry for a set of work clothes and another set for after work. They virtually never fit' (Laqueur 1992, 191). Generalising, he asked

[w]hat were the issues topmost on the agenda of the kibbutz assembly – the main decision making body in theory, if not always in practice? There was a constant tug-of-war between the radicals, who put the stress on the collective concerns and interests, and the liberals – a term not widely used at the time – who believed that the emphasis in kibbutz life was gradually bound to shift to the private sphere, the family. (Laqueur 1992, 200)

Laqueur, after noting that at one point the kibbutz assembly had passed a resolution against families having a second child (this was in time of war), pointed out that '[t]he interference of the collective in the life of the individual went very far' (Laqueur 1992, 201).

Putting together the various accounts from within and without the Kibbutz the implication seems clear. The decision to seek membership in the Kibbutz remains a serious and life-changing decision for the individual concerned. However, it no longer has the implications for loss of personal autonomy that it may once have done, and it certainly does not have the implications for loss of personal autonomy that joining the Bruderhof or the IG has. Even on the issue raised in the novel by Gur, Near notes that by '1979 more than half the kibbutz students said that they themselves had chosen their course of study, without prompting from the kibbutz authorities; and this proportion grew over the coming years' (Near 1997, 308, fn 98). Personal autonomy is an important issue, though in some ways quite hard to quantify and assess – and indeed the IG and the Bruderhof have very different perspectives on it to the 'conventional wisdom' of bourgeois society and perhaps to the more 'liberal' minded (in Laqueur's sense) kibbutznikim.

LIVING STANDARDS

More easily assessed is standard of living. We saw that the IG renounced the 'mendicant order' approach for a fairly comfortable urban lifestyle. The situation here has varied over time. One might well expect that conditions in Palestine in the 1910s and 1920s would be fairly primitive. However, this was still also the case in the early 1940s, as Laqueur's account makes clear (Laqueur 1992, 188–95). This was true for living conditions (tents and shacks with corrugated iron roofs), food (Laqueur's aversion to kibbutz mamaliga, a Romanian dish, being powerfully expressed), clothing, furniture and working conditions. It is important not to exaggerate this. However, clearly conditions in the Kibbutz even after thirty years of pioneering were tough by today's standards and even some standards of the day. The position today is different. Just to give one example from Near's account, he describes colour television as 'now a standard piece of equipment in every kibbutz home' (Near 1997, 349). The quality of food, accommodation and clothing is reasonable by the standards of the West. Laqueur's account of a visit to Hazorea in the 1960s suggested that a transformation had occurred in the period between the 1940s and the 1960s (Laqueur 1992, 207–08). However, this transformation brought a paradox, well described by Near. Writing of the period after 1948 he states,

> [t]he fact that the kibbutz shared the growing prosperity of the country in the following decades put it somewhere in the top (mainly Ashkenazi) half of Israeli society in terms of standard of living. The contrast with the relative poverty of the neighbouring immigrant towns, many of whose inhabitants worked as hired labourers in the kibbutzim, emphasized the status of the kibbutz as part of the middle, perhaps even the upper class . . . socialists, dedicated to the building of a classless society, had become part of the privileged class. (Near 1997, 332–33)[3]

Near's argument is rather strongly reinforced by a reading of the members' page of the Kibbutz Tamuz website. This is an urban kibbutz and hence extremely atypical in many ways. Despite this, it is interesting to examine the brief descriptions given there, which present a community of highly educated 'middle-class' professionals.[4]

NEW MEMBERS AND EDUCATION

We can now examine where new members, or rather inhabitants, come from. The leaflet produced by the government and Yad Tabenkim broke down population change in 1998. 1998 saw a net decrease of 700 inhabitants; this figure is derived from balancing gains and losses. The gains included new births, 1,700; entrants from other locations in Israel, 4,200; and new immigrants to the country, 2,600. The losses included deaths, 800; persons leaving for other locations in Israel, 8,000. These figures are not membership figures, but they do show us the statistical picture of the movement's situation in 1998. (Note that the breakdown is of main, not all, components in population change.) The failure of the movement to recruit the children of members as members in their own right has been an issue of concern for some time. Indeed, Moshe Kerem indicates that this has been such an important issue for the Kibbutz that '[s]everal years ago, we sought the advice of the late Professor Lawrence Kohlberg of Harvard University about the large numbers of kibbutz-born young people who opt to leave' (Leichman and Paz 1994, 241). Perhaps a few kibbutznikim have been casting an interested eye over the Bruderhof and the IG during the last 15 years or so because two important problems identified in this account of the Kibbutz – retention of the children of members, and apathy towards communal affairs within kibbutzim – have been areas where the Bruderhof and IG could be seen as having done rather better than the Kibbutz.

This leads on to a consideration of Kibbutz education. We noted the Children's House phenomenon, which is now dead in its classical form. However, the

Kibbutz had to educate its children as well as giving them somewhere to sleep at night. In very schematic terms, Avrahami summed up the Kibbutz's educational provision. He noted that in most kibbutzim there existed educational institutions, from nurseries right through to schools. Youth were usually educated at regional schools (which in the Kibbutz Artzi tradition were boarding schools). The movement also operated adult education centres, along with two teacher-training colleges (Avrahami 1998, 11–12). Near shows that the present structure of Kibbutz education is the outcome of historical trends in which the various movements adopted different policies. While there was general, though not universal, agreement that a kibbutz with sufficient children should have a primary school, there were differences over whether there should be a secondary school on each kibbutz, or whether the regional system, strongly favoured by Artzi, should operate. (Near indicates that the primary schools became part of the state system in 1953. Near 1997, 303.) Near notes that by the time the Kibbutz had moved into the final period he examined, 1977 to 1995, almost all high schools were regional, and a majority of the elementary schools were organised on this system (Near 1997, 350).

Such are the nuts and bolts – very briefly – of the Kibbutz educational system. However, the educational system needs to be examined from another angle too, and this is the angle of pedagogy. Were Kibbutz schools supposed simply to be like any other school in Israel, or were they supposed to be different? Were they underpinned by a specific pedagogic method, like Steiner schools? This is a far-reaching question. While it is clear that there was no attempt to enforce a specific pedagogic system on all Kibbutz schools in the early days of the movement, there is also little doubt that the educators of the early Kibbutz did attempt to develop an educational system which would be appropriate to the Kibbutz and which learned from the 'Reformpädagogik' movement of the first part of the twentieth century. (Franz-Michael Konrad uses the term 'progressive education' as an English equivalent. Fölling and Fölling-Albers 1999, 83.) Konrad shows how educators influenced by figures such as Siegfried Bernfeld and John Dewey played an important role in the emerging Kibbutz education system in the 1920s (Fölling and Fölling-Albers 1999, 89). He notes, for instance, how a former member of the *Jerubaal* circle around Bernfeld was responsible for founding a school initiated by three neighbouring kibbutzim. 'Beth Alpha was based on the idea of children's society and in this respect can doubtless serve as a model for kibbutz education' (Fölling and Fölling-Albers 1999, 89). David Merron puts this into terms that should make it clearer for a British reader. 'We had our own project-based curriculum, influenced by ideas similar to those of A. S. Neil, which promoted an all-round development of the child and not just academic excellence' (Merron 1999, 76–77).

The 'children's society', which was seen by Near as an aim of Kibbutz educators (Near 1997, 337), is a fairly obvious descendent of the 'Jugendkultur' propounded by Gustav Wyneken at the time he influenced the German Youth

Movement. However, this educational experimentation withered. Near points out that one of the most controversial changes to Kibbutz education, which had happened in most schools by the end of the 1970s despite being opposed by the educational leaders of all the Kibbutz movements, was the inclusion of preparation for the national matriculation examination in the Kibbutz school programme, this being a prerequisite for university entrance. 'Thus over this period [1954–1977] the kibbutz school became much more like the non-kibbutz school than it had been in its first flowering' (Near 1997, 305). Near shows that in the post-1977 period, these trends continued, despite some experimentation in teaching methods and subject material. He identifies the increase in non-kibbutznik, hired teachers as a factor in this change, and notes also the difficulty in maintaining the classic children's society in the face of the development of a 'moratorium' in which adolescents spent some time off kibbutz (Near 1997, 350–51). The trends Near pointed to in brief were the subject of a conference in Regensburg, Germany, in July 1998. The volume that emerged from this conference is an essential reference point for further consideration of the issue of education in the Kibbutz, both from a historical point of view, and also in terms of contemporary developments. The title of the volume sums up its contents very nicely: *The Transformation of Collective Education in the Kibbutz. The End of Utopia?* (Fölling and Fölling-Albers 1999).

HISTORY

Origins
We can now move on to a consideration of historical aspects of the Kibbutz. However, it needs to be made very clear that this can only be a rather brief summary of some specific points in Kibbutz history, notably those issues that connect most strongly with the overall themes of this book. Henry Near's recently published two-volume history of the movement is around 800 pages long, and is in itself something of a work of synthesis. This fact reinforces the limitations of what is being attempted here.

What, then, are the origins of the Kibbutz? We have seen that reasonably precise answers can be given to this question in respect of the Bruderhof and the IG. With the Kibbutz, the question is far harder to answer, but it is important to give it some thought. One could suggest that the Kibbutz was the product of the Second Aliya, or wave of immigration. (The pre-World War II Aliyot were First Aliya, 1882–1903; Second Aliya, 1904–1914; Third Aliya, 1918–1923; Fourth Aliya, 1924–1928; Fifth Aliya, 1929–1936; and Sixth Aliya, 1936–1939. The word Aliya means 'ascent', and Aliyot is the plural. The dates here were given by Avrahami – Avrahami 1998, 22 – but see Warhurst 1999, 54 for a slightly different dating of the Aliyot.) Given the claimed 'birthday' of the Kibbutz in 1910, we can see that it was born right in the middle of the Second Aliya. Laqueur, in his history of Zionism, suggests that

[t]he second immigration was by no means a homogeneous group, even though almost all were young, unmarried and came from Russia. The main contingent came from White Russia, eastern Poland and Lithuania. They had all grown up in a traditional Jewish environment and spoke Yiddish, but all knew at least some Hebrew . . . But there were also substantial numbers from south Russia, the sons and daughters of assimilated families higher up on the social ladder, who knew only Russian. (Laqueur 1972, 279)

Of this Second Aliya, Near notes '[t]hey created the Labour Zionist movement and laid the ideological and structural foundations of the State of Israel. One of those foundations was the Kibbutz' (Near 1992, 11).

The creation of the Kibbutz could be seen as almost being accidental. Laqueur argued that the 'first collective settlements came into being not according to any preconceived pattern but by trial and error' (Laqueur 1972, 288). There was some 'baggage' of socio-political thinking brought to them, however. Laqueur himself noted that the Russian pioneers had sometimes lived communally prior to emigration (prefiguring the later kibbutz aliya). Indeed, there were 'communes' actually in Palestine from 1904 onwards, as Near shows (see Near 1992, 18 et seq.). These seem to have been groups of immigrants pooling resources as a way of dealing with the problems they faced in the new country. From around 1910 to the early 1920s, the term kvutza was used to describe communal groups, some of which were permanently settled, and some of which were organised for specific purposes and for a limited period of time. From the confusion of the kvutzot described by Near in the first chapter of his first volume the Kibbutz eventually emerged, with the term Kibbutz only actually starting to be used in the early 1920s. Crucial in this early phase were the key moves made by the Degania group, according to Near. These were the combination of community of consumption with communal production, and the decision to settle permanently in one place. By making these two moves – along with one or two other pathbreaking innovations – the Degania group made an important contribution to the future of the Kibbutz, and according to Near merit their historical title as 'mother of the *kvutzot*' as a result (Near 1992, 54. See also Baratz 1954 for an account of Degania by one of its original members.) Was Laqueur correct in his characterisation of the role of trial and error? Near agrees with him, although he does point out that some groups in fact came to Palestine with quite well-thought-out schemes for communal living, citing the group around Josef Trumpeldor, for instance. Paradoxically, these groups found their ideology useless when confronted with the realities of life. Near suggests that the less ideological groups who didn't have blueprints but did have a positive attitude to the idea of community were the ones who prospered because they could be flexible in their approach (Near 1992, 56–57). Martin Buber, writing in 1945, summed up this line of argument as follows: the founders of the Kibbutz 'did not, as everywhere else in the history of co-operative settlements, bring a plan with them, a plan which the concrete situation could only fill out, not modify; the ideal gave an impetus but no dogma, it stimulated but did not dictate' (Buber 1958, 143).

Whatever the ideologies that the pioneers of the Second Aliya brought to the construction of the early kvutzot, for all of them the kvutza was an expression of the notion of the 'conquest of labour'. This phrase had two meanings. The first was that Jewish workers should be doing as wide a range of jobs as was possible. If a Jewish farmer in Palestine was hiring workers, according to this argument, then those workers should be Jewish. The second meaning was rather different. It was that there was a moral imperative for Jews in Palestine to conquer themselves for labour – to become workers despite the horrendous difficulties that the conditions and climate imposed upon them in this task (Near 1992, 17). The 'icon' who embodied this phrase was Aaron David Gordon, who had become an agricultural labourer in his late 40s after a life in the Ukraine of white-collar work.

Movements in the Kibbutz

The next historical issue that we need to consider is the question of whether settlements should be small or large. This is bound up with the complex organisational and political issues facing the Kibbutz movement in the aftermath of World War I. The issue was one of the factors in the gradual crystallisation of the different Kibbutz movements in the 1920s. One section of the movement was in favour of keeping settlements small and intimate. This eventually organised itself into the Hever Hakvutzot (Federation of Kvutzot) in 1929. It was based upon the small kvutza that had not joined in with the other movements that had started to form slightly earlier. This wing of the movement not only wanted to keep the communal settlements small, but unlike all the others to be mentioned it also restricted itself to agricultural work. The embodiment of the opposite view, namely that the communal settlement should in no way limit itself, was a movement called Kibbutz Me'uhad (the United Kibbutz). This was formed in 1927 and was primarily based upon a body that had been called Kibbutz Ein Harod. Kibbutz Ein Harod gives us an indication of where the term Kibbutz derives from. Ein Harod was one kibbutz initially, but had gradually started to form itself into a sort of kibbutz federation. Near indicates that in the aftermath of World War I a new vocabulary had grown up in communal Jewish Palestine (Near 1992, 67). A kvutza now meant only a settled communal group. An unsettled communal group was now a pluga, and a group of plugot with a common administration was a havura or a kibbutz. Ein Harod was a split from the first countrywide Kibbutz in this sense, the Gedud Ha'avoda. This was a body that existed between 1920 and 1927. Its name meant Labour Battalion, and its aim was no less than to organise the entire Jewish working class in Palestine into one large commune. Steernhell examines the Gedud, and the campaign waged against it by labour Zionist politicians such as David Ben-Gurion, seeing the Gedud as a serious, if limited, socialist challenge to the ideologies of labour Zionism (Steernhell 1998, 212–13. Mitchell Cohen also considered the Gedud. See Cohen 1987, Ch. 5.) The key ideologist of the idea of the large communal settlement, Shlomo Lavi, had been a member of the Gedud. Within Ein Harod, Lavi debated with another ideologist, Yitzhak Tabenkin, who felt that Lavi was limited in his vision to Ein Harod. Ein Harod would expand in Lavi's view – incorporating the allied plugot – but Tabenkin also took the notion of a country-wide Kibbutz to heart and so wanted to see kibbutzim throughout Palestine expanding and providing workplaces for Jewish pioneers.

A view that differed from both that of the Kibbutz Me'uhad and that of the Hever Hakvutzot was the position of the Kibbutz Artzi of the Hashomer Hatzair movement. Founded in April 1927, it 'did not aspire to indefinite expansion' according to Near (Near 1992, 151). This was because it wanted to create 'organic' kibbutzim that would be composed only of those who had been educated through the Youth Movement. Kibbutz Me'uhad wanted to provide places for anyone who wanted to come, and its work with the Hechalutz movement in the diaspora reflected this, as we have seen. Artzi was different in this respect, and this reflected as well in its concept of 'ideological collectivism'. This is summarised by Near as follows:

> [t]hey [Artzi] therefore adopted the principle of 'ideological collectivism', defined as 'a framework for continuous ideological action and discussion': a constant search for consensus, a reluctance to reach decisions opposed by a substantial minority, and a readiness to defer the resolution of conflicts or to reach compromises for the sake of movement unity – all this backed by unanimous support for the general movement line once a decision had been made. (Near 1992, 152)

Merron gave an insider description of 'ideological collectivism'. 'Since our lives were collective in every way, it seemed quite natural to hold common ideological beliefs which strengthened our social, economic and cultural cohesion' (Merron 1999, 120). The specific nature of the Hashomer Hatzair pioneers was shown in the book *Kehilatenyu (Our Community)*. This was based on the diaries of the members of the Betanya Commune of the movement. A seminal text for understanding the early Kibbutz, let alone just Hashomer Hatzair, it has unfortunately never been translated into English (though see extracts in Yassour 1995 and Leichman and Paz 1994).

Near provides a useful table that summarises these debates in a brief and comprehensible format (Near 1992, 160–61). Readers wishing to delve further into these debates, which are obscure but important for determining the long-term development of the Kibbutz, should also see the excellent source book produced at Kibbutz Merhavia by Professor Avraham Yassour, *The History of the Kibbutz, a Selection of Sources 1905–1929* (Yassour 1995). This includes much useful material on the kvutzot, Hashomer Hatzair and Gedud Ha'avoda, and has an article on the large kvutza by Shlomo Lavi. Very little of this material is available elsewhere in English.

The situation that had evolved by the end of the 1920s, namely a Kibbutz movement that was divided into a number of different federations, persisted until recently, with the 2000 merger bringing most kibbutzim into one movement. Without going into all aspects of the history of the various divisions in the Kibbutz, it is important to consider some key points that arise from it. It should initially be reiterated that this is a major area of distinction between the three movements being studied; the Bruderhof and the Integrierte Gemeinde are unified bodies and always have been. Admittedly they are far smaller than the Kibbutz, and in the early phases of their history were very small bodies indeed. However, in the 1920s the Kibbutz was not a large institution, growing from 3,899 members in total in 1927 to 8,674 in 1935 (Near 1992, 189). 1927 was the year that the 'big' federations were formed, and the membership in that year is perhaps comparable to that of the Bruderhof at its high points of the late 1950s and the present day.

If we start by considering the present day, there were until recently three main federations in the Kibbutz: Takam, Artzi and Dati. In terms of continuity Artzi and Dati were the two most straightforward. Artzi was founded in 1927 as the Kibbutz expression of the Hashomer Hatzair youth movement. Dati was founded in 1935, although there had been some earlier kibbutzim of a religious orientation. Near showed that the main basis for Dati was the German section of Bachad (an abbreviation of the Hebrew for the term League of Religious Pioneers). This in turn was based on German Jewish youth movement groups such as Esra (Near 1992, 288–92). Takam represents the continuation of the Kibbutz Me'uhad and Hever Hakvutzot. However, its formation in 1981 came after an earlier split in Me'uhad, in which a minority left in 1951 and merged with the Hever Hakvutzot to form the Ihud Hakvutzot Vehakibbutzim (the League of Kvutza and Kibbutzim; short form Ihud). Me'uhad merged in 1981 with Ihud to form Takam. (The anglicisations of the Hebrew terms used above and henceforward are the ones used by Near. Other authors use their own variants.) The importance of this history lies in what it tells us of the ideology of the Kibbutz.

The splits and splinterings, along with the unifications, do not, paradoxically, really have very much to do with issues of Kibbutz organisation. Otherwise, why would a section of Me'uhad have merged with the Hever to form the Ihud? These represented the traditions that argued for the large and the small kibbutz respectively. The splits and disunity of the Kibbutz reflected, rather, political wranglings. Perhaps this is why the 1951 Me'uhad split was especially disruptive. Laqueur described it graphically.

> Separate dining halls and kindergartens were established for members of the rival factions and their offspring, and when these palliatives did not help, old

established and flourishing kibbutzim such as Givat Haim, Ashdot Ya'akov and Ein Harod were divided, separate settlements being set up, sometimes no more than a mile apart. (Laqueur 1972, 323–24)

Amia Lieblich, in her study of one kibbutz, *Kibbutz Makom*, has presented testimonies from both sides of the Me'uhad split (Lieblich 1981, Part 2, 'The Division'). Least affected of the movements by this political wrangling was Dati. Dati grew out of the Mizrachi (and especially the Hapoel Hamizrachi workers' strand) tradition of religious Zionism. In the period after the declaration of Israeli independence the Dati federation formed, according to Near, a dovish faction in the National Religious Party. However, elements within it (and especially in its youth movement, B'nei Akiva) were influenced by the rightist Gush Emunim (Bloc of the Faithful) movement, which advocated Jewish settlement in the Occupied Territories (Near 1997, 261. See also Arian 1998, 130.) Even in Dati, however, there was evidence for the relevance of Near's argument about the roots of the Kibbutz in socialist thinking. The memoirs of the anarchist Augustin Souchy include a couple of pages about his visit to Kibbutz Yavneh in 1951. He was delighted to find that the members of this Dati kibbutz had been inspired by the ideas of Gustav Landauer (Souchy 1992, 163–64. See also Yaacov Zur's article on 'The Religious Kibbutz Movement' for confirmation of the existence of socialist thinking in Dati in Gorni 1987, 117–23.) Souchy knew something of Landauer's ideas, as he had belonged to Landauer's Sozialistisches Bund in the pre-World War I period (Souchy 1992, Ch. 1).

The other grouping that was consistent in its politics was the Kibbutz Artzi. From the point of view of this book, Artzi is an extremely interesting movement. It was based, as we have seen, on the Hashomer Hatzair youth movement. This movement was founded in Galicia, but profoundly influenced by the ideas of sections of the German Youth Movement and the Jewish youth movement. Shomrim (as the movement's members were known) made their way to Palestine from the start of the Third Aliya. The first communal experiment of note connected with the movement was Betanya, in 1920 and 1921, the community that produced the *Kehilatenyu* diary. By the start of 1926 there were 550 shomrim in Palestine, and by the end of that year they had two established kibbutzim. Artzi was founded the following year. Hashomer Hatzair remained active in the diaspora as well. It was thus a movement that had established kibbutzim in Palestine, remained a youth movement in the diaspora, and which had its model of ideological collectivism. It remained politically unaffiliated with any of the existing Zionist-socialist parties. From the mid-1930s it had an urban political ally, the Socialist League. After a process of debate lasting some years, a Hashomer Hatzair party was formed officially in 1946 (Near 1997, 69).

The political basis of this party was Marxist. In this it reflected the ideology of the Hashomer Hatzair movement as a whole, which had adopted Marxism around 1924. A key leader of the movement, Meir Yaari, had called on the movement to take this step and disavow its earlier anarchistic orientation at this time (Oved 2000, 48). Oved suggests that prior to this phase of its ideological evolution, 'Landauer's influence was first felt among the members of the *Hashomer Hatzair* youth movement who had emigrated to Palestine and lived as a cooperative community at Bitaniya Illit' (Oved 2000, 48). Oved's judgement is interesting, as it bears out a comment made in interview with Chaim Seeligmann, who noted that it was the Shomrim who had read Landauer more closely than the members of his own movement, Habonim.[5] It is also interesting to note that Avraham Ben-Shalom, an early Hashomer Hatzair leader, pointed to a change in the basis of the movement around 1924, suggesting it was the end of the movement's phase of being a free youth movement (Ben-Shalom 1937, 32).

Whatever had been the case in the past, the movement was determinedly Marxist by 1946, and the German invasion of the Soviet Union in 1942 strengthened the hand of those in the movement who wanted to shift policy in an even more pro-Soviet direction. The most lasting 'label' of the Artzi political expression is Mapam (United Workers' Party), which still exists, but as part of the Meretz coalition. Over time its pro-Soviet stance withered. Aside from its clear and Marxist-socialist political stance, there was another distinctive feature of the Zionism of Hashomer Hatzair: this was its advocacy of a 'bi-national' approach to the future of Palestine. Hashomer Hatzair was concerned to ensure that an accommodation with the Arabs in Palestine was reached. In the 1930s this was expressed in the concern for a future that could be characterised as a 'bi-national society'. In the 1940s it was expressed in the demand for a bi-national state, meaning a state that would accommodate both the Jewish and Palestinian peoples, and accordingly not the specifically 'Jewish' state of the more conventional Zionists (see Near 1997, 71–72 for the specifics of Hashomer Hatzair's bi-nationalism). The Hashomer Hatzair viewpoint was in some respects quite close to that of Martin Buber. A recent book from a determinedly 'orthodox' Zionist point of view suggests that Buber was the most prominent of a group of largely German-background thinkers who promulgated a doctrine that has gradually replaced real Zionism as the ideology of the political and cultural elite in Israel. This doctrine looks something like 'bi-nationalism', and Hashomer Hatzair is something of a 'bit part' player in the story told by the author, Yoram Hazony, a former adviser to Benjamin Netanyahu, the Likud politician. (Hazony places the formation of Hashomer Hatzair in Vienna in 1916, which fits nicely with his overall thesis, but is wrong; it was formed in 1913 in Galicia. Hazony 2000, 199.)

Although its origins were in Poland, Hashomer Hatzair spread widely and became a substantial movement. Jehuda Reinharz suggested that by the late 1920s it had around 38,000 members in Eastern Europe along with its four kibbutzim (Reinharz 1986, 178). The founding of Artzi in 1927 led to expansion into new territory such as Hungary, France and the USA, and by around 1930 the movement started to be active in German-Jewish youth circles. Reinharz's portrayal of its activities in Germany affords us a clear idea of the educational activities and 'bund' life of the movement. This is important for understanding Artzi, as the key idea of Artzi was that its kibbutzim would be 'organic' because the members would all have gone through this process of education and activity. Reinharz indicates that the movement divided its membership into age groups (shichvot). These were Bnei Midbar (9–12 years old); Zofim, sub-divided into Zofim Zeirim (12–13) and Zofim (14–15); and Bogrim, again sub-divided into Zofim Bogrim (16–17) and Bogrim (18 and over). Reinharz suggests that the sub-divisions were developed in 1933–34 for educational purposes. The units in the Zofim were not co-educational (Reinharz 1987, 187–88). Reinharz suggests that the practice in other youth movements in Germany at the time was for co-educational groups. This may have been true in the Jewish youth movement, but in the general German Youth Movement of the Bündische period this was not the case, and the shomrim were accordingly in line with German practice. If we compare the structure that Reinharz outlines with that of the German bünde described by Laqueur, it is clear that even without the sub-divisions, the age groups do not conform to those that Laqueur portrayed.

Reinharz outlines the educational programmes that the movement followed. The Bnei Midbar worked using an emotional approach based on customs, symbols and commandments of the movement. The Zofim programme was based upon character-building and establishing the basis for a Marxist-Zionist world-view. The Bogrim worked on deepening their understanding of the ideological and political foundations of Hashomer Hatzair in the light of the world and Palestinian situation. Reinharz lists some of the authors studied. The Zofim worked on texts such as the *Communist Manifesto*, and writings by Kropotkin and Landauer. The Bogrim worked on Marx, Lenin, Plekhanov and the Austro-Marxists Victor Adler and Otto Bauer. They also worked on Max Weber. In the field of psychology they looked at the writings of Alfred Adler, Freud, Reich, Manes Sperber and Bernfeld. They also attended lectures by the likes of Martin Buber (Reinharz 1986, 188–89). This was the educational system that the Hashomer Hatzair constructed, and which it intended would be the bedrock of the Kibbutz Artzi. Its 'organic' kibbutzim would be built by members who had gone through this educational process.

This leaves us to consider the politics of the groupings – Me'uhad and the Hever – that would eventually become the Takam movement. Ben-Rafael argues that the Hever was the least political of the major kibbutz movements (Ben-Rafael 1997, 130). Me'uhad on the other hand was very much involved politically. The leading figure in Me'uhad, Yitzhak Tabenkin, personified the connections of the movement to one of the two Zionist-socialist political parties that merged in 1930; he had been secretary of the party, Ahdut Ha'avoda (Labour Unity) prior to joining Kibbutz Ein Harod in 1921. The connections with this party were not formal, but rather of a personal and political nature (Near 1992, 204–05). Ahdut merged in 1930 with Hapoel Hatzair (the Young Worker) to form Mapai, the Workers' Party. Hapoel Hatzair was the party that A. D. Gordon had belonged to, and had some personal and political connections with the Hever (generally supporting the small kvutza idea). Ahdut was certainly not a dogmatic Marxist party, but was more influenced by Marxist ideas than Hapoel, which was positively anti-Marxist. (Mapai is sometimes called the Labour Party in the literature, but this was actually formally founded in 1967.)

Within Mapai the Kibbutz Me'uhad came to play a significant role. In effect it became a sort of 'left opposition' to the leadership of David Ben-Gurion and Berl Katznelson. This was particularly apparent in the years between 1938 and 1944 when Me'uhad, along with some mainly Tel Aviv-based urban allies, was the basis of the oppositionist Si'a Beit (Faction B) in Mapai. This faction left Mapai in 1944 to found a new Zionist-socialist party, l'Ahdut Ha'avoda – the Movement for Labour Unity (Near 1992, 353–58). This body united with the Hashomer Hatzair party in 1948 to form the United Workers' Party – Mapam. In some ways this was a unity that ignored some basic differences. Artzi and Me'uhad had historically represented different approaches to the building of the Kibbutz. They also had different views over the correct political structure that Zionists should aim at building, Hashomer Hatzair favouring the bi-national state and Me'uhad 'militant action against the mandatory power and the establishment of a Jewish state over the whole of Palestine' (Laqueur 1972, 334). The two factions seem to have co-existed in Mapam rather than merging, and the merged party only lasted until 1954. Laqueur suggested that an important reason for the disintegration was the unwillingness of the Ahdut Ha'avoda (i.e. Me'uhad) grouping to accept the enthusiasm for the Soviet Union that prevailed in the Hashomer Hatzair, citing the growing anti-Israeli and anti-Semitic nature of Soviet policy in the latter days of Stalin. An important incident in laying this bare was the 1952 arrest and imprisonment in Czechoslovakia of Mordechai Oren, ironically a leading light in Hashomer Hatzair (Laqueur 1972, 334). Ahdut Ha'avoda became an independent party again, until 1967, when it merged with Mapai and another splinter group, Rafi, to form the Israeli Labour Party. We can now 'place' the 1951 defectors from Me'uhad who helped to found the Ihud. They were a pro-Mapai grouping, although the way in which the Ihud conducted itself politically meant that the small Ha'oved Hatzioni movement of six kibbutzim was able to join it. This movement had political links to the Progressive Party, later known as the Independent Liberals (Near 1997, 251).

In political terms, what did all this shuffling by Me'uhad's leaders actually mean? One factor was power politics, relating to the extremely proportional nature of representation in the Knesset, Israel's Parliament. This meant that there was a proliferation of parties, and that governments tended to be based on coalitions. Smallish parties could bargain their way into governmental coalitions and perhaps do some useful deals for those they represented. Near noted that '[f]rom 1958 onwards Ahdut Ha'avoda was a regular partner in government coalitions' (Near 1997, 255). This was less of a factor in the pre-state period immediately after the split from Mapai, however. Ben-Rafael saw Me'uhad as having a sort of schizophrenic political heritage. It had developed the idea of the large Kibbutz, which would, in due course, absorb the whole of the working class in the creation of a socialist society. This was its 'mass politics' side, linked to social democratic politics, as against Leninist elitism. However, over time it came to see that the Kibbutz was not going to attract the majority of workers in Israel. Thus it developed an 'elitist' approach that held that only the politically conscious were capable of joining the Kibbutz. 'Hence, soon enough, this movement was torn apart by two opposed tendencies: on the one hand, and in accordance with its social democrat perspective, it was willing to be an integral part of the "revolutionary masses", while on the other hand it developed a self-image which insisted on the unique value of its own contribution' (Ben-Rafael 1997, 131). Ben-Rafael analyses the tensions in and around Me'uhad from the mid-1930s to the mid-1950s in this light, but notes that 'the Kibbutz Ha-Meuchad's breakup went together with a shift in ideological perspectives from the original social-democratic outlook to Leninism' (Ben-Rafael 1997, 131). Hence, in Ben-Rafael's view, we need to read the vicissitudes of the Me'uhad in terms of a journey into what he calls Leninism, but which may perhaps more properly be called Stalinism. Ultimately the movement rowed back from this position, as exemplified in the formation of the Labour Party and the Takam. Laqueur's point regarding the inherent problems in the united Mapam – after the 1954 split the name was kept by the Hashomer Hatzair remnant – over what could be called the 'Arab Question' retained its importance for many years. Near noted the hawkish line that Me'uhad took in Israeli politics in the aftermath of the Six-Day War of 1967. Yitzhak Tabenkin became 'one of the leaders of the Movement for Greater Israel, which supported the retention and settlement of the territories conquered in the war' (Near 1997, 255). The majority in Me'uhad initially supported him on this issue.

From this account it will be understood that the Kibbutz has been a divided entity. The divisions have concerned issues of actual import to the way of life in the Kibbutz (for instance, small or large settlements), religion and politics. The result was that for the bulk of the twentieth century the Kibbutz was divided into a number of different movements. The differences between the movements can, in some measure, be seen as 'ideological', but in other respects this term is hardly appropriate. From the point of view of this book, however, there was a very significant result of the splits within the Kibbutz. This was that in the diaspora (and from our point of view, most importantly among young German-speaking Jewry) different youth movement bodies 'lined up' with different Kibbutz movements. The obvious example is the close organic connection between Kibbutz Artzi and the Hashomer Hatzair youth movement. A useful general summary of these links for a particular period is to be found in the table Near uses to summarise the Kibbutz in the 1920s and 1930s (Near 1992, 160–61). This gives a list of the various youth movements connected to the different Kibbutz movements.

Some of these are not youth movements in the narrowly defined sense that has been used in this book; for instance, Hechalutz is listed in the column for Me'uhad. As was shown in an earlier chapter, Hechalutz was determined not to be a youth movement. It attempted, rather, to prepare a wide range of young people to take their places in the 'large' kibbutzim. On the other hand, Habonim is also in the Me'uhad column. This body, in Germany, represented a merger of several former youth movement organisations including the Jung-Jüdischer Wanderbund/Brith Haolim and the main body of Kadima, Ring Jüdischer Wander- und Pfadfinderbünde. Connected with the Hever Hakvutzot was the Gordonia youth movement. This is an interesting example of the swirling currents of ideas and practice in the diaspora youth at the time. It was established in Galicia around 1923–24 and led by Pinhas Lubianker (later Lavon). Near stated that 'it rejected the concept of "youth culture" as propounded by Hashomer Hatzair and many of the smaller youth movements' (Near 1992, 122). However, this body, established by supporters of Hapoel Hatzair and named after Aaron David Gordon, 'used many of the educational methods developed by Hashomer Hatzair' (Near 1992, 123). 'Youth culture' and the educational methods Near refers to can be seen as part of the legacy to the shomrim of the German Youth Movement, picked up at the time of their leaders' stay in Vienna. A German organisation, Maccabi Hatzair also developed links with the Hever, but its relationship with that body was determined for some time by its adherence to certain Youth Movement attitudes. It merged with Gordonia in 1941 (Near 1992, 274–77).

Chaim Seeligmann, kibbutznik since the mid-1930s and prior to that a member of the Jung-Jüdischer Wanderbund and Habonim, was accordingly correct when he entitled one of his lectures to the Integrierte Gemeinde 'Die Jüdische Jugendbewegung- Eine Wurzel der Kibbuzim' ('The Jewish Youth Movement – a root of the Kibbutz') (Seeligmann 1998, 103). However, it was only one of several roots, and also we need to keep in mind that there were a variety of movements of Jewish youth linked to a number of Kibbutz federations in various ways. (The close connections between Artzi and Hashomer Hatzair were eventually shadowed by the Hever–Gordonia links, but were in turn different in nature to the Habonim–Me'uhad links.) This is clearly a complicated pattern of historical events that is very different to the Youth Movement connections of the IG and the Bruderhof.

To conclude our consideration of a number of specific issues in Kibbutz history, it is worth considering the overall pattern of growth of the Kibbutz (see Table 1). The table shows a pattern of growth which saw a massive expansion of the movement in the 1920s, 1930s and 1940s, followed by a slower but still evident expansion until the 1990s, when the figures peak and then start to fall back. This is the context for the next part of our consideration of the Kibbutz, which will focus on what has become known simply as 'the Crisis'.

Table 1   The Growth of the Kibbutz

Year	Kibbutzim	Population
1910		First kibbutz founded
1920	12	805
1930	29	3,900
1940	82	26,500
1950	214	67,500
1960	229	77,950
1970	229	85,100
1980	255	111,200
1990	270	125,100
1995	269	123,900
1998	267	115,500

(Table based on figures given in Avrahami 1998, 25, and on figures for 1998 from Central Bureau of Statistics and Yad Tabenkin 2000)

THE CRISIS

The Crisis has come to dominate discussion of the Kibbutz at an academic level and is also a focus of attention in the movement. Some indicators can be found in recent editions of *Kibbutz Trends* (an English-language magazine). In spring 1999 it reprinted an article from *Hakibbutz* published in autumn 1998 and written by *Hakibbutz*'s former editor Ezra Dalomi. 'It's a waste of time and effort, *chaverim*. The end is near. Next year the kibbutz movement will celebrate its ninetieth birthday, but it probably won't get up to a hundred' (Dalomi 1999, 25). The magazine printed a few of the responses that the article provoked – some opposing and some supporting Dalomi's apocalyptic vision. Likewise, at the end of 2001 it reprinted a further article and responses from *Hakibbutz*, this time the main piece being by Ayala Gilad (originally published in May 2001), and simply if starkly called 'Kibbutz: The End' (Gilad 2001). Some kibbutznikim are evidently 'thinking the unthinkable', a point dramatised by articles appearing in the London press in the wake of the dissolution of Kibbutz Mishmar David, one of which was simply called 'Death of the Kibbutz' (Wheatcroft 2001). Another straw in the wind is to be found in the fall/winter 1999 edition of *Kibbutz Trends*, with a report on a conference at Kibbutz Yavne establishing the 'Communal Stream' within the movement. Attended by 200, this included representatives from kibbutzim in all the then three movements. This stream can be seen as representing those in the Kibbutz who wish to hold to what they see as the traditional values of the movement. *Kibbutz Trends* published a number of critical responses to the holding of the conference, along with a reply from Mordechai Hayut of the 'Communal Stream' (Armoni et al. 1999). This all goes to show the

depth of feeling about 'the Crisis'. Yet the crisis is not something that has happened recently. Perhaps the definitive academic account in English is Eliezer Ben-
Rafael's *Crisis and Transformation. The Kibbutz at Century's End* (Ben-Rafael
1997). This book emerged from a research project financed by Yad Tabenkin, the
research centre of Takam. Ben-Rafael starts the book by writing, '[i]n 1985, eight
years after a dramatic political setback, a sudden economic crisis shook the entire
kibbutz movement to its foundations' (Ben-Rafael 1997, 1). We are, accordingly,
at the time of writing, over 15 years into the crisis, which Ben-Rafael links to the
1977 election of the Likud (rightist) government in Israel. The crisis is a long-
standing one, and as the articles in *Kibbutz Trends* mentioned indicate, its rever-
berations still dog the Kibbutz. A contrasting work to Ben-Rafael's that is also
largely focused on the crisis is Daniel Gavron's *The Kibbutz. Awakening from
Utopia* (Gavron 2000). While containing a good deal of solid information, the
strength of this work is its focus on the ways in which a number of specific kibbutzim are reacting to the crisis. Apart from an introduction and conclusion, it
has twelve chapters, and ten of these are devoted to 'case studies' of specific kibbutzim (one kibbutz examined is Kibbutz Tamuz, an urban kibbutz).

A full account of the crisis is beyond the scope of this study – though hopefully the references given will enable interested readers to find out more about it
should they wish to. A brief consideration of this crisis is important for this book
for two reasons. The first is that to omit an account would be grossly misleading,
as the present-day reality of the Kibbutz is framed by this crisis. The second is to
note certain responses to the crisis that have had some aspects of their origins in
the youth movements, which are still extant, in both Israel itself and in the diaspora. If the Kibbutz is to be renewed, might the renewal have a base in the ideas
of the contemporary chalutzo-Zionist youth movements?

It could be suggested that the crisis has two main aspects. For the sake of simplicity we could call these the 'objective' and the 'subjective' aspects. Utilising
Ben-Rafael's account, we can start our consideration of the crisis by examining
its 'objective' aspect, by which is meant the events and their consequences at a
concrete and quantifiable level. As we noted, the Likud government of Prime
Minister Menachem Begin was elected in 1977. This ended a period that started
with the foundation of the state of Israel in 1948 in which one or more of the
various parties to which the different Kibbutz movements were linked had been
in power. The 1977 election led to '14 years of uninterrupted government' (Ben-
Rafael 1997, 38) for the right in Israel (although from 1984 until the end of the
1980s there were in fact national unity governments with Labour participation).
This affected the Kibbutz in two ways. First, there was a diminution in the
number of kibbutznikim in Parliament, and a total absence of kibbutznikim
from government. Under Labour and its predecessors there had always been one
or two cabinet positions held by them. However it also led to a loss of a less
obvious power: '[i]t dislodged the federations from longstanding political positions – in the Ministries of Agriculture, Education, or Commerce and Industry,

and even the Ministry of Defence – where their presence had been strong through representatives and institutionalized lobbying' (Ben-Rafael 1997, 38).

At a political level, Ben-Rafael suggests that this resulted in a delegitimation of the Kibbutz, noting Begin's characterisation of the kibbutznikim as 'millionaires', and his casting the blame on the Kibbutz for the problems of the underprivileged towns near the kibbutzim (Ben-Rafael 1997, 38). This is in the context of the Israeli right having a power base in the poor Sephardi masses who saw the Kibbutz as part of the Ashkenazi middle and upper classes – an irony we earlier noted. Ben-Rafael insists that '[t]his growing remoteness from the corridors of power, and thus from resources, is a major factor in the mid-1980s economic crisis' (Ben-Rafael 1997, 39). Before considering the economic crisis referred to, it is worth picking up the hidden message in the comment by Ben-Rafael. This is that the Kibbutz was playing the system in its political activities, that it was using its political power to benefit itself. Ben-Rafael in a later section of his book quoted a non-kibbutznik, who stated, 'Kibbutz members who speak on behalf of the movement forget that they stand for crucial social values; instead they defend conservatism and vested interests at their worst, and this for plain opportunist reasons. The kibbutz movement behaves as an interest group moved by mere political and selfish ambitions' (Arye Shirom, quoted in Ben-Rafael 1997, 138). Perhaps Begin and his impoverished constituency had a point.

How can the economic crisis of the mid-1980s be characterised? Again, Ben-Rafael is to the point. 'The financial debt of numerous kibbutzim went up by tens of percents between 1984 and 1988 as the country's unprecedented inflation took them by surprise' (Ben-Rafael 1997, 39). In monetary terms, Ben-Rafael spells the situation out. 'The anti-inflationary policy of the government, which required a drastic rise in interest rates, multiplied the debt of the kibbutzim to the banks – from three billion shekels in 1984, to over seven billion in 1988. . . . Throughout the kibbutz movement, factories and financial funds collapsed' (Ben-Rafael 1997, 39). Ben-Rafael adduced some other economic circumstances that also contributed to the situation the Kibbutz faced: an agricultural crisis, over-speedy industrialisation by the kibbutzim in the 1970s, and over-investment in members' accommodation in the early 1980s in order to facilitate the end of the children's houses, among others. Nothing, however, 'should dismiss the kibbutz economic leadership from accusations of incompetence' (Ben-Rafael 1997, 39). A deal to convert short-term debts into long-term loans affecting 55 kibbutzim in 1988 prefigured a major deal between the banks, the government and the Takam and Artzi federations in 1989. This saw the writing off of some debts, the rescheduling of others, and involved a loan to the kibbutzim. In return the kibbutzim agreed to sell off some assets, and ended the mutual liability of the kibbutzim and their federations (Ben-Rafael 1997, 40). This process of negotiation was not helped by a financial scandal in Takam, which saw allegations of illegal and unethical behaviour.

These two, interrelated problems (the economic crisis and the loss of political clout) can be seen as the two sides of the objective aspect of the crisis in the

Kibbutz. This led into the subjective aspect of the crisis. Again, Ben-Rafael puts it succinctly: '[f]or the kibbutzniks as a whole, however, the economic crisis also revealed a more basic crisis in kibbutz ideology and social structures. In other words, in kibbutz identity' (Ben-Rafael 1997, 40). For Ben-Rafael, the 'crisis amounted, indeed, to nothing less than a thorough questioning and a restatement of the notion of kibbutz' (Ben-Rafael 1997, 41). He suggests that it occurred because the 'objective' crisis led to a questioning of the whole rationale for Kibbutz in the eyes of the kibbutznikim themselves. We may, perhaps, then rename the 'subjective' crisis, and suggest that it could be seen as an 'existential' crisis of the Kibbutz. Voices demanding radical changes in Kibbutz made themselves heard, and equally opponents of change argued back. Ben-Rafael produced a table (Ben-Rafael 1997, 42) showing a selection of some of the changes that were on the agenda in 1991. This includes 24 separate changes, and among these we can find ideas such as the abolition of the communal dining room, abolition of rotating senior jobs, financial rewards for extra work, general differential financial rewarding, and the separation of the economy from the community. Ben-Rafael noted of the 24 changes that '[i]f all these changes would be implemented in one kibbutz, it would become indistinguishable from a non-kibbutz village' (Ben-Rafael 1997, 42). Chris Warhurst, an English commentator, suggested in an article published in *Kibbutz Trends* that '[d]ifferential allowances do not liberate kibbutzim, they eradicate them' (Warhurst 1993, 50). This judgement is based upon his view of the Kibbutz as a specific mode of production. (His view, drawing upon Marxist and neo-Marxist political economy, has been expounded at length in his recent book. See Warhurst 1999, especially 71–74.)

The crisis has affected the tone of life on the Kibbutz. The consideration of this issue is a particular strength of Gavron's book (Gavron 2000). Ben-Rafael suggests that the debates around these issues were not conducted with joy and enthusiasm by the kibbutznikim. Rather, there was a general loss of resolve in the kibbutz. 'For many members, the feeling of crisis cast doubt on the justification of past efforts and sacrifice on behalf of the ideals of community life, which had meant years ago abandoning promising careers outside the kibbutz' (Ben-Rafael 1997, 43). He suggests that even a decade after the crisis 'the feeling of self-confidence and of confidence in the kibbutz has not been recovered yet' (Ben-Rafael 1997, 43). The evidence cited from *Kibbutz Trends* in the years subsequent to the publication of Ben-Rafael's book indicates that, to some extent at least, his judgement still stands. This also needs to be set in the context of the downturn in Kibbutz membership that started in the early 1990s and which recent figures suggest is still continuing. This trend can be seen as being linked to the 'existential' aspects of the crisis.

Most of the recent sources used for this book's consideration of the Kibbutz reflect the crisis to a greater or lesser extent. Avrahami's brief introductory pamphlet (Avrahami 1998) ends with a rather downbeat couple of pages reflecting the new situation. Leichman and Paz's excellent anthology includes a solid chapter of readings on 'Crisis and Challenge', although this is not a dominant feature of the book. Even the second volume of Near's history ends with a chapter that is focused on the crisis. It would clearly be beyond the scope of this book to attempt to provide a comprehensive account of all aspects of this crisis, and indeed of all possible explanations for the 'existential' aspects of the crisis. A good, brief introduction to the academic study of the crisis is to be found in Ben-Rafael's chapter, 'The Kibbutz beyond Utopia', in Fölling and Fölling-Albers 1999. This acts as a summary of his own book and of the work of others on the crisis.

THE URBAN KIBBUTZ

From the point of view of this book, it is interesting to consider a possible response to the crisis in the Kibbutz that goes beyond the defeatism of an Ezra Dalomi or the 'back to basics' of the 'Communal Stream'. This is the formation of a new type of Kibbutz; the Urban Kibbutz. Urban kibbutzim are located in the cities and towns of Israel rather than, as was traditionally the case, the rural areas. Some traditional kibbutzim became urban, or perhaps suburban, as a result of the process of urban expansion rather than as a conscious decision, which is the case with this 'new generation' of kibbutzim (for this process see Kahana's comments in Fiedler 1995, 118–19). The idea for the Urban Kibbutz 'started, or was renewed in the eighties' (Catholic Integrated Community 1997, 81) according to Yftach Goldman of Kibbutz Tamuz in a presentation to the Urfeld Circle in December 1996. Goldman and Amram Shlomi of Kibbutz Migvan both gave presentations at this meeting. Both being urban kibbutzim, Tamuz was Takam affiliated, and Migvan was Artzi. Tamuz is in the town Beth Shemesh, and was started in 1987, and Migvan is in Sderot. Tamuz's website indicated the existence of two further urban kibbutzim, both in Jerusalem and both religious. This statement is outdated, as there is now the Habonim-Dror urban kibbutz Kvutsat Yovel in Jerusalem, a key part of a small but developing network of urban communes based upon the Ha'Noar Ha'Oved Ve'Halomed labour Zionist youth movement. This network is starting to organise itself into a movement, the Magal Hakvutzot.[6] Tamuz had been based in rented apartments between 1987 and August 1999. It then moved to a new, permanent location.[7] Tamuz is one of the kibbutzim featured in Gavron's book (Gavron 2000, Ch. 11) and his consideration there is a useful source for material on this kibbutz.

The presentations of Goldman and Shlomi to the Circle were both fairly schematic. The main shared points were a stress on a process of mutual learning within the urban kibbutzim and a need for a stronger involvement of the kibbutzim in Israeli society (Goldman's contribution is on pp. 80–83, and Shlomi's on pp. 86–87 of Catholic Integrated Community 1997. Shlomi's presentation is followed by some discussion.) Shlomi indicated a disappointment with the extent to which the Kibbutz was realising its beliefs as one of the factors that led to the start of Kibbutz Migvan (Catholic Integrated Community 1997, 86). The Tamuz website indicates a similar concern, though it is phrased differently. Tamuz suggested that a section of the membership of the traditional Kibbutz were staying put simply because they found it easier than having to face city life. They had lost any sense of community, and of the meaning of Kibbutz. Those who had retained a concern for this were constantly having to fight within the Kibbutz for what they believed in.

The structure of Kibbutz Tamuz is based around the members working at their own professions. As it notes on the website, 'Once you are a candidate, your salary goes directly to the kibbutz and you receive a budget based on the size of your family, like everyone else on the kibbutz.'[8] Tamuz is much smaller than traditional kibbutzim, and it claims that this means that it cannot afford to lose a sense of community. It also means that the kibbutz works on the basis of direct democracy. It also claims on its website that it gives 'a lot more freedom to the individual than the traditional kibbutz, and that helps as well.' (It is clear from the website that Tamuz has some members who had previously been at traditional kibbutzim, and Migvan seems to have been mainly built by young people who had been in traditional kibbutzim.) The point regarding freedom of the individual in the context of Tamuz is borne out by the following comment by Yftach Goldman in his speech to the Urfeld Circle:

> every individual, in each of his decisions, remains sovereign to decide where he wants to go. The community cannot decide for me, on no occasion. The community did not decide for me to go to Rome this week. The community would not make a decision for me, whether or not, I will go to study philosophy, and at which university. All decisions, that have to do with my own life, should be made by me. (Catholic Integrated Community 1997, 80)

This indicates that the Urban Kibbutz is a departure in many ways from the traditional idea of Kibbutz, although within the context of a commitment to what the urban kibbutzim see as the core values of the Kibbutz. The Urban Kibbutz recalls the 'communes' that were the precursors of the Kibbutz and the Kvutza in pre-World War I Ottoman Palestine. Interestingly, in this context, one of the urban kibbuztim, Kvusat Yovel, has put Muki Tsur's account of the early days of the Kibbutz, 'The Intimate Kibbutz' on its website.[9] For commentators who see the Kibbutz as a specific 'mode of production' (e.g. Warhurst 1999) and who stress the combination of collective living and collective production that characterised the traditional Kibbutz, the urban kibbutzim, with their lack of production departments, will represent a falling away from crucial aspects of what they have seen as being the core of the Kibbutz. Clearly, we see here a possible conflict between different visions of just what were, and indeed are, the central values of the Kibbutz. In its stress on the freedom of the individual, an urban kibbutz such as Tamuz is at the other end of the spectrum of communal life to a movement like the Bruderhof. It even differs on this point from earlier versions of Kibbutz orthodoxy, though not present-day (and perhaps long-standing) practice.

All this is very interesting, and may come to represent an important trend in the Kibbutz over the next few years. What has it got to do with the main themes of this book? Simply, the idea has been taken up by sectors of the still extant chalutzo-Zionist youth movement of the diaspora. A report in *Kibbutz Trends* on the recent celebration of the 70th anniversary of the British section of the Habonim movement – now called Habonim-Dror – ended by noting, '[t]oday however, the movement is looking for new directions. The year program in Israel is no longer kibbutz based, and the most recent aliyah group from the UK is working to create a new urban kibbutz community, something that they see as a response to the true current needs of Israeli society' (Anon 1999, 71). The organisations that we examined in the context of the building of the Kibbutz in its earlier phases are now getting involved in the building of a rather different type of Kibbutz at the start of a new century.

This is apparent from the website of Kvutsat Yovel, an urban kibbutz in Jerusalem. The kvutsat is the direct outcome of the activities of members of Habonim-Dror from a number of English-speaking countries and in 2000 it had around 12 members. The website suggests that in fact no Habonim-Dror kibbutzim were built or developed in the 1990s at all. Hence the title of the page, 'Kvutsat Yovel: Habonim Dror is back in business – the Kibbutz building business!'[10] The page also details the related activities of the Israeli youth movement that Habonim-Dror has connections with, Ha'Noar Ha'Oved Ve'Halomed. Several hundred post-army 'graduates' (bogrim) of the movement have, according to the page, been building a network of 'next generation' kibbutzim and communes for some years. The page mentions Kibbutz Eshbal, which although in a remote, rural area, does not undertake agricultural or industrial work. Rather its members work with Arab and Russian youth and Bedouin women, teach, run seminars in Poland, staff a Holocaust museum and run a boarding school for what are called 'Ethiopian hard-cases'.[11] Yovel itself is also described on the website, where an article that originally appeared in the Israeli newpaper *Ha'Aretz* on 23 February 2001 can be found. Some interesting points emerge in this article, which suggests that the Urban Kibbutz may actually be quite a broad church. The article includes statements that Yovel's members do not wish to see it grow much larger than the dozen or so it had at the time of writing. The kvutsat intends to function through consensus rather than voting on issues. All members' salaries go into a joint bank account, with all members having their own cash card. Finally, unlike Tamuz, Yovel does not yet have a purpose-built site.[12]

The picture, then, is of a small, emergent trend within labour Zionist youth who are reinventing Kibbutz in ways that they see as being more relevant to contemporary Israel. Only time will tell whether this trend, coalescing as the Magal Hakvutzot, becomes important. Small numbers are no indication of the likely outcome of the enterprise, and should not be taken as a harbinger of likely failure. All the movements examined in this study are now substantially bigger than they were when they started. These new kibbutznikim argue that they are applying the old principles in a new context: 'former general-secretary of Habonim and new immigrant James Rosenhead believes that, "the values of Habonim – socialism, Zionism and Judaism have not changed – just the methods of applying them are different."'[13]

CONCLUSION: THE KIBBUTZ AND ISRAELI SOCIETY

We can conclude this consideration of the Kibbutz by returning to the two issues that shape this book as a whole. The sheer size of the Kibbutz as compared with the other movements, and also the fact that the Kibbutz shares a commitment to Zionism with the mainstream of Israeli society, means that it should be seen as much less of a 'fringe' institution than the Bruderhof and the Integrierte Gemeinde. In large measure we have seen how the Kibbutz has created an 'alternative society' throughout this chapter. If we leave the newer urban kibbutzim on one side for this summary, we might suggest that this 'alternative society' is rural, though by virtue of the size of Israel many of the kibbutzim will be easily accessible from the cities. It is a fairly open society, with members now having access to television as well as radio and newspapers. This has been widespread in respect of radio since the end of World War II (Laqueur 1992, 200–01). Indeed, it positively desires interaction with Israeli society as a whole, believing that it has a message for it – or at least this is the 'official' story. The Kibbutz society has a relatively sophisticated 'superstructure' of institutions: it has its own educational systems, for instance, and it has a number of federations with the attendant bureaucracy, and so on.

The economy is, as we saw, no longer simply an agricultural one. There is an important industrial sector, and a significant service sector, although the latter would appear to be largely focused on the needs of the kibbutznikim. There is no obvious effort to be self-sufficient. Indeed, Stanley Maron – scholar and kibbutznik – indicated that there never really was.

> Although given some consideration in the beginning, the idea of a self-sufficient or autarkic community was given up at an early stage, and instead the kibbutz pursued a policy of seeking integration in the surrounding economy through systems of co-operative marketing and purchasing that largely did away with the need for direct contact between individual kibbutz members and the surrounding market. (Maron 1993, 35)

The kibbutzim were consciously part of the Zionist enterprise, and their aim was never simply to feed themselves, but was always to contribute to the viability of the Jewish community in Palestine and subsequently the State of Israel (they performed this task alongside another form of agricultural co-operation, the mosh-avim). Kibbutz society and economy have changed significantly over time, as has been indicated in this chapter. Perhaps most crucially, Kibbutz society can today be characterised as a society in crisis, a characterisation valid since the mid-1980s. For the first time in its history, the 1990s saw a protracted turning of the tide of its growth, and the Kibbutz is today a movement in numerical decline, although it is too early to say whether this is going to be a 'blip' or a long-term trend.

We can now consider the interaction of the Kibbutz with Israeli society as a whole, and indeed its impact upon that society. As noted, at least in theory, the Kibbutz saw itself as being a movement with a message for Israeli society. One of the complaints made by the urban kibbutznikim against the traditional Kibbutz was precisely that it had ceased to take that message to the wider Israeli society, and get involved in attempting to change society. One may presume from the tone of the urban kibbutznikim that by this they did not mean to suggest a revival of that self-serving 'interest group' activity which we saw that the movement can be accused of having undertaken, perhaps as a consequence of its gradual accretion of economic and political power between 1948 and 1977. Other than the mission to create a socialist society in Israel, there are three other areas in which we can consider the impact of the Kibbutz: its contribution militarily, economically, and finally in terms of the 'national psyche' of Israel.

Beginning with the military contribution of the Kibbutz, we are thrown back to the pre-state period between 1910 (the start of the Kibbutz) and 1948, when the state was declared. This is the period of the Yishuv, or pre-state Jewish community. Ben-Rafael described the security role of the kibbutzim in the period of the Arab Revolt of 1936 to 1939. This was when the 'Wall and Tower' (Choma u-Migdal in Hebrew) strategy was employed, a strategy that involved the kibbut-zim to a large extent. This strategy 'consisted of quasi-military operations which installed groups of settlers on sites formerly acquired by the Jewish Authorities, to serve as armed posts in hostile zones. Fifty-two settlements were created in this manner during 1938–1939, and of these 37 were kibbutzim' (Ben-Rafael 1997, 35). Why use kibbutzim in this context? Maron summed up the position:

> Political and security considerations now became more important than those of economic viability. Clearly, kibbutzim were the most expedient way of set-tling remote areas quickly and cheaply, and of assuring safe and flexible arrangements for the reception of new immigrants. Kibbutz members were willing to endure hardships and confront dangers more than most of the civilian population, which preferred the comforts and security of urban life. (Maron 1993, 13)

Maron gives a telling characterisation of the Kibbutz of that period. 'In those years of dedication to fulfilling national tasks, kibbutzim were like semi-military camps mostly made up of tents or wooden huts centred around the communal kitchen and dining room' (Maron 1993, 65). This could be seen as tending to bear out the characterisation of the Kibbutz given by Steernhell in his 'revisionist' account. Indeed, even someone dedicated to attempting to refute Steernhell would have to acknowledge that this part of the history of the Kibbutz was concerned with the forging of national sovereignty. An opponent of Steernhell would have to argue that there was no conflict here with the aim of bringing about a social revolution.

This was far from being the Kibbutz's only military contribution to Israeli society. In the period that Israelis call the War of Independence (Palestinians doubtless would not see it in those terms) between November 1947 and March 1949, there are two points that can be made. The first is that, as might be expected from our consideration of the 'Wall and Tower' period, the kibbutzim were fully involved in the fighting. The second is that there was an extremely close relationship between the Palmach (described by Near as the mobilised force of the Hagana – the 'official' Jewish defence forces – as against the 'unofficial' forces such as the Irgun Zva'I Leumi and the Lehi or Stern Gang that were linked to the Revisionist Zionists) and the Kibbutz. The dismantling of the Palmach and the downgrading of Israel Galili from his key position in the military command structure in May 1948 were seen as political blows by the Kibbutz movement. Indeed, a sort of 'substitute' had to be given to the movement by David Ben-Gurion in the form of the Nahal (No'ar Halutzi Lohem – Pioneering and Fighting Youth), an army section drawn from graduates of the Kibbutz-connected youth movements that worked closely with the movement. This still exists. Near's chapter on 'The War of Independence' (Near 1997, Ch. 5) is vital reading on the role of the Kibbutz in this phase of Israel's military history.

Ben-Rafael indicates that, as part of the Kibbutz's perception of itself as an 'elite' in Israeli society, ready to shoulder tasks of general import, the movement has continued to play an important role in the Israeli military. 'One may also recall here the fact that sons of kibbutzim are encouraged by the federations as well as by the public opinion of their communities to volunteer for special tasks during their military service, which explains, for instance, the high rate of kibbutzniks in the airforces, low rank officers, and soldiers of elite units' (Ben-Rafael 1997, 211). He points out that for a long period nearly 50 per cent of Israeli fighter pilots were kibbutznikim, and that this was encouraged by the kibbutzim despite the problems of the length of service and possibility of well-paid subsequent posts in El-Al. He suggests as well that the high proportion of kibbutznikim in elite units means that proportionally in wars the kibbutznikim are often the most affected section of society, offering figures from the Yom Kippur War of 1973 (Ben-Rafael 1997, 245–46). Near shows that there was an over-representation of kibbutnikim in the dead of the War of Independence (Near 1997, 117–18).

Moving on, we can consider the overall contribution of the Kibbutz to the economy of Israel. In the Kibbutz agricultural sector, using 38 per cent of Israeli agricultural land, 27 per cent of the Israeli agricultural workforce produced 33 per cent of Israeli agricultural value added in 1997. The overall position regarding industry was that in 1996 in the Kibbutz's 360 factories and 11 regional corporations, 8.6 per cent of the Israeli industrial workforce produced 10.2 per cent of Israeli industrial income, a gross industrial product of 8.3 per cent of the Israeli industrial gross product and 9.4 per cent of Israeli industrial exports (all figures from Central Bureau of Statistics and Yad Tabenkin 2000). The figures show that the movement remains an important economic player in Israel despite the crisis. This is especially true of agriculture, even though this is becoming progressively less important in terms of work within the kibbutzim. When all is said and done, these figures are probably now more important to the movement itself than to the country as a whole. Israel is no longer in the pioneering period. Thanks in no small measure to the Kibbutz (and the moshavim) it ensured that it could feed itself in the period after independence. As Freddie Kahana put it, '[n]ational goals are changing, agriculture is losing its mythical value' (in Fiedler 1995, 117).

The final aspect of Kibbutz interaction with Israel as a whole is the question of its impact on what might be called the 'national psyche'. This is admittedly a vague term that might lead us into very deep waters if pursued relentlessly. Nevertheless, it is worth considering the issue because there is some evidence that the Kibbutz did, indeed, have something of an impact on how Israel saw itself. In discussing the War of Independence, Near illustrates this point well. 'Just as the caricaturist's picture of the young man in the kibbutznik's "dunce's cap" (*kova tembel*) had become the symbol of the Israeli in his social and national manifestations, so the Palmachnik in his Balaclava helmet (*kova gerev*), his informal style of uniform, and his beard became the symbol of the Israeli at war' (Near 1997, 120). Remembering that the Palmach was, as we saw, very closely linked to the Kibbutz, it seems that, if Near is correct, the Kibbutz at this point was burned into the imagination of Israel. Having said this, only shortly after the War of Independence David Ben-Gurion, Prime Minister of the new State of Israel, attacked the Kibbutz vigorously for its failure – in his view – to do enough for new immigrants to the country (Near 1997, 182–84 for this episode). At this point the main leader of the Hever Hakvutzot detected a sea change in public opinion, from sympathy for the movement to indifference and even hostility – and this was seen as spreading into the Labour movement (Near 1997, 182). This was, perhaps, a difficulty caused for the Kibbutz by the mamlachtiut ideology adopted by Labour politicians. Mamlachtiut, according to Near, means something like 'statism', although he suggests that this word does not really convey the full force of the word. Mamlachtiut was associated with Ben-Gurion in particular, and the younger politicians who worked with him (see Near 1997, 182–86, and also Cohen 1987, 220–27 for the young generation of Labour politicians around Ben-Gurion). In this context the Kibbutz might have diminished in importance in the minds of these politicians in their desire to use the mechanism of the state instead of the voluntary bodies of the Yishuv period.

The picture today is very different from the period when the Kibbutz held an honoured place in the 'national psyche'. A number of recent studies point in the same direction. Eric Cohen notes of the whole period of statehood, '[c]oncomitantly, many of the utopian and innovative ideas of an earlier period also lost their vitality and the institutions embodying them gradually declined in national importance. The principal example of that decline is the collective settlement, the kibbutz, which was stripped of much of its centrality in the new state' (in Wistrich and Ohana 1995, 207). Gabriel Shefer made some similar comments, in the course of a discussion of 'Israeli personality and the weakening of collective identities and loyalties':

> [t]his weakening process accelerated since the mid-1980s, and, with the notable exception of the religious segment, still continues . . . Few Israelis seriously believe in notions such as 'one integrated society', 'homogeneous culture', 'pioneering', 'mutual responsibility', or 'Israel is a model society and state.' If it exists at all, the 'Israeli Personality' is a strange mix of nationalist, religious, xenophobic, selfish and individualistic attributes. Not surprisingly, the popularity of the old ideological camps, parties, and the kibbutz and Moshav movements has waned. (in Levi-Faur et al. 1999, 62)

Shefer went on to consider the crisis that the overall workers' movement, the Histadrut, has been plunged into, especially at elite level. His argument was summarised succinctly. 'Regardless of "ethnic" or class background, the trend among young Israelis is toward individualism and personal fulfillment' (Levi-Faur et al. 1999, 63). The traditional values of the Kibbutz are accordingly, if these authors are correct, now no longer a major part of the Israeli psyche. Appropriate to the era of the Yishuv, they are now old hat. The young advocates of the Urban Kibbutz might well face a difficult task to spread interest in the face of this mindset. That said, some commentators have recently suggested that individualism is, in fact, in decline in contemporary society. This view will be examined in the final chapter, and clearly if these commentators are correct, the picture might look rather different than the one painted by Shefer and Cohen.

It might be suggested that the evidence of the changes in the Kibbutz indicates that the Kibbutz is not immune from the trends that we have examined. The crisis in the movement has seen a questioning of its whole rationale. A section, at least, has advocated changes that will make the Kibbutz a more 'privatised' type of community. In this respect, the Kibbutz seems to be following trends in the national self-image rather than setting them, which as a self-declared elite it might wish to do.

Perhaps we are witnessing the final death knell of those institutions that Near suggested were built by the people of the Second Aliya, and which he argued formed the basis of the State of Israel, among which he named the Kibbutz, although the Histadrut could equally be seen in this light (Near 1992, 11). For Near there was clearly a positive value in these institutions. Steernhell also stressed the importance for Israeli history and society of these institutions, and of the social group that created them, which he calls the 'labor elite' (Steernhell 1998, 4. By labor he indicates that he means the 'central' trend in the labour movement, for instance Mapai.) He also includes in this elite people from the later Third Aliya. He even suggests that from around 1935 'the labor movement provided Israeli society with such a strong model of development that even after its fall from power in 1977 no real changes occurred in the economic, social and cultural life of Israel' (Steernhell 1998, 4–5). Whatever may have been the case in the immediate aftermath of the 1977 elections, as social institutions the creations of labour Zionism such as the Kibbutz, the Moshav and the Histadrut are in crisis today. The day of the kibbutznik as the self-image of the Israeli has long gone.

It does not really make much sense to call Israeli society a 'host' to the Kibbutz in the way that British society is 'host' to the Bruderhof, or German society 'host' to the IG. The Kibbutz was a crucial factor in the forging of Israeli society, and the Kibbutz has never seen itself as being 'apart' from Israeli society in the way that the other movements examined, whatever their intentions towards social change, have tended to see themselves vis-à-vis their 'hosts'. The Kibbutz sought to lead Israeli society, and in that it failed some decades ago. Perhaps this is where the ambiguity which Oved has discussed in respect of the relations between a commune and the society it is situated in might be seen as arising in the case of the Kibbutz. The Kibbutz has always seen itself as part of Israel (and the Yishuv before 1948), and it has sought to lead it towards socialism. It felt itself, according to kibbutznik commentators such as Ben-Rafael, to be an elite within Israel. Yet the reality was rather different, as Near showed. Despite the rhetoric of socialism, it ended up as part of the richer section of society, and acted, on the basis of evidence adduced by Ben-Rafael, like an interest group within society. For the young urban kibbutznikim a further charge was that it had lost its drive to be involved in Israeli society. The ambiguity here is between rhetoric and reality; socialist vanguard for a changed society on paper, as against the reality of a group of fairly rich people looking out for their own interest. Both characterisations are caricatures, but the polarities do give us a way of thinking about the relationship between the Kibbutz and Israel.

Whether it can survive in its present form seems a live question in a way that is not even on the agenda for the smaller movements, which might appear a paradox. It is not a paradox, however, when we recall that the Kibbutz is a far less coherent movement in terms of world-view than the Bruderhof and the IG. It is pluralistic in ways that they are not. That will mean that it has to try to establish a degree of unity among people who are not necessarily committed to very much beyond a bare minimum in the way of shared beliefs. In time of crisis, this

can be seen to be a difficult task. And it is only the starting point for the movement as it battles to come to terms with its future.

NOTES

1   Information sent to Mike Tyldesley by Professor Yaacov Oved, 23 November 2000.
    Professor Oved is a member of Kibbutz Palmachim. He indicated that his kibbutz
    procedure, described here, is fairly typical.
2   See http://tamuz.org.il/english/praxis_join.html
3   See Arian 1998, 32–36 for a discussion of the Ashkenazi–Sephardi distinction.
    Crudely, in this context it relates to whether one's origins were in Europe – Ashkenazi
    – or Asia and Africa – Sephardi. Sylvie Bijaoui and Avi Egosi indicate in a piece
    dating from the mid-1980s that what they term 'Oriental' members of the Kibbutz
    formed around 10 per cent of the membership (Gorni et al. 1987, 533). Simons and
    Ingram present arguments that suggest that the relatively lower involvement of
    Sephardi Israelis, as compared with Ashkenazim, is more to do with the opportunity
    structure created by the State of Israel for immigrants in the post-1948 period than
    with alleged cultural prejudices held by Sephardim against co-operative and commu-
    nal life (Simons and Ingram 2000).
4   See http://tamuz.org.il/english/praxis_members.html
5   Discussion between Mike Tyldesley and Chaim Seeligmann, Yad Tabenkin, Israel, 11
    April 2000.
6   Information from James Grant-Rosenhead to Mike Tyldesley, 25 March 2002.
7   See http://www.tamuz.org.il/english/praxis_housing.html for details and picture.
8   http://www.tamuz.org.il/english/praxis_join.html
9   http://207.21.194.249/kvutsatyovel/netscape/intimatekibbutz.htm. Tsur had been a
    member of a group of young kibbutznikim concerned to review aspects of the
    Kibbutz, the Shdemot circle. See Gad Ufaz's article in Urian and Karsh 1999.
10 http://207.21.194.249/kvutsatyovel/netscape/wlzm.htm
11 More on Eshbal can be found on the website, which features an article by Neil Harris,
    originally published in *Kibbutz Trends*, called 'Kibbutz Crossroads. Kibbutz
    Renaissance, 1998', http://207.21.194.249/kvutsatyovel/netscape/eshbal.htm
12 http://207.21.194.249/kvutsatyovel/netscape/haaretzyovel.htm
13 http://207.21.194.249/kvutsatyovel/netscape/changes.htm, an article originally
    printed in *Ha'aretz* magazine in October 1999.

Chapter 6

Comparative Findings

ISSUES

We are now in a position to draw some comparative conclusions regarding the three movements that have been considered in this book. Two questions have been returned to constantly throughout. These have been, first, what impact has been made on the 'host' societies by the movement concerned? This can be seen as part of a more general question, namely, how can the interactions between the movements and their 'host' societies be characterised? The second question was, broadly, how have the movements attempted to construct 'alternative societies' and 'alternative economies'? Some comments have been made regarding these questions in the chapters dealing with the movements, and these will be now be brought into comparative focus.

These are, however, not the only questions and issues that need to be considered in this chapter. In the course of the discussion two further issues have arisen that appertain to all the movements, and which can also be considered comparatively. The first of these could be identified as the 'individual–collective' dichotomy within the movements. This issue concerns the extent to which individual members of the movements have personal autonomy, or putting it the other way around, the extent to which the collectivity that they form part of impinges upon and determines their lives. Another way of thinking about this issue is to pose it as a question: what is the distinction between private and communal spheres in the movement? Are certain issues seen as matters that are to be determined by an individual by their own private judgement, or are they to be discussed by the whole collective? It seems a reasonable working hypothesis that in movements of communal living the communal sphere will incorporate issues that in ordinary 'bourgeois' life would form part of the personal sphere. However, we might ask how far the process of moving issues from the personal sphere into the communal sphere goes in the specific instances we are considering.

The second issue that requires comparative consideration is the way in which the movements now perceive their relationship with the German Youth Movement. The relationships were different: to restate briefly the two most divergent examples among the three considered, the Integrierte Gemeinde in effect forms the direct continuation of a specific Youth Movement bund, whereas the Youth Movement was merely one of several roots of the Kibbutz. The question of the connection does not need to be re-opened. However, we have seen in the discussions of the three movements that they now have different views of their relationship to the Youth Movement. These will be comparatively considered, and then analysed. The analysis is necessary because there might be an element of post hoc rationalisation in the way in which the movements now view this relationship. It may be presented in a way that is influenced more by the ideological needs of the communities today than by academic standards of historical accuracy. No hypothesis is presented in advance of a consideration of this issue, but the self-understanding of the movements will be subject to some critical consideration. These four issues will, accordingly, be the focus for this chapter.

THE MOVEMENTS AND THEIR HOSTS

The starting point, then, is the consideration of the impact upon the 'host' societies of the movements. In considering this question, it is clear that the Kibbutz is a completely different case to the other two movements, for a number of reasons. The first is that the Kibbutz is much larger than the other two movements. More importantly, it was one of the key bodies in the creation of the society that hosts it. The Kibbutz was instrumental in the agricultural sector in the Yishuv and the newly independent State of Israel. Later, it was also home to an important industrial sector. In terms of security, the Kibbutz acted as a stronghold in the 1930s (in some areas for many years longer) and subsequently supplied important human resources to the armed forces of the Yishuv and the state. The Kibbutz was also involved in the political process. The Labour Party, Mapam, Ahdut Ha' avoda, the National Religious Party and even the Independent Liberal or Progressive Party all see or saw involvement from the Kibbutz. Ben-Rafael notes that in that first Knesset (Israeli Parliament) of 120 members, 20 were kibbutznikim. However, he goes on to point out that by the late 1970s this figure had dropped to five or six (Ben-Rafael 1997, 37). Quoting Near, we saw that there was a period in which the Kibbutz was an important part of the self-image of Israeli society and of the image Israeli society presented to the outside world. On both counts this is no longer the case. To summarise, the impact of the Kibbutz on Israel has been enormous. However, this was mainly in the past; for some time now it has been fading. This was clearly the case by the mid-1970s, and is perhaps a part of the 'crisis' that engulfed the movement for a considerable part of the 1980s and the 1990s, and that continues into the new century.

The extent to which the old standing of the Kibbutz has ended appears to disconcert some sections of the Kibbutz, who regard this changed circumstance as the result of ingratitude on the part of the wider Israeli society. A potent image of this mentality is the evocation of the poem 'A Kibbutz Backyard' by Natan

Alterman. Ezra Dalomi in the previously cited article 'It's a waste of time, Chaverim', states:

> [a]t a time when bank directors receive a salary of almost half a million shekels a month and benefits worth millions, when the unproductive ultra-religious sector is given billions, no resources can be found for trifles such as the provision of reasonable security for veteran members, founders of settlements, builders of the country. (Dalomi 1999, 26)

He then goes on to evoke Alterman's image of the Kibbutz as a wretched drudge, implying a movement that did the hard work and is now spurned. Amos Oz, in an interview with Muki Tsur (published in 1994 but dating from some years previously) put it slightly differently. 'In his poem "A Kibbutz Backyard" Natan Alterman in reference to the kibbutz says: "Throughout the history of the Jewish people there was never a more obedient servant . . ." We kibbutzniks have always been the first to fill an obligation' (in Leichman and Paz 1994, 124). Some kibbutznikim clearly feel that the movement's standing in Israeli society is no longer that warranted by its historical record.

In considering the impact of the Bruderhof on its 'host' societies, we should first summarise what 'hosts' it has had. In its initial phase (1920–1937) Germany was its host, and there have been two subsequent phases in Germany (1956–1961 and 1989–1995). It has been in England from 1937 to the present day with a short gap between 1966 and 1971. It was in Paraguay between 1941 and 1961, along with Uruguay between 1952 to 1960. The USA has hosted the Bruderhof from 1954 to the present day, and it has been active in Australia from 2000. This is an obviously more complicated pattern than that of the Kibbutz. Examining the movement's history, it is clear that in some of these locations its impact has been so limited as to have been neglible. This seems to be true of the years in South America. Oved noted that '[i]t must be borne in mind that the people of the Primavera Bruderhof lived in isolation. A wide barrier separated them from the native Paraguayans with whom they came into contact' (Oved 1996, 128). The major exception to this judgement must be the hospital that the movement ran, and which was open to the local population, described by Oved (1996, 130–32). However, rather than considering the instances in which the Bruderhof has failed to make an impression, it might be more productive to consider some instances in which it can be shown that the Bruderhof has made a real, if limited, impact upon its host societies.

The first such example is the impact it made in its early period in Germany on the circles of Religious Socialists and other 'seekers'. Of the latter, Baum points out that in the second year of the Bruderhof's existence, 1921, there were over 2,500 visitors to the commune (Baum 1998, 132). Regarding the Religious Socialists, Eberhard Arnold's involvement in Neuwerk and its precursors obviously meant that he was a part of a substantial network. Bruderhof member

Marjorie Hindley notes of the Tambach conference of September 1919 that 'there were present among others Carl Mennicke, Paul Tillich, Heinrich Schultheis, Gerhard Günther, Emil Fuchs, Eugen Diederichs, Eugen Rosenstock-Huessy, Edward Thurneysen, Eberhard Arnold and Karl Barth' (Hindley 1993, 208). Barth attended instead of Leonhard Ragaz, the prominent Swiss Religious Socialist. Baum's biography of Arnold shows that Ragaz was well acquainted with the Bruderhof, having had a rather stormy relationship with it in the years before its departure for England (Baum 1998). Hindley's list includes many of the key figures of twentieth-century German Protestant theology. Frank Gordon's examination of the relationship between Protestantism and socialism in the Weimar Republic includes the observation that the largest organised body of Protestant Christian Socialists, the Bund religiöser Sozialisten, grew to a membership of 25,000 by 1928 (Gordon 1988, 438). The Bruderhof through its links with this milieu undoubtedly made an impact, and in these circles Eberhard Arnold was a figure of some standing. Indeed, one might suggest that this, along with the German background of many of the Bruderhofers, makes it rather strange that the movement has had no lasting success in re-establishing itself in post-World War II Germany. The daughter of the expelled Bruderhof leader Hans Zumpe suggested that there may have been an estrangement between the Bruderhof and circles that had been friendly to it in the Weimar period, possibly a contributory factor in the immediate post-war years.

> My father also looked up some old Bruderhof friends. Most of them were disappointed that the Bruderhof had left in 1937. 'We needed you right here in Germany,' many of them said. 'But you left. Many died in the gas chambers for their faith and beliefs, but you chose the easy way, and that was to leave! If you want to be the "light of the world," how can you stop shining when times get bad? We have no need for your lovely talks and writings, because you left us when we needed you the most.' (Bohlken-Zumpe 1993, 98)

A second instance is the influence that the Bruderhof had on the circles of the British pacifist movement in the period just before and during World War II in England. In the 1930s this was a substantial movement and from 1934 it had an organisational focus in the Peace Pledge Union (PPU). Members took a 'pledge' that stated 'I renounce war and never again will I support or sanction another, and I will do all in my power to persuade others to do the same' (Morrison 1962, 17). The PPU's 'official' history indicated that it collected about 150,000 such pledges (Morrison 1962, 17–18). With the advent of World War II, and indeed in reality perhaps for a couple of years prior to this, many of its activists had started to turn to the idea of living in community. This was so much the case that in March 1941 the PPU's weekly *Peace News* started to publish a monthly supplement covering community projects, as Andrew Rigby has noted in his important account of World War II pacifist communities (Rigby in Coates et al. 1993. See also Hardy 2000, 41–52 for an account of this wave of pacifist community formation.)

Hardy's recent account of the Bruderhof in England shows the extent to which the Bruderhof was a beacon for pacifists and others interested in community life in England at this time.

> Ashton Keynes was a mecca for visitors in search of their own salvation as well as those with a broader interest in finding solutions to society's ills. The Bruderhof encouraged such visits . . . Sometimes it all seemed overwhelming: the Workers' Educational Association organized a visit by 300 with an interest in community, while another group, the Folk House, brought ninety from Bristol. (Hardy 2000, 188–89)

Hardy also showed that the Bruderhof actually went out into the country to spread the word, publishing a journal, *The Plough*, and sending speakers to over 50 meetings, mainly in big cities, in 1938 (Hardy 2000, 188). The Bruderhof at this stage was also involved in conferences that met to discuss community living, and from which, in 1937, the Community Service Committee sprang (Hardy 2000, 194–97). Hardy's overall conclusion on this period in the Bruderhof's history seems reasonable. 'The Bruderhof communities, for instance, became focal points for a much wider range of spiritually related experiments in a troubled period' (Hardy 2000, 273).

The third and final example focuses on the post-World War II period in the USA. While undoubtedly consolidated by the setting up of the Woodcrest Bruderhof in 1954, this phase of influence actually rather pre-dated this, with some North Americans making the journey to Paraguay to visit the bruderhof there. Rubin discusses this, noting the example of Bob and Shirley Wagoner, who visited Primavera in 1953. They came from a background in the Church of the Brethren, an Anabaptist church (Rubin 2000, 85–86). Rubin suggests that the 'theology of Arnoldism would enjoy a warm reception from American intentional communities, Anabaptists and Friends committed to the new evangelicalism of the Fourth Great Awakening in America' (Rubin 2000, 89). Rubin is a very hostile witness on Bruderhof issues, but Mow's account of this period, from an 'official' Bruderhof standpoint, bears it out (Mow 1991, but note Chapter 1 where Mow makes it clear that he was from a Brethren background). Another confirmation is to be found in the Jacksons' account of the Reba Place Fellowship, a Christian community with a Mennonite (and thus Anabaptist) background. They pointed out that John Miller, a key figure in Reba Place's early years, in the autumn of 1956 'made a trip to Woodcrest, the Society of Brothers' (Jackson and Jackson 1987, 33). This trip made an impression upon him according to the Jacksons' account. The Bruderhof in fact, as the various accounts all show, absorbed in whole or in part several largely, though not exclusively, Christian communities in this period. Again, the milieu we are discussing was not, in the North American context, a large one. However, the result of this phase was that the Bruderhof established itself in the hearts and minds of radical Christians in North America, and it has kept that place to this day.

We have seen three examples in which the Bruderhof established a presence in the thinking of minority, indeed dissident, sections of opinion. This is important in one crucial respect. If the Kibbutz was able to use the waves of immigration into Israel, and the diaspora youth movements in particular, as sources for new members, and if the Integrierte Gemeinde has been able to recruit from among theological students, we could suggest that the Bruderhof's impact in the various milieux described has been one factor in its continuing ability to recruit new members from non-Bruderhof backgrounds. Other than this impact, it would be hard to suggest how else it has really influenced host societies. There is the minor matter of localised impact; the sale of agricultural produce from the Wheathill Bruderhof at Digbeth market in Birmingham in the 1950s is an example. The late Stanley Fletcher, a former 'tramp preacher', often spoke on these occasions. A further possible exception is the success of its products, most notably Community Playthings.

The Integrierte Gemeinde is the hardest community to discuss in the context of examining the impact upon its 'host' society. By and large its 'host' has been Germany, and specifically what was West Germany. Its expansion into Italy, Austria and Tanzania has come relatively recently. We have noted that the movement has in membership Catholic theologians who had held positions in universities (Rudolf Pesch and Gerhard Lohfink), and that, perhaps as a result, recruitment to the movement from among theology students has occurred. We have also noted the strong connections that the community has forged with Cardinal Joseph Ratzinger, a bond that perhaps acts as a shield for them within the Roman Catholic Church (although this also might tend to incur disapproval from sections of the Church in Germany for whom Ratzinger is a less than sympathetic figure). We also observed that the community has undertaken the pastoring of a couple of parishes for the diocesan authorities concerned, providing parish priests at a time when the Church in Germany is finding it hard to recruit. None of this, it must be said, is indicative of any great impact upon German society.

The impact made seems to be mainly confined to circles interested in the Roman Catholic Church, a point underscored by the involvement of the community with the Catholic daily *Tagespost*. Even here, it has to be said that the *Tagespost* is a very small circulation newspaper. The community also appears to have forged good links with the Jewish community in Germany, notably in Munich. It has attempted to widen its influence on German society. A double page in its history shows the 'guests and friends of the first years', featuring photographs from the 1970s. This is notable because two Lutheran professors and the important Catholic theologian Karl Rahner are pictured. Rahner is seen as a rather more liberal figure than Ratzinger, and he had a background in the Catholic youth movement (Integrated Community 1996, 102–03).

Other than these fairly minimal points there is little evidence for any impact by the IG on German society. This may be because the movement is comparatively young. It has effectively only been in its present form since the late 1960s, as against 1920 for the Bruderhof and 1910 for the Kibbutz. In addition, one might suggest that the emphasis on theology in the IG might militate against a major impact on German society. Although the IG clearly intends to influence German society, when talking to its members one picks up the impression that it is not in an undue hurry to do so. It is resigned to being a minority trend in society, and indeed in the Church, and seems to be more concerned with ensuring that those people who are attracted to it are equipped with an adequate grasp of what it is about. This obviously means theology, and theology is not the hottest topic in today's Germany. This impression is heavily reinforced by Bernhard Koch's recent discussion in the community's newspaper of the 'principle of the small number' (Koch 2000, 3). Finally the rather protean nature of the community over time has seen it metamorphose on a number of occasions. It started as a bund for Catholic girls in post-war West Germany. By the late 1960s it was largely focusing on the radicalised student body of that era. Perhaps the community has 'moved on' too often in the past to have made a lasting impact on any specific section of society.

We can now consider the broader issue of the interaction of the movements with their host societies. The starting point for this consideration must be to reiterate that these communities are, in Oved's terms 'involved' rather than 'secluded' organisations. They all wish to bring about change in society. Perhaps, however, we need to recall the point that Oved made, which is that he has always found ambiguity in the relations of communities and their 'host' societies, whatever relationship they were seeking.

In the chapter on the Bruderhof we noted that the movement's ideology, as developed by Eberhard Arnold, exhibited a definite desire to be a factor in social change. This would not be through conventional political means. The Bruderhof's members do not, for instance, vote in elections, although Mow's account indicated that a serious discussion was held on the question of whether this practice was to be changed in the context of the Johnson–Goldwater presidential election of 1964 (Mow 1991, 233–35). The following comment from Arnold, made in 1933, shows that although the Bruderhof is not prepared to use conventional political means, it is still concerned with the underlying issues of politics.

> We have to find a different way. It is a very modest way because we refuse to attempt the reform of social conditions by political means. We abstain from all efforts to improve conditions by legislation; we refrain from playing any kind of role in the civic order of society. It may look as though we were withdrawing and isolating ourselves, as though we were turning our backs on society. In fact we are building up a life that is disengaged from the established churches

> with their autonomy and self-sufficiency. (Hutterian Society of Brothers and
> Yoder 1984, 201–02)

The Bruderhof, accordingly, does not see itself as withdrawing from society. Its attempts to build its life in community are its contributions to the resolution of the social questions that trouble society. Its recent turn towards rather more 'upfront' campaigning needs to be seen in the light of this comment of Arnold's. At base, its involvement in campaigns such as those against the death penalty in the USA is not an effort to secure the election of particular parties, in the way that Kibbutz movements sponsored parties, for the simple reason that it does not sponsor parties. Rather, it should be seen as an aspect of the movement's witness to Christian values, a witness that is most essentially represented by its attempts to live in community, attempts that succeed to the extent they do, in the Bruderhof's view, thanks to the grace of God rather than their own efforts.

However, there is, as we saw, another side to the Bruderhof's interaction with its 'host' societies. This was shown in the quotation from Heini Arnold indicating the need for the movement to cut itself off from the corrupt generation that surrounded it – and that such separation cannot be done sharply enough. Oved observes that the ambivalence in relationships between 'involved' communities and their 'host' societies arises from the fact that they need to build their communal group, and that this objectively removed them from society (Gorni et al. 1987, 150). This seems a useful insight into the Bruderhof's condition for two reasons. The first is that the Bruderhof has become – twice – a multinational, even multicontinental movement with a complex set of connections linking a number of communities that cohere as one overall organism. The building of this movement is no mean feat, and to have done it twice in the space of two generations, with the debacle of 1961 as a mid-point, is in many ways quite remarkable. The energy required to build and sustain this movement will surely have been such as to require a certain degree of focus on internal issues at times. The second reason is that the ideology of the movement is so central to its way of life, and poses such demands upon the community, that some introspection must be inevitable at times. New recruits need to be educated into the movement's ideas. Unanimity has to be achieved within the bruderhofs. Stands have to be taken by the movement as a whole on issues. One can only speculate as to the difficulties caused within the movement by the estrangement from the Hutterian Brethren, for instance, given the centrality of that connection in Eberhard Arnold's ideology. Interestingly, both Zablocki and Oved in their books on the Bruderhof indicate that the movement became most introverted in the years that followed the Great Crisis. This is exactly what one might expect given Oved's comments. This was when the movement needed to concentrate strongly upon building up (or perhaps rebuilding) its communal structures. Zablocki suggests that the Bruderhof now saw itself as a church among churches, and that it repudiated its 'social movement' phase (Zablocki 1980, 110). Oved is even clearer. 'But there was another aspect to the new conditions that had been created: the Bruderhof began to concentrate on their internal problems and distance themselves from those of surrounding society' (Oved 1996, 244).

In respect of the Bruderhof, then, the interactions with the host society are ambiguous. The movement is, in a sense, on the horns of the dilemma faced by any movement for social change: it wants to change society because it sees serious problems with that society. However, to be too open to the outside might result in vulnerability to influences of a pernicious sort.

Moving on to the Integrierte Gemeinde, we should again stress the point that it is an 'involved' rather than a 'secluded' community. Moreover, the IG is not based in communes outside the cities of its 'host' society (true of the bulk of the kibbutzim as well as of the bruderhofs). Rather, it is a community based mainly in urban Germany, especially in Munich. Hence, it is physically located in the mainstream of its 'host' in a way that is not the case for either of the other movements. The IG is rather different to the other communities in another respect in that its interactions with its 'host' are mediated by the institution of the Roman Catholic Church, which is the context for some of its activities. The likelihood of an encounter with the movement is far greater within the context of that Church than outside it.

The extent to which the IG feels that it is a part of the wider society can be seen by paying a little more attention to their critique of the Bruderhof as 'Rechabites'. Arnold Stötzel, in developing this analogy, starts by pointing out that the Prophet Jeremiah discussed the Rechabites with great respect. The Rechabites clung to a tented way of life at a time when the rest of Israel was moving on from this. However, Jeremiah, for all his respect, did not ask the whole of Israel to turn back history, or halt it by following the practices of the Rechabites. Stötzel suggests that this is, in effect, what the Bruderhof was demanding of the IG. He continued: '[d]oubtless the majority in Israel were also spoilt and infected by the role models of the Canaanite culture, later in the time of the Maccabees of the Hellenistic world culture – just like we and our children are spoilt and infected by the conveniences of the world of consumerism and individualism' (Catholic Integrated Community 1997, 26). Going on to consider the (then) recent shooting of Prime Minister Rabin, he said of the Rechabites and the Bruderhof, '[t]hey may live more perfect and purer; but they remove themselves from these questions. They, so to speak, place themselves in the lee of history; they distance themselves from the "world" and do not allow Israel to clarify who it is and what its task is' (Catholic Integrated Community 1997, 26). The implication of this rather sophisticated and roundabout critique of the Bruderhof is clear. The Bruderhof may well lock itself away and stay 'pure'. 'We' (the IG and the Kibbutz?) on the other hand, are in the mainstream of society, exposing ourselves to the dangers posed by this choice, but able thereby to get involved in the important issues.

What is perhaps most interesting about this critique is that it comes in an article in which Stötzel suggests that the IG intended to live in freedom, separate from the heathen but under the same conditions of the secular world as them. Even in an article containing such a sharp statement of the 'involved' nature of the IG, there is a reminder of the ambiguity of their approach. The heathens outside – and it is not immediately clear whether they are outside the IG or the Church – have to be kept at a distance. The risks of being spoiled and infected will be taken – but only up to a point. Oved's expected ambiguity is found again. In fact, with the IG the ambiguities are rather interesting. What are their feelings towards their fellow Catholics? Are they within the fold or outside it? The question is worth posing because of the polarised nature of contemporary Catholicism, and the positioning of the IG firmly in a specific camp. Equally, one might suggest that simply being in the midst of the city does not necessarily mean that one cannot be a 'Rechabite'. That said, the IG clearly intends to be an 'involved' community, and this is how it should be judged.

The Kibbutz is certainly not a 'Rechabite' community, even if in its early days members lived in tents in the very country where the Rechabites themselves camped. The Kibbutz always intended to influence Israeli society, and indeed to actually bring that society about. There are some important points to be made concerning the relationship between the Kibbutz and Israeli society, which can perhaps give something of an overview to what has already been written.

A useful starting point here is a recent article by Hagai Ben Gurion on 'Communication: Influencing Change on Kibbutz'. Ben Gurion starts with a statement that gives what might be called a 'mythological' view of the Kibbutz.

> During its first fifty years, the kibbutz operated as a closed ideological society, without influence of its surroundings, with independent member selection, judging its behaviour by its own internal systems and moral codes, conscience and ideological values which developed into the isolation of a sect, separate from the surrounding culture. As a closed and dominant society – with an elitist image of justice, equality, culture and economic success – this influence was always externally directed, that is from the kibbutz to the outside community, without affecting the kibbutz community. (Ben Gurion 2000, 23)

Ben Gurion suggests that the Kibbutz interacted with Israeli society in a sort of 'one-way' exchange, influencing the wider society but not being influenced by it.

What makes this view mythological? First, and most importantly, Ben Gurion offers a clear statement of just how kibbutznikim believe the process of interaction between itself and Israeli society proceeded. Slightly later in the piece he discusses the mechanisms for this influence, mentioning the press, governing authorities, the Palmach, the Nahal, and youth groups inter alia. He then says, 'These frameworks carried a strong influence, always positive, to Israeli society, especially the higher strata' (Ben Gurion 2000, 23). In this view the Kibbutz was the elite of Israeli society, certainly until 1960 or so. It was an unequivocal force for good, uncontaminated by the rather less adequate values, mores and lifestyle of Israeli society outside its boundaries. To call this a mythological view is not to say it is wrong, rather it is to stress that it is the embodiment of a certain self-image, which is more important for its prevalence among kibbutznikim than for its empirical validity. However, the second, less important reason why it might be called mythological is that it might well be empirically invalid. The evidence adduced in our discussion so far suggests that its claims cannot be taken seriously for the years following World War II. Here we might note Laqueur's comments about returning soldiers bringing radios that became their own property. Laqueur noted that 'eventually everyone got his or her radio, unless, of course, the person did not want it' (Laqueur 1992, 201). If everyone who lived on a kibbutz who wanted one had a radio by the mid- to late 1940s, then Ben Gurion's argument seems rather exaggerated.

However, if Ben Gurion is not necessarily correct in his statement, his characterisation of the Kibbutz does help us to consider the interaction between the Kibbutz and Israel. While the Kibbutz is an 'involved' community, the ambiguity that we can find in its relationship with Israel could be summed up as 'do as I say, not as I do'. For all the fine words about positive, unsullied influences, building socialism, justice, equality and the like, a case can be made that the Kibbutz came to act as a privileged interest group that had an elitist practice, not in the moral sense that Ben Gurion invokes, but in a rather darker sense. This was, of course, the point that was played upon by Menachem Begin in the election of 1977. This view is, no doubt, just as much a myth – in both senses – as Ben Gurion's view. However, there is the critique made by some members of the urban kibbutzim to be considered here, that the Kibbutz has left its beliefs behind in practice and lost its desire to influence Israeli society.

ALTERNATIVE SOCIETIES

Turning next to the nature of the alternative societies and economies created by the movements, we can again see contrasts and similarities. All three of the movements are characterised by the fact that they do not really aim at a position of complete self-sufficiency. This is, of course, only to be expected in that, as substantial movements with a reasonable (if, in the case of the Bruderhof, frugal) material standard of living, it would be extremely hard for them to achieve self-sufficiency to anything like an absolute extent. However, there are differences in the extent to which the movements have created a degree of self-sufficiency.

If we consider the Kibbutz first, we saw that the movement had considered and rejected the idea of an economically self-sufficient society. The Kibbutz economy was, and indeed is, part of the overall Israeli economy. However, there may be an extent of social self-sufficiency that does merit consideration. Stanley Maron, in noting the rejection of economic autarky by the Kibbutz, did point out that the way in which the Kibbutz was integrated into the surrounding economy largely did away with the need for contact between the individual kibbutznikim and that surrounding economy (Maron 1993, 35). Maron's comment suggests the possibility of a situation in which there was a smallish number of members involved in economic interaction with the wider society, along with some involved in, for example, political work, while large numbers might for all intents and purposes be 'cut off' from the wider society and economy. Whatever the case in the past, the sheer numbers of kibbutznikim now involved in working off-site (11,000 out of 72,000 employed residents), along with the large number of non-kibbutznikim now working on the Kibbutz (one-third of the 91,000 workers), mean that at the economic level, and almost inevitably at the social level, the interchange and interaction between the two economies and workforces have increased. While it may be possible to live a life with little or no contact with mainstream Israel on the Kibbutz, it must clearly be harder to do so than it was in the past. In this respect the alternative society and economy of the Kibbutz has clearly become more 'porous'.

In the main, Kibbutz society remains rural, although the Kibbutz economy is becoming more an industrial economy. Whether it retains the pioneering aspect that was clearly a facet of Kibbutz life in the Yishuv period, and in some parts of Israel in the state period, is open to question. In some areas this is possibly still a factor. Kahana's comments about the increasingly urbanised nature of Israel come into play here. It is unlikely that many kibbutzim other than those in the Negev and perhaps the Golan Heights are very far from a major urban settlement. The Urban Kibbutz represents, perhaps, an attempt to grasp the urban nature of Israeli society and develop an alternative society, if not economy, within that context. It is, as yet, too soon to comment on the alternative society in the process of creation by the Urban Kibbutz. It looks to be combining the pioneer spirit of the original Kibbutz movement with a shift away from the combination of communalised work and life that the original movement created. Self-sufficiency of an economic type is not, here, even on the agenda.

The alternative society and economy of the Bruderhof is, arguably, comparable to that of the Kibbutz. The bruderhofs are rural in location. The movement's economy is integrated in certain ways into that of the surrounding society (i.e. via sales of Community Playthings on the one hand and the purchase of required supplies on the other). While the Bruderhof has this economic interchange with the outside society, it is possible that a relatively small percentage of the membership is involved in direct contact with persons outside the community, as may have been the case with the Kibbutz in the past. A major difference, however, is that the Bruderhof does not have the interchange of labour with the outside community. Very few, if any, bruderhofers go out to work in the main economy, and very few people come in to work on the bruderhof, although there are visitors and other minor exceptions.

In this respect, there is a degree of self-sufficiency about Bruderhof society – as against its economy – that marks it off from Kibbutz society. This can be further enhanced by the members' lack of means for finding out about the world outside. Whereas the kibbutznik has the ability to access television, radio and newspapers at will, this is far from the case at the bruderhof. Bruderhof society is accordingly characterisable by a considerable degree of self-containment. It is clearly possible for a Bruderhof member to have little contact with the outside society, other than by meeting guests at the community. In the chapter on the Bruderhof we saw why this situation can be justified by the movement's ideology. The Bruderhof has an extremely rich and involved internal life. This does not necessarily conflict with its commitment to social change, but it does emphasise the pertinence of Oved's comments about the ambiguities of communal life. These are also brought out sharply by an article in the Australian newspaper, *The Age*, in March 2001, which characterised the movement as a wealthy sect and stressing its success at 'wealth-creation'. The article hints that the move into Australia was made on business grounds: 'Like many businesses, the Bruderhof, which has members from Japan and Korea, wanted a Pacific Rim presence.'[1]

Finally, we can consider the Integrierte Gemeinde's alternative society and economy. As has been pointed out on several occasions in this study, the common life of the IG takes a radically different form to that of the Bruderhof and the mainstream Kibbutz. (There seem to be a number of points of comparability between the form adopted by the IG and that of the Urban Kibbutz). By and large, the IG is based in urban Germany and, accordingly, its alternative society and economy are intermingled with urban German society. At an economic level, the IG cannot aspire to self-sufficiency, as it does not live in a communal form in the manner of the Bruderhof or the Kibbutz. Its economic enterprises, not actually owned by the community but by members, take the form of companies in the market. It seems likely that to some extent the workforce may be drawn from the IG, and this obviously contributes to the social solidarity of the IG. This, however, will be the extent to which the IG constructs an alternative economy for its members.

At a social level, the members of the IG are brought together by a number of means: the 'table communities', the 'geographical communities', the feasts, the integration houses, the enterprises, and perhaps the schools. The alternative society can, accordingly, be characterised as one in which members come together to live their common life in a number of different ways, by contrast with the commune structure of the other movements. It seems possible that considerable numbers of IG members will be able to live and work largely with their fellow members, and given the high demands placed upon members this may lead to something like the level of social self-sufficiency that is exhibited by the Bruderhof being reproduced in the suburbs or centre of Munich. However, it should be reiterated that IG members generally seem to be more concerned with external news and current events than bruderhofers (reading newspapers, for instance, and thus keeping up with events in the 'world'). They are also involved in external bodies in a way that is, perhaps, more comparable to the Kibbutz than the Bruderhof: hence, their involvement in church institutions, and their participation in political parties.

We can summarise by suggesting that the movements have all created societies and economies that are radically different from their surroundings, and that all three are different from one another. While it is difficult to generalise, it seems that the main comparative finding is that the alternative societies of the Bruderhof and the IG make more demands upon their members, and they seem to be, at least potentially, more marked off from the outside societies they find themselves in than does the Kibbutz.

PERSONAL AUTONOMY AND THE COMMUNAL SPHERE

The two further issues that arose in the course of examining the three movements may now be considered. The first of these is the question of the extent of personal autonomy afforded to members of the movements. In this respect the Bruderhof stands out. The words of Hardy Arnold in his letter to Henri Lasserre are a useful starting point in thinking about this issue, as are some comments made by J. C. Arnold. In 1939, Hardy Arnold (Eberhard Arnold's eldest son) argued that while not 'totalitarian' in a political or cultural sense, the Bruderhof was totalitarian in the fullest sense of the word because God demanded the whole person (see Thomson 1949, 78). At a practical level, we saw in Chapter 5 J. C. Arnold's 1996 argument that, contrary to the widely held belief that the healthiest relationship is the most private, the Bruderhof believes that issues such as marriage and engagement are concerns of the whole church – meaning in this context the whole 'brotherhood' within the community – and not just the individuals concerned (Arnold 1996a, 91). Taken together, these two statements suggest that there has been a degree of continuity in the approach of the Bruderhof over time. God demands the whole person, surrendered into the community of believers, and that community has to concern itself with every aspect of life. The extent to which this is the case can be gathered from a reading of J. C. Arnold's *A Plea for Purity*, which shows that the Bruderhof has a 'line' on issues of sexuality that goes far into what would ordinarily be considered private matters, and much further than issues of engagement, marriage, contraception and abortion (J. C. Arnold 1996a, 65).

We suggested earlier in this chapter that a reasonable working hypothesis was that in situations of communal living, aspects of life firmly in the private sphere in ordinary bourgeois society might well transfer into the communal sphere. In respect of the Bruderhof this hypothesis seems to be well and truly borne out. Arguably Hardy Arnold's statement indicates in theory that there is no private sphere at the Bruderhof, and examples chosen from J. C. Arnold's text simply go to show that in practice the Bruderhof is as good as its word. The determination to eliminate the private sphere is not something that can only be extrapolated from the words of Hardy and J. C. Arnold. It is stated very clearly in one of the key texts of the movement, *Why We Live in Community*, by Eberhard Arnold. 'When working men and women voluntarily join hands to renounce everything that is self-willed, isolated, or private, their alliances become signposts to the ultimate unity of all people' (Eberhard Arnold 1995, 6). From a hostile point of view, this destruction of the private sphere is confirmed by a former member of the Bruderhof, quoted by Zablocki: '[i]t is difficult to convey the degree to which the Bruderhof demanded and got conformity in the most private attitudes and feelings' (Zablocki 1980, 238). In passing, we might note that this does not seem to be an uncommon approach in groups attempting to live a Christian communal life. In the Jacksons' account of the Reba Place Fellowship, Chapter 16, 'A Crooked Line', is devoted to problems that the Fellowship perceived to have arisen from its adoption of a similar approach. The next chapter starts: '[t]he light did not dawn all at once about how the individual's free will had been eroded at the Fellowship' (Jackson and Jackson 1987, 251). To sum up, we need to be very clear that when a writer such as Merrill Mow from the Bruderhof uses the chapter heading 'Of one mind' (Mow 1991, 200), it is not meant as an analogy. The Bruderhof is deadly serious in this respect, and we should assume that it means precisely what it says. This is all part of the abnegation of the self.

Is this destruction of the private sphere shared by the other two movements that we have examined? Before examining those movements, it is worth noting that the communal movement described by Mark Roseman, the Bund, Gemeinschaft für sozialistisches Leben, which also emerged from the German Youth Movement, engaged in practices that tended to eliminate the personal sphere. Roseman notes of the Bund that '[i]ts members were engaged in the experiment of creating a moral community, and there was a tradition of open discussion about relationships' (Roseman 2001, 367. Roseman's account indicates that the Bund was founded in 1924, and that while it survived the Nazi era – the focus of his book – it declined in the post-war period. On his account it appears to survive as a group of ageing veterans.) Moving on to the Kibbutz, the answer to the question is that in certain parts of the movement, and at certain times in its history, something rather similar to the Bruderhof approach was tried, although it is no longer attempted today in any significant way. Laqueur's account of a kibbutz in the 1940s pointed to a conflict between the 'radicals' who wished to stress the collective interest and the 'liberals' who believed that the emphasis of Kibbutz life would shift into the private sphere over time (Laqueur 1992, 200). Evidence of the situation in the late 1920s and early 1930s can be found in Ruth Bondy's biography of the Italian Socialist Zionist and kibbutznik, Enzo Sereni, who lived at Kibbutz Givat Brenner. 'Within the kibbutz Enzo insisted on individual freedom for himself and for others, in matters of opinion, conduct and needs' (Bondy 1978, 89). Bondy suggested that this led him to favour the Kibbutz Me'uhad policy of building large kibbutzim that would grow and absorb new members. 'The sectarian, closed and suffocating atmosphere prevailing in small, "organic" kibbutzim such as were advocated by Hashomer Hatzair, with their public confessions and constant examination of what goes on within the members' souls shocked him' (Bondy 1978, 90). Sereni's opinions, while interesting, are not at issue here. The point is that clearly, in his view, the type of kibbutzim being built by the shomrim were encroaching on the private sphere to an alarming degree.

Muki Tsur's article on 'The Intimate Kibbutz' indicated that the kibbutzim of the early days of the movement shared the atmosphere that so concerned Sereni, and moreover Tsur makes no attempt to suggest that any one trend was more or less involved. He wrote, rather, of the 'various Jewish youth movements which had sprung up since 1912' (in Leichman and Paz 1994, 13) and whose members went to Eretz Israel in the years following World War I. This was the phase of what he called the 'Intimate Kibbutz'. He says of this:

> [f]rom the basic assumptions of honesty and confidence in each member and a general distrust of formally structured systems, a mode of daily living had to be worked out through trial and error. The experimentation extended to every sphere of the individual's and the group's life, and the results of these experiments were largely to set the patterns for kibbutz life in the future. (Leichman and Paz 1994, 13)

This life was 'governed' by an assembly without rules and without agendas, which could be convened at any time by any member to discuss any issue. Tsur suggested that '"[t]he table", i.e., the roundtable of dinner and debate, was omnipotent. Its powers lay in the concept of the kibbutz as a family' (Leichman and Paz 1994, 13). This passage points to some very interesting parallels with the Integrierte Gemeinde. Tsur described this as an 'effort to base the society on feelings' (Leichman and Paz 1994, 16). In this it was rather different from the Bruderhof; one might suggest that it was an effort to build the community on eros, rather than agape. However, at a practical level we might argue that the early Kibbutz, as considered by Tsur, seems to have obliterated the private sphere in a way that compares to the Bruderhof. This judgement is borne out by Daniel Gavron's account of the early days at the first kibbutz, Degania. 'Yosef Bussell spoke out about the need for partnership in the raising of the children. "There must be no privacy," he said, according to an early protocol of Degania. "All privacy interferes with our communal life. All of us are obligated to participate in the expense of raising the children – not just the parents"' (Gavron 2000, 26).

However, the private–communal distinctions returned to Kibbutz society. It is evident that if the 'large kibbutz' policy of Kibbutz Me'uhad was to be followed, then the type of commune based upon intense emotions as described by Tsur was destined to end. Kibbutz Artzi, with its selective recruitment through the Hashomer Hatzair youth movement, could perhaps retain aspects of the elimination of the private sphere, reinforcing it with the notion of 'ideological collectivism'. However, we need to recall here that Laqueur's kibbutz, Kibbutz Hazorea, was an Artzi kibbutz. Also, Merron's memoirs portray the same sort of tensions that Laqueur pointed to (see Merron 1999, 34 et seq. for a portrayal of the debate at Merron's kibbutz in the early 1960s). In interview, Merron suggested that ideological collectivism, although clearly affecting issues to do with an individual's weltanschauung, did not reach into personal lives. Indeed, he suggested that the concept within Hashomer Hatzair of Hagshamah Atzmit (personal realisation) meant that there was an incumbency on the individual to realise their ideals, and a recognition that this could not be achieved through group mechanisms.[2] Evidence examined in the chapter on the Kibbutz suggests that the trend to allow the growth of the private sphere continued, and indeed perhaps gathered momentum during the crisis. Maybe for some this was part of what they saw as the end of the Kibbutz as previously understood, or a reason for seeing that efforts to continue were 'a waste of time'. Interestingly, while some facets of the Urban Kibbutz phenomenon suggest an effort to return to the 'Intimate Kibbutz' tradition (for instance, use of the term kvutsat, and a desire to keep the kibbutz small), it is notable that representatives of this new wave specifically stated that they intended to safeguard members' individual freedom. Accordingly, we might suggest that on this issue we have a major disparity between the Kibbutz and the Bruderhof. The Kibbutz today does seem to be happy to preserve a sphere of individual autonomy – which its structures will mean is narrower than in 'bourgeois society' – whereas the Bruderhof, as in the past, wishes to create a community without a private sphere at all. With the Kibbutz, it seems unlikely that the kind of utter destruction of privacy envisaged by the Bruderhof was seriously contemplated other than in the earliest period of its life.

It is actually more difficult to be clear about the IG in this context than it is with the Bruderhof and the Kibbutz. The type of material published by the IG is rather different to that produced by the Bruderhof, which tends to shy away from the theological that is the leitmotif of the IG. Accordingly, the sort of direct and straightforward statements of the type we have seen about this issue from the pens of leading Bruderhof figures tend not to be what we get from the IG. What we can do is interrogate some statements from IG sources to see if we can draw any conclusions. A starting point could be a statement by Rudolf Pesch that we have already noted in another context: 'The assembly of those who are called into it is the decision making body of the Community' (Urfelder Kreis 1996, 71). From the same Urfeld Circle discussion two further points of note can be mentioned. First, Traudl Wallbrecher pointed out that the responsibility for the community is carried by the assembly, and not by the priest alone. Second, Rudolf Pesch pointed to the way in which the IG worked on the basis of unanimity, a point reiterated by Traudl Wallbrecher, and which caused some debate on the part of kibbutznikim present at the meeting (Urfelder Kreis 1996, 72–74).

These points can be amplified by examining the discussion of the apostolic and post-apostolic assembly that we find in Gerhard Lohfink's *Does God Need the Church?* (Lohfink 1999, 233–36). Among the points that Lohfink makes about the assembly are the following: '[t]he community assembly is also the place of brotherly and sisterly correction' (Lohfink 1999, 234). In the assembly the sinner must be brought to the right way. 'Without correction there can be no serious life in faith, for isolated Christians are not in a position to free themselves from their self-deceptions' (Lohfink 1999, 234). This is a voluntary thing: the freedom of the individual must be respected and they should be spoken to only if they permit it and want to be helped. However, we might ask whether a lack of willingness to be helped and to be spoken to might indicate unfitness to be within the assembly. Lohfink was clear that this should not involve scapegoating. All members should examine whether they have contributed to the failure of the brother or sister concerned. Lohfink's second point followed from this: 'the assembly is not only the place of mutual correction; it is also the place of constant reconciliation' (Lohfink 1999, 235). Because the assembly is where worship and life come together, it is also where new beginnings can be made and genuine conversion can occur. Lohfink's third point about assemblies was simple. 'The assembly gains its power from its unanimity' (Lohfink 1999, 25). These are not the only points that Lohfink made about assemblies in the church of apostolic and post-apostolic times (broadly the period prior to Christianity becoming the religion of the Roman Empire). However, they are the most crucial for our purposes here.

It seems reasonable to assume that the picture Lohfink painted of these assemblies represents a sort of manifesto for how the assemblies of the Integrated Community should function in the present. We can see from both his, Wallbrecher's and Pesch's accounts that the assemblies will function on the basis of unanimity, in this respect being similar to the Brotherhood in the Bruderhof, but sharply different from the general meeting of the Kibbutz. They will also have responsibility for mutually correcting the sins of the members of the assemblies. In this respect it is important to bear in mind the comment of Wallbrecher that the responsibility for the community is carried by the assembly and not by the priest alone. For lay Catholics the question of sins would be between themselves and their priest in the confession box. However, the assembly has a function – if Lohfink's model is applied in the present – for mutual correction of sins. Hence, the IG member's conduct becomes an issue for the community, as well as for the individual and their priest. Perhaps this does not mean that the private sphere is obliterated, but what it does mean is that all aspects of life covered by the Catechism of the Catholic Church are catapulted from the private sphere (private between the individual Catholic and a priest who does not discuss issues raised in confession with a third party) into the communal sphere. This is to some extent speculative, but it seems reasonable to conclude that if the assemblies described by Lohfink are meant to be programmatic for the IG today, then the private sphere of IG members will be significantly circumscribed. Why is it reasonable to see Lohfink's description as programmatic? The following statement by the IG sheds some light here:

> [t]his unique people [i.e. the People of God] seeks its salvation neither in the
> form of a theocracy nor in integralism nor in the state-religion, but in the figure
> of the community church of the beginning, born at Pentecost out of the

Synagogue: the Church, experienced and described in the New Testament as the culmination of previous and present history, and given as the measure for all times. (Integrated Community 1996, 38)

As the IG does not speak in the same way that Eberhard Arnold did, we need to be tentative in concluding on this issue. However, it does seem reasonable to gather from what has been examined that the IG has an approach that will see a narrowing of the private sphere for its members, with issues going into the communal sphere that perhaps even other Catholics would normally see as being private. The assemblies seem to have the function of mutual correction of sins, and this means that they will become the place at which issues that are private for those living in the 'bourgeois' order will be opened up to fellow members of the community. So, to summarise, we find that two of the three movements (one definitely, one tentatively) do close down the private sphere for their members, while the other – the Kibbutz – may have to a greater or lesser extent attempted to do so in the past. With the Kibbutz, it seems evident that once the move towards the large kibbutzim associated with the Kibbutz Me'uhad was made in the early 1920s, the resurgence of the private sphere was to some extent guaranteed in the long run. It is also notable that the Urban Kibbutz appears to be unconcerned about reviving the types of practice associated with the Intimate Kibbutz in this area of activity. What there is to report upon suggests rather a concern for individual freedom in a communal context.

CONTEMPORARY ESTIMATIONS OF THE YOUTH MOVEMENT

The fourth and final area for comparative consideration is that of the standing of the German Youth Movement in the communal movements today. There is a wide disparity here. Perhaps the easiest movement to deal with is the Kibbutz. We saw that historians of and commentators on the Kibbutz who are members of that movement are quite clear about the contribution of the various youth movements to its development. The likes of Near, Seeligmann, Salinger and others have shown the connections in their work, indicating that there were youth movements that had ideological connections to the German Youth Movement (the 'chalutzo-Zionist' section of the German-Jewish youth movement, along with some others from outside Germany such as Hashomer Hatzair) and others that were alien to that tradition (notably Hechalutz other than, perhaps, in Germany). All these movements are seen as part of the variegated roots of the Kibbutz. The writers do not feel constrained to make statements about the overall worth or otherwise of the Youth Movement (although Seeligmann and Salinger seem broadly favourable, which is hardly surprising given their backgrounds).

This is very different from the approaches taken by the other movements. The Bruderhof and the Integrierte Gemeinde take very different stands on the Youth Movement. Considering first the Bruderhof, the movement has a generally favourable view. This was shown perhaps most graphically in the material derived from an interview with Bruderhof veterans. The veterans interviewed indicated that for them the Youth Movement was still a living impulse, with certain of its practices being lived out at the Bruderhof in the present. The Hohe Meissner was seen by them as a continuing inspiration. The appropriation of certain Youth Movement forms by the Nazis did not 'contaminate' the memory of the movement for them. They continued to sing happily the songs of the Youth Movement, which retained for them the original meaning. Eberhard Arnold, as well as participating in the movement, developed a view of it in which the religious aspect was stressed, along with its role as a 'school' for community. While this was an individual slant upon the movement, we did observe that there were reasons to suggest that it had some merit. Notably, there were grounds for support to be found in the work of Borinski and Milch, which could be seen as important given Borinski's role in the Youth Movement.

However, is the Bruderhof's positive stance towards the Youth Movement the whole story here? If we consider J. C. Arnold's *A Plea for Purity* it might be suggested that in some ways the movement today ignores certain crucial principles of the Youth Movement. We have already noted Arnold's comment in his book that the Bruderhof rejects the prevalent idea that the most healthy relationship is the most private, and that questions of engagement and marriage are issues for the whole church. The next sentences are important in the context of this discussion.

> Therefore, when young men and women in our communities feel drawn to one another, they turn first to their parents and ministers. From this moment on their relationship is placed under the care of the church. Our young people do not regard this step as an imposition, nor do they feel that they are being chaperoned. On the contrary, they are grateful for the possibility of guidance in an area where immaturity and impurity bring misery to so many. (J. C. Arnold 1996a, 91)

This follows a discussion of dating practices in modern society which includes the straightforward statement '[b]ecause of this, we reject conventional dating in our communities' (J. C. Arnold 1996a, 89). It may well be that in some respects the practices of the Bruderhof in this field are not dissimilar to those of sections of the Youth Movement at certain points in time. However, the crucial point is that whatever practices the Youth Movement adopted, those practices were adopted by the young people themselves, independently shaping their own lives, as the Meissner Formula put it. For instance, Bondy's biography of Enzo Sereni shows that the Jewish youth movement in Germany at times followed principles quite similar to Arnold's and the Bruderhof's, whereas at times it followed practices that the Bruderhof would doubtless find unacceptable. But, to reiterate, they decided their practices themselves, as young people (Bondy 1978, 107).

While the Bruderhof and its members continue to cherish the memory of the Youth Movement, and indeed even argue that they live out some of its ideals, there are ways in which this identification can be seen as limited. Does the Bruderhof accept the full implications of the Meissner Formula? Given the overriding commitment to Christianity on its part, could it apply it to its own children? Perhaps choosing to live at the Bruderhof was the way in which some people actually lived the Meissner Formula in their own lives. However, J. C. Arnold's approach suggests that the movement's moral outlook trumps the formula as far as young people living at the Bruderhof today are concerned. In summary, the movement more or less has to affirm the Youth Movement. Not to do so would be to throw off the vision of Eberhard Arnold. However, one might suggest that it is Eberhard Arnold's vision of the movement that is ultimately being affirmed. While it is a vision that can be supported, it is one man's view, and it is the view of a deeply committed and partisan figure who never pretended to be anything other.

By contrast, the Integrierte Gemeinde tends to take a rather negative view of the Youth Movement. We saw in Chapter 4 that the IG today sees the community as a 'new thing', which has left the Youth Movement behind. Even as early as the foundation of the Junger Bund, there was a view expressed that it would be wrong to take up either bourgeois or Romantic forms again; we can read the term 'Romantic' as perhaps being synonymous with Youth Movement. Indeed, the leaving behind of the Heliand Bund has been described in these terms by Bernhard Koch: '[l]ike in 1947–48 the exodus from the traditional youth movement' (Koch 1999, 14). The need of the hour was to leave behind the Youth Movement and to move on into something new.

Again, is this all that is to be said? We need to bear in mind the extent to which the IG did in fact recruit people who had been involved in the traditional Catholic youth movement. Obviously the Wallbrechers were examples, but equally Gerhard Lohfink had some experience of the movement (Lohfink 1999, 313). However, the major point which raises concerns about the validity of the view that the IG simply left the Youth Movement behind is the comment made about Fr Goergen and Romano Guardini referred to in Chapter 2. An official IG publication suggested that by leaving the IG at the time that it started to evolve the practice of Integration, Goergen abandoned Guardini's vision. Guardini was also specifically noted as the spiritual mentor of the Catholic youth movement. As indicated, the inference to be drawn from this passage is that in at least some respects the IG sees itself as embodying Guardini's vision. It might be further suggested that it cannot both embody Guardini's vision and also represent a radical shift away from the traditional Catholic youth movement, which was mentored and partially created by Guardini. This is, perhaps, a relatively minor point. However, it needs to be mentioned and perhaps given some force because it is a theological point, and theology is very important for the IG.

This discussion can be ended by noting that there is a sort of 'aftertaste' of the Youth Movement in all three of the movements. In the Kibbutz this takes the form of the children's society and its involvement with youth movements active in both the diaspora and the wider Israeli society (both of these features appear to survive in very much attenuated forms in the present day). At the Bruderhof, there is a grouping for unmarried members of the movement, the Shalom group. According to Eggers the result is a group with a membership aged – roughly – between 18 and 50. In describing a meeting, he suggests, '[a]bout eighty young people (more or less) are present' (Eggers 1988, 127). Characterising the group, he notes that they 'have their own choir and discussion groups. They hike together or take weekend trips. Surely many a bruderhof marriage was kindled on a shalom trip' (Eggers 1988, 127). The description suggests that the group has an affinity with the Youth Movement, while the comment about marriages perhaps suggests the limits of the autonomy of the group, given the Bruderhof's clearly stated policy in this area. Finally, there appears perhaps to be an attempt to formalise young people's activities within the IG around the concept of a 'youth diaconate'. An article in *Community Today* by Thomas Wallbrecher discussed the idea, and was prefaced by the following remark:

> [y]outh diaconate means the free decision of a young adult from the age of 18–25 years to learn and practise, in a way suited to his age, following Jesus and serving the Church in the build-up of communities and during this time directing the questions of his personal life towards the main concerns. This time shall also contribute towards clarifying whether someone wants to serve today's gathering movement of Jesus as a married person, as unmarried or as a priest, to clarify what his calling is. At the end of the 70's and the beginning of the 80's young people had these ideas for the first time.' (Wallbrecher 2000, 14)

The sense of the article and some discussion that follows it suggest that the notion of youth diaconate may have fallen into disuse in the IG, and that efforts may be being made to revive it. It might serve as a rather more structured form for the activities of the younger members in the IG that currently appear to be fairly informal, if nonetheless vigorous. A good description of an example of these 'informal' activities can be found in *Easter in Israel*, a brochure about meetings in Israel between young kibbutznikim and young members of the IG (Catholic Integrated Community 1999).

NOTES

1   See http://www.theage.com.au/news/2001/03/26/ffxs 5faopkc.html
2   Interview of David Merron by Mike Tyldesley, London, 4 April 2001. Merron was a member of Hashomer Hatzair from 1948, and lived on a kibbutz from 1956 to 1973.

Chapter 7

Against the Stream?

'Above all: *Gemeinschaft*, which literally means Community, but which sounds deeply mystical and supernatural to a German ear' (Halkett 1939, 94). G. R. Halkett's words form a useful starting point for this conclusion. They link the notion of community with German sensibility, and they perhaps inevitably call to mind the work of Ferdinand Tönnies, *Gemeinschaft und Gesellschaft*, where the notion of community was developed and defended under the guise of impartial social science. The three movements that we have considered in this book all take the form of communities, and all have roots in German culture. Halkett's comment appears to place the whole subject into question. For him there is something deeply problematic about this German talk of *Gemeinschaft*. We saw what he felt it led into. To conclude, we might consider some questions raised by our discussions. Have we been considering backward-looking, Romantic movements that seek to (re)create an illusion, fighting against the mainstream of modern life? Do their histories and ideologies tell us something of significance about German, and indeed perhaps European, life and culture in the twentieth century? Let us start by addressing the issue of whether they were backward-looking. Perhaps the best way to face this is to consider their relationship to Romanticism.

ROMANTICISM AND UTOPIA

Earlier in this book the political breadth of the neo-Romantic trend was highlighted by reference to arguments advanced by Michael Löwy. It is to Löwy's work that we can now return in order to probe a little further into what this might mean in the context of the movements studied in this book. In work done jointly with Robert Sayre, Löwy developed a clear conception of Romanticism taken not simply as a literary phenomenon, but also as a social movement. 'At the root of the Romantic worldview is a hostility towards present reality, a rejection of the present that is often quasi-total and heavily charged with emotion . . . Moreover the Romantic sensibility perceives in the present reality – more or less consciously and explicitly – essential characteristics of modern capitalism' (Sayre and Löwy 1984, 54–55). In other words, this was no rejection of an abstract 'present', but a specific rejection of the capitalist present. All the varied trends of Romantic anti-capitalism in effect protest against what Marxists would call the all-powerful nature in capitalist society of exchange value – of money and market relations. This means that they protested against reification, and 'as a corollary of gener-alized reification, social fragmentation and the radical isolation of the individual in society' (Sayre and Löwy 1984, 55). In Romanticism, for Sayre and Löwy, this rejection is connected to a feeling that in the modern world something precious has been lost. 'The Romantic soul longs to return home, and it is precisely the *nostalgia* for what has been lost that is at the center of the Romantic anti-capitalist vision' (Sayre and Löwy 1984, 56). The past that is the object of this nostalgia may be real or wholly legendary; regardless, it is always idealised. 'The Romantic vision takes a moment of the real past in which negative traits of cap-italism were lacking or were attenuated, and in which human values crushed under capitalism existed still, and *transforms it into a utopia*, making it an incar-nation of Romantic aspirations' (Sayre and Löwy 1984, 56, italics in original). Accordingly, Sayre and Löwy point to the paradox that the Romantic orienta-tion to the past functions, in their view, also as an orientation to the future. The image of a desired future is inscribed into a nostalgic vision of the past. In the book that developed from their 1984 article, they actually put this connection the other way around. 'Without nostalgia for the past there can exist no authentic dream of the future. In this sense, *utopia will be romantic or it will not be at all*' (Löwy and Sayre 1992, 303, my translation, italics in original).

In the work of Löwy and Sayre, then, we find a very tight linkage between the concepts of Romanticism and Utopianism. We need to reiterate that Löwy did not see any political homogeneity in Romanticism. In both the article and their book Löwy and Sayre develop a typology that ranges from Fascist to Revolutionary and/or Utopian Romanticism, the fifth variant of which is Libertarian Romanticism whose most typical representative was Gustav Landauer (Sayre and Löwy 1984, 84). So, in using their analysis to consider the movements, we are not reducing them to a non-existent political, or any other, lowest common denominator. Rather, we can draw out a point that might not be obvious immediately. This is that nostalgia for a past is present in the ideology of all the three movements we have considered, however much they may in some cases balk at being called Romantic or Utopian.

The most straightforward case is that of the Bruderhof. We saw that the move-ment makes reference to the 'Early Church' or the 'Jerusalem Church' in its state-ments. For Eberhard Arnold and subsequent bruderhofers, the Early Church was the paradigm of real Christianity (Baum 1998, 57). It is what Christianity was, what it should be, and what, with God's grace, it might become again. What does the movement mean by the 'Early Church'? Simply the Church as recorded in the New Testament, especially in the Acts of the Apostles. Crucially, it was a com-munal church in which life was lived in common and property was shared (Acts 2:44 and 4:32). The Bruderhof accordingly envisages a future that is based at least in part upon nostalgia for a past, in that the Early Church is seen as a pattern for a future society. The movement's attitude to present-day society as shown in, for instance, the book *A Plea for Purity* (J. C. Arnold 1996a) is one of radical rejection in which the categories noted by Sayre and Löwy in their characterisation of the Romantic critique of the contemporary world – social fragmentation, the radical isolation of the individual – are identified as endemic and attacked. In terms of the Sayre–Löwy analysis, the Bruderhof is a good example of a Romantic, Utopian anti-capitalist movement, although it would be reluctant to accept this terminology, with the exception of the anti-capitalist element. Utopianism and Romanticism would be terms that allow for the possibility of human action being able to accomplish desirable change and for the Bruderhof that could not be acceptable. Such change will only result from the grace of God and any other view is a humanist illusion.

If we turn to the Integrierte Gemeinde, we have seen the way in which the movement characterises itself as something 'new'. Discussing its evolution in the 1960s, the movement commented, '[a]nd she [Traudl Wallbrecher] searched for similar new ways for the Community. A secular institute? A house sharing fellowship? A commune? The New could not be any of these...' (Integrated Community 1996, 85). Alongside this stress on the new we find an argument that there is a need for a 'Theology after the Age of the Enlightenment' (Urfelder Kreis 1996, 23). Ludwig Wiemer made it clear that this is in the context of an acceptance of the Enlightenment. 'And hereby we feel completely in accord with the Jewish-Christian tradition which always sided with the Enlightenment' (Urfelder Kreis 1996, 23). This stress on the new, along with a positive approach to the Enlightenment, with all that that implies about culture, suggests a rather different approach than that taken by the Bruderhof, and one that has scant space for nostalgia. This suggestion is reinforced by a sub-heading in an article by Arnold Stötzel: 'No basis for early Church romanticism'. This section included the argument that '[t]o return to the early Church would mean fishing in vain for an imaginary picture which does not exist' (Integrated Community 1996, 52).

This is, however, not quite the whole story. Recall that the IG sees itself as advocate for 'God's forgotten solution', the 'international People of God, consisting of Jews and Christians' (Integrated Community 1996, 38). Moreover,

> [t]his unique people seeks its salvation neither in the form of a theocracy nor in integralism nor in the state-religion, but in the figure of the community Church of the beginning, born at Pentecost out of the Synagogue: the Church, experienced and described as the culmination of previous and present history, and given as the measure for all times. (Integrated Community 1996, 52)

Stötzel continued: '[t]he cause and concern of the beginning always brings about the New only when the new hour is tied to the origin' (Integrated Community 1996, 52). He ended, '"Back to the roots", "God always creates something new":

both together enabled over and over again a survival of the Church as one unique
structure in the world to whom "God's solution" has been entrusted, however
torn and wounded the Church may be' (Integrated Community 1996, 52). In this
context we can see why Gerhard Lohfink argued that the

> Integrated Community has neither been founded nor been started by those,
> who were there right from the outset. It would never occur to Mrs Traudl
> Wallbrecher, to see herself as 'donor' or 'founder' of the Integrated
> Community; together with a few others she went the way she was called to
> go . . . Since Jesus there is nothing that needs to be instituted or founded or put
> into the world anew. We can only re-discover, find again, bring back to life
> again, what has been there all along. (Integrated Community 1996, 201–02)

The IG accordingly battles against a Romantic identification with the primitive
Church. However, its stress on the new, which cannot be underestimated as an
element in its practice and a crucial factor in its willingness to 'reinvent' its structures, is combined with a concern for the point of origin of Christianity. This
works out in the shape of a nostalgia, but one that is subtly different from the
Bruderhof's. The nostalgia is for the point at which the Church emerges from the
Synagogue, a point when the Jewish root of Christianity was indisputably
evident. One could suggest that this is simply another way of looking at the Early
Church of the Bruderhof's position. The key difference, however, is in the emphasis placed upon the Jewish roots of the Church by the IG. For the Bruderhof, by
contrast, the most important point about the Early Church lies in its communal-
ity. This is also important for the IG, but here we must consider what is most
crucial for its ideology. For the IG, despite its protestations, there is a nostalgic
view of the past that informs its view of the future. The future in the IG's view
will, with God's grace, lie with the international People of God consisting of Jews
and Christians. Although it would be as reluctant as the Bruderhof to see this as
a Utopia, in the terms of Löwy and Sayre's argument it could be seen as such.
That it is combined with a distinctly unfavourable view of present-day society,
again one which like the Bruderhof's could be seen as stressing social fragmentation and the radical isolation of the individual in the current social order, can
be seen by a number of collages that were put into one of its publications, that
feature press cuttings with headlines such as 'Consumerism, unbridled hedonism,
anarchic leniency', 'Morally Amoral' and 'Amusing Ourselves to Death'
(Integrated Community 1996, 22–25, 30–31. The latter two pages were devoted
to material from Catholic sources, with an implication that something is amiss in
the Church.) This again suggests the sort of Romantic sense of loss that Sayre
and Löwy discuss.

Turning to the Kibbutz, we saw that Henry Near suggested – and our examination largely bore his thesis out – that the twin ideological underpinnings of the
movement have been Zionism and socialism. Neither appears, at first sight, to be

a promising source for the nostalgia Löwy and Sayre described. In the case of socialism, its intellectual dynamo in the twentieth century was without doubt Marxism. Kibbutz socialism always had a strong element of Marxism, even if this was not the whole story. Certainly the Artzi tradition saw itself in these terms, and the Me'uhad tradition was also strongly influenced by Marxism. Löwy and Sayre pointed to the category of Marxist Romanticism, focusing mainly, though not exclusively, on Ernst Bloch (Sayre and Löwy 1984, 85–87). They might well have been justified in suggesting this as a line of enquiry; however, it seems reasonable to suggest that most Marxists in the twentieth century would have denied any connection with Utopianism, Romanticism, or any form of nostalgia for pre-capitalist social formations. Similarly, Zionism might be seen initially as an unlikely source of Romantic nostalgia. For a start, it is an extremely recent phenomenon. Laqueur in his history of Zionism noted that '[t]he term Zionism was first used publicly by Nathan Birnbaum at a discussion meeting in Vienna on the evening of 23 January 1892' (Laqueur 1972, xiii). While there was something of a pre-history prior to that date, it was not very extensive, and Laqueur argued further that '[t]he emergence of Zionism in the 1880s and 1890s can be understood only against the general background of European and Jewish history since the French Revolution on the one hand, and the spread of modern antisemitism on the other' (Laqueur 1972, xiii). On this reading, Zionism is a national movement concerned with the creation of a Jewish state (or national home in some versions), at least in part as a reaction to recent tendencies that endangered Jews in the diaspora. This can be seen as an almost quintessentially modernist project with little room for nostalgia. Laqueur pointed out that Ahad Ha'am, the Russian 'cultural Zionist' thinker, attacked mainstream Zionist Theodor Herzl's presentation of the Zionist case in the novel *Altneuland* on the grounds that he was concerned with creating just another, typical modern state with no specific Jewish features (Laqueur 1972, 132–33).

However, perhaps there is a little more room in Zionism for the fusion of nostalgia and Utopia than might immediately seem likely. If Zionism was about the creation of a Jewish nation state (and its most influential versions were), and if this was to be done in hostile surroundings, then a harking back to shared myths among the pioneers of the new state might be expected. The obvious reference point was the pre-diaspora situation of Jewry. After all, the Jews had, in the past, had their own 'state'. This they knew because sources such as biblical scriptures told them so, and moreover told them where it had been situated. The power of this memory is shown by the Uganda controversy within the Zionist movement. As Laqueur noted, in 1902 Herzl became involved in discussions with the British government. One issue on the agenda was the possibility of Jewish colonisation in the then British-ruled territory of Uganda, in East Africa. Even though Herzl made it clear that this was not intended as a replacement for Jewish self-determination in Palestine, this proposal caused a major furore within the Zionist movement. Zionism definitively rejected the idea at the seventh congress of the movement in 1905, with some of those prepared to consider it leaving the Zionist movement to form the Territorialist movement (Laqueur 1972, 127–37). Territorialism, led by Israel Zangwill, argued that there were no connections between the vital interests of the Jewish people and Palestine, placing no value on 'historical rights' to Palestine. The Territorialists formulated plans for settlement in various places around the world, none of which came to anything. Territorialism ended formally in the 1920s, although similar movements survived into the post-World War II world, before the idea finally vanished (Laqueur 1972, 414). This story is important because it can be argued that if Zionism was simply about the construction of a Jewish state – Ahad Ha'am's typical modern state – then perhaps Territorialism had a degree of logic. Given the situation of East European Jewry in the early years of the twentieth century, with the pogroms and persecution they faced, perhaps the crucial task was to get the Jewish home started in some way to give them shelter. The answer given by Zionists was yes, but only in Palestine.

In this respect, we can see a nostalgia that fuelled a vision of the desired future: the nostalgia for Eretz Israel. Nothing else would do. In this, it could be argued, Zionism was consistent with the desire for restoration embodied in the words of the Passover ceremony: 'God grant we do it time and again, Pure One, Dweller in height august, Raise up the folk of countless dust! Soon lead the stem shoots of thy ward, Redeemed and singing, Zionward. Next Year In Jerusalem!' (Regelson 1981, 53). It is certainly true that some religious Jews regard Zionism as unacceptable because it seeks to accomplish this goal by human action, rather than trusting to the Messiah. But it is worth noting Abraham Regelson's words at the start of his English translation of the Passover Haggadah. He suggests that the redemption of Israel from Egypt 'is the archetype – the first great historical instance and everlastingly inspiring example – of all liberations of oppressed and enslaved peoples' (Regelson 1981, 5). He suggests that '[t]he aim of the Seder on the night of Passover is to bring the events and miracles of the outgoing from Egypt into present immediacy, so that each of the celebrants, old and young, is made to feel "as though he had personally come out of Egypt"' (Regelson 1981, 5). This surely suggests that Zionism touched upon a view of a golden age embodied in the ceremonies of diaspora Jewry. This is not to say that Zionism simply took over diaspora Jewish memory. As Yael Zerubavel pointed out in *Recovered Roots*, '[t]he predominantly secular Zionist movement turned away from traditional Jewish memory in order to construct its own countermemory of the Jewish past' (Zerubavel 1995, 14–15). This counter-memory was, she argued, the framework for legitimising the Zionist view of the future. For all the differences between Zionists, they were united in their view of the past. 'In spite of the diversity, followers of Zionism shared some fundamental views about the Jewish past and the present: they regarded Jewish life in exile as inherently regressive and repressive, and believed in the need to promote some form of revival of Jewish life as experienced in antiquity' (Zerubavel 1995, 14).

If, then, there was a Romantic-Utopian element to Zionism, can we find something similar in the other tap-root of the Kibbutz – socialism? Despite Löwy's best efforts, we need to look outside the Marxist tradition, and to the man he saw as the key figure in the Libertarian version of Revolutionary Romanticism, Gustav Landauer. We have already seen that Landauer was a figure of some importance for sections of the Kibbutz. We also noted Löwy's suggestion that Landauer's work was replete with references to the Romantic poets. Indeed, so significant is the Romantic element in Landauer's work that Eugene Lunn included chapters in his biography of Landauer called 'The Socialist as Romantic' and 'The Romantic as Socialist' (Lunn 1973). Rolf Kauffeldt's essay on 'The Idea of a New Bund (Gustav Landauer)' is also extremely interesting on this question (in Frank 1988. See in particular p.168 et seq. Unfortunately this material is not available in English.) Landauer's socialism was decidedly anti-Marxist, and Landauer was especially clear that socialism did not require a given level of technical development in society. As he put it in the January 1919 foreword to the republished *Aufruf zum Sozialismus*, 'socialism is possible and necessary in every form of economy and technology' (Landauer 1978, 25). Landauer's vision of history did not see linear development or dialectical processes powered by class struggles or the production process. For Landauer there was a process of rise and decline that was determined by another factor. 'We say that nations have their golden ages, the high points of their culture, and that they descend again from their pinnacles . . . Nations reach their periods of greatness and maintain them when they are dominated by one spirit' (Landauer 1978, 35). Landauer's historical vision is best developed in his book *The Revolution* of 1907. This has never been translated into English (Landauer 1974 is a French edition).

Landauer is a paradigmatic example of Sayre and Löwy's argument: a revolutionary whose vision of a socialist future was powered by a strong vision of the past. Arguably his viewpoint might have been more useful in giving the early kibbutznikim a 'licence' to commence the building of socialism in the feudal conditions of Ottoman and mandate Palestine than Marxist historical dialectics, certainly in their more 'orthodox' versions. We have noted already that German Socialist-Zionists consulted with him on practical issues concerning the construction of communal settlements. Interestingly, one source for his socialist vision was the biblical tradition. After a passage in which he makes clear that he does not dogmatically favour any particular type of ownership system in a socialist society, Landauer argues, '[n]o final security measures for the millennium or for eternity are to be made, but a great, comprehensive equalization and the creation of the will to repeat this equalization periodically' (Landauer 1978, 129). Landauer then quotes what might be seen as his source for this important notion: Leviticus Chapter 25, which deals with the Jubilee year and similar issues (Landauer 1978, 129–30). Landauer's socialism accordingly draws upon the traditional, 'Mosaic' social order decreed in the scriptures. Perhaps this indicates that for kibbutznik and other Jewish socialists there may have been a looking backward that was unique to them, namely a recollection of the traditions of social justice inscribed in the scriptures and theoretically the framework for the earlier, independent Jewish commonwealth.

In terms of attitude towards contemporary society, it is perhaps clear that there will be a rather different approach on the part of the Kibbutz than that taken by the Bruderhof and the IG. The overt 'moralism' of the religious movements is unlikely to be a major factor in the way most kibbutznikim will approach their fellow Israelis. However, in the consideration of the Kibbutz we have noted two linked traits that perhaps perform a similar function in the Kibbutz ideology. These were the self-ascription to the Kibbutz of an 'elite' function in Israeli society, and also the view, often expressed with a quotation from Alterman's poem 'A Kibbutz Backyard', that in some ways Israel had failed to appreciate just what the Kibbutz had done for it. Although the 'existential' aspect of the Kibbutz crisis has perhaps knocked the extent to which the Kibbutz regards itself as a model for Israeli society quite seriously, there can be little doubt that, historically, the Kibbutz has been concerned with overcoming social fragmentation and the radical isolation of the individual in bourgeois society.

ROMANTICISM AND EUROPEAN IDENTITY

Löwy and Sayre have developed an approach to Romanticism that is highly political and no doubt controversial. It affords us insight into the movements we have examined by leading us to consider the relationship of past, present and future in their thought, a consideration that has only been started here. One further point that is very strongly reinforced by considering the movements through the prism of Löwy and Sayre's approach to Romanticism is their European identity. The Romantic tradition that they identify, in all its ramifications, is one that is essentially European. In saying this, we must use the word in a sense that is not narrowly construed. Sayre and Löwy identify a variant of Revolutionary Romanticism they call 'Populist Romanticism' (Sayre and Löwy 1984, 80). Many of the key figures that they identify with this trend are Russian. They also identify a number of English Romantic writers, and so both the 'far ends' of Europe should be seen as included here, even if the overwhelming majority of the writers they analyse are German or French. They also allude to a number of North American writers, but the writers they mention (T. S. Eliot, Ezra Pound, the Southern Agrarians) were all European Americans. North American culture and thought should not be seen as European in its entirety, but an important aspect of it is European. These thinkers are part of the European element in North American thought, and we might well see the Bruderhof's communities in North America as likewise belonging to the European aspect of North American culture. The only non-European thinkers mentioned by Sayre and Löwy are two Marxist Romantics, Li-Ta-Chao from China and J. C. Mariategui in Peru (Sayre and Löwy 1984, 85), who are seen as exemplars of 'Third World' Marxist thinkers looking to the pre-capitalist traditions of their countries as a possible basis for a revolutionary movement, a move not made by the Kibbutz. Moreover, perhaps Löwy and Sayre's analysis can assist us in a consideration of the identity of the Kibbutz. If North American culture and thought can be seen as having a European aspect, then the same can also be said of Israeli culture and thought. The shifting tides of immigration to Israel and Palestine over the last century, and especially since 1948, have meant that the role and position within Israeli society of that European aspect have changed. Arguably the Kibbutz is one of the institutional embodiments of the European aspect of Israeli culture; the figures for 'Oriental' participation in the Kibbutz certainly indicated that numerically the Kibbutz was and has remained – for whatever reason – a primarily 'Ashkenazi' phenomenon. Even if the movements examined in this study have or have had bases in Asia, North and South America and Africa, as well as Europe, they can still be seen as culturally European when viewed in this light. (See Kockel 1999 for a discussion of the question of Europe and European identity. Chapter 1 is perhaps most important on these points, but Chapter 2 should also be examined.)

A GERMAN IDEOLOGY?

It is, of course, possible to be rather more specific. We have seen that these movements have a root (even if in the case of the Kibbutz it is but one root among several) in the German Youth Movement. We can now perhaps consider whether the background of the movements in German culture is purely contingent, or whether there is more to it than that, and indeed whether these movements help us to understand the German experience of the twentieth century. A useful starting point here are the arguments of Louis Dumont, most notably those put forward in his book *German Ideology*. For Dumont, German ideology constituted 'a national variant, among others, of modern ideology' (Dumont 1994, 17). In other words, for Dumont there was (in the period before 1933, the end point for his research) a specifically German way of looking at the world, and its formative period was in the 'extraordinary blossoming of German thought between 1770 and 1830' (Dumont 1994, 17). We can see that this suggests a distinct Romantic colouring in Dumont's German ideology, a point that he has acknowledged (Dumont 1994, 20).

Dumont sees modernity in terms of an ideological pattern that he calls the 'individual configuration', corresponding historically to trends set in motion by the Enlightenment. Although shared in Western Europe in the nineteenth century, there were national variations. In particular, Dumont argues that in the years between 1770 and 1830 'a process of estrangement between Germany and its Western neighbours' developed, because for Dumont the German Enlightenment was, unlike its Western equivalents, religious (Dumont 1994, 19). At a practical level what does this mean? Dumont suggests that to some extent it could be summarised by what he identifies as predominant views taken in France and Germany. 'The one proclaims "I am a man by nature, and a Frenchman by accident," the other confesses: "I am essentially a German, and I am a man through my being a German"' (Dumont 1994, 3).

Dumont argues that an examination of German literature from Goethe to Thomas Mann indicates a characteristic and, at first sight, puzzling duality. On the one hand we find a survival in modern times of the community, in other words a holistic feeling and orientation. On the other hand he points to a pronounced inner development of individuality. Accordingly, he gives us a formula for German ideology: '[c]ommunity holism + self-cultivating individualism' (Dumont 1994, 20). Considering the views of Ernst Troeltsch, he picks out a slogan from a 1916 work, '*state socialism and culture individualism*' (Dumont 1994, 40). Dumont argues that state socialism in this context can be seen as holistic in that it is an attitude that values the whole at the expense of the individual. The devotion to the whole that Troeltsch sees as so valuable is, for Dumont, freely given. 'This spontaneous adhesion to the social whole is exactly what Tönnies called "spontaneous will" (*Naturwille*), for him the characteristic trait of the community or *Gemeinschaft* as opposed to the "arbitrary will" (*Kürwille*) of the individual subject in the society. (*Gesellschaft*)' (Dumont 1994, 41). What of the other term in Troeltsch's slogan, culture individualism, which evidently connects to Dumont's self-cultivating individualism? 'We have here what might be called German individualism, characterized by two very marked traits: on the one hand the closing up of the self vis-à-vis the external world, and on the other the activity of construction or education of the self, the famous *Bildung* which is more or less identical with culture' (Dumont 1994, 43). For Dumont this purely internal individualism left the surrounding holism standing. Again, he points to Tönnies' conceptual formulae: 'the individualism of *Bildung* is located on the level of community (*Gemeinschaft*), which is union, cultural belonging, and has nothing to do with the level of society (*Gesellschaft*), which is division, the struggle of particular interests' (Dumont 1994, 44).

This gives us a rather schematic understanding of what Dumont means by the German ideology, yet from what did this diverge? Dumont offers the following characterisation of the 'individual configuration', which is the core of modern ideology in his view. He suggests that

> we might take as its general features or architectonic elements the following: individualism (as opposed to holism), primacy of the relations of men to things (as against the relations between men), absolute distinction between subject and object (opposed to a merely relative, fluctuating distinction), segregation of values from facts and ideas (opposed to their indistinction or close association), distribution of knowledge into independent, homologous, and homogeneous planes or disciplines. (Dumont 1994, 7)

This, Dumont suggests, was in fact exceptional in human history and the opposed holistic ideology is the general type that has prevailed (this is a controversial idea in anthropology: see Rapport and Overing 2000, 183). To recap, Dumont sees the German ideology as a variant of the modern ideology in which there was a crucial admixture of holism that continued to hold sway.

Clearly, none of the movements that we have considered constitutes a simple and straightforward 'example' of Dumont's German ideology. Dumont is dealing with trends and tendencies and attempting to create a heuristic device, and so such a 'fit' is extremely unlikely. Dumont's work does, however, suggest that the ideologies of the movements we have examined have proximity at certain points to his posited German ideology, even if they do not share the nationalistic elements of his model as developed more fully in his book. Is it fanciful, perhaps, to suggest that the movements developed 'variants' on Dumont's German ideology, most especially in their stress on the need for a variety of voluntaristic community holism as an answer to social fragmentation and the isolation of the individual? We might also suggest that the self-cultivating individualism of Dumont's German ideology has a parallel in the very decision to join one or other of these movements. Unless born into them, in which case different factors come into play, such a decision marks members out as being prepared to stand strongly against the prevalent social norms, and possibly risk scorn from friends and family. (A possible exception here might have been found in the chalutzo-Zionist youth movements of Nazi Germany.)

It is interesting to note just how close to some of the concerns of a central figure in Dumont's argument the ideas of the movements are. In the above account, the name of Ferdinand Tönnies appears on several occasions, with his Gemeinschaft–Gesellschaft and Naturwille–Kürwille distinctions. Tönnies (1855–1935) is most famous for his book *Gemeinschaft und Gesellschaft* (1887; English translations: Tönnies 1955; 2001). This has been rendered into English as *Community and Society*, *Community and Association* and most recently *Community and Civil Society*. Tönnies was seen by Sayre and Löwy as a 'Resigned Romantic'. In his main work he attempted to be objective, but his nostalgia for Gemeinschaft shone through, along with his tragic conviction that there was no return to it – hence the resigned nature of his Romanticism (Sayre and Löwy 1984, 72–74).

This view of Tönnies might, however, be revised in the light of Harry Liebersohn's account of Tönnies's activities. Tönnies had desired to create communities not altogether dissimilar to the ones created by the movements considered in this study. Liebersohn noted that,

> [t]o Lily Braun, one of the founders [of the German Ethical Society], Tönnies wrote in 1892 that for over ten years he had believed the time had come to found communities without superstition (that is, non-religious communities), in which individuals would work and live together. The Ethical movement, his letter implied, would be this postreligious community. (Liebersohn 1988, 37)

If we note that it was between 1881 and 1887 that Tönnies worked on the man-uscript of *Gemeinschaft und Gesellschaft* (Liebersohn 1988, 27), we can see that the implication of the letter to Braun is that during all the period in which the book was being written, and until at least five years after it appeared, the 'resigned' Tönnies was in fact interested in founding something that sounds rather like a commune, though his hopes for the Ethical movement as a seedbed of community never came to fruition. Some of Jose Harris's editorial comments in her English version of *Gemeinschaft und Gesellschaft* tend to bear out Liebersohn's 'activist' view of Tönnies (Tönnies 2001, xxiv, xxix).

Moreover, it is arguable that Ferdinand Tönnies exercised direct influence on at least one of the communal movements we have considered in this book, the Bruderhof. Julius Rubin suggests that 'Eberhard Arnold's sociological vision of *Gemeinde* represents a backward-looking rejection of modernity founded upon two models of community: Ferdinand Toennies's romanticization of the Germanic medieval village (*Gemeinschaft*) and the *ekklesia* of the Apostolic Church' (Rubin 2000, 55). Rubin reiterates this point on the next page of his book: 'Eberhard Arnold was greatly influenced by Toennies's pessimistic critique of modernity and plan for social reconstruction through organic community' (Rubin 2000, 56). Rubin adduces no textual or other evidence from Arnold to back up this line of argument. However, this does not necessarily indicate that it is unfounded. Rubin indicates that Tönnies was in correspondence with Carl Friedrich Arnold (Rubin 2000, 56), a professor at the University of Breslau, who was Eberhard's father. Rubin's cited source for this point was Harry Liebersohn. Liebersohn's account indicated that apart from their correspondence, Tönnies and Carl Arnold did actually meet and were friends in their student days (Liebersohn 1988, 36). This does suggest a distinct possibility that Tönnies formed part of Eberhard Arnold's intellectual universe.

A DIONYSIAN REVOLT?

In evaluating the movements, then, we can perhaps see them as a revolt against the spirit of their age, if 'Gesellschaft' can be used as a summary name for that spirit. Given their German roots, that this revolt took a communal form is not altogether surprising in the light of Dumont's account of German ideology. Also, given Dumont's comments, it is not surprising that we can find in them an attempt to attack the social fragmentation and radical isolation of the individual that were the hallmark of the Gesellschaft type of social formation, increasingly characteristic, for some commentators, of the real world of the early twentieth century. Liebersohn summarises Tönnies's view as follows: '[i]n contrast to local-ized *Gemeinschaft*, *Gesellschaft* pushed ever further outward, encompassing all parts of the globe, dissolving traditional communal relations and creating a uni-versal class of workers who were formally free but oppressed by marketplace con-ditions' (Liebersohn 1988, 29). Another way of putting this might be to suggest that the movements we are considering can be seen as part of a Dionysian revolt against an Apollonian age. This formulation borrows from the terminology used by Friedrich Nietzsche in his first major work, *The Birth of Tragedy* (Nietzsche 2000). Initially it might seem rather strange to use this type of language, but for Tönnies *The Birth of Tragedy* was a text of central importance and there were connections for him between Gemeinschaft and the Dionysian. Moreover, a number of thinkers connected to the movements considered in this study can be linked to the thought of Nietzsche. It is also fitting when we note the importance for Romanticism of the figure of Dionysus, magisterially established by Manfred Frank (Frank 1989–90).

The starting point here is to understand what Nietzsche meant by the terms Apollonian and Dionysian, derived from the two Greek deities Apollo and Dionysus. Nietzsche posed the Apollonian and Dionysian in terms of the opposed artistic worlds of the dream (Apollonian) and intoxication (Dionysian) (Nietzsche 2000, 21). Putting it differently, he suggested that 'Apollo might even be described as the magnificent divine image of the *principium individuationis*, through whose gestures and looks all the pleasure and wisdom and beauty of "appearance" speak to us' (Nietzsche 2000, 22). By contrast, '[w]hen we add to this horror the blissful rapture which rises up from the innermost depths of man, even of nature, as a result of the very same collapse of the *principium individuationis*, we steal a glimpse into the essence of the *Dionysian*' (Nietzsche 2000, 22). Nietzsche further argued that either under the influence of narcotic drink or in the approach of spring, Dionysian impulses awaken in humans, 'which in their heightened forms cause the subjective to dwindle to complete self-oblivion' (Nietzsche 2000, 22). He suggested that '[u]nder the spell of the Dionysian it is not only the bond between man and man which is re-established: nature in its estranged, hostile, or subjugated forms also celebrates its reconciliation with its prodigal son, man' (Nietzsche 2000, 22). In introducing Nietzsche's text, Douglas Smith makes clear that for Nietzsche himself, the two drives are 'as complementary as they are antagonistic' (Nietzsche 2000, xix). Without this equilibrium, there are likely to be ill-effects from the working of one of the drives.

The details of Nietzsche's arguments in *The Birth of Tragedy*, with its parallels between ancient Greece and his own Germany and the visions he entertained for a reformed German culture, need not detain us here. Rather, most important is what some of Nietzsche's readers made of his ideas. As suggested above, some of these readers were members of, or were influential on, the movements examined in this book. There has, for instance, been something of a debate as to the extent or otherwise of Nietzsche's impact on the German Youth Movement in its various phases (Laqueur 1962; Thomas 1983; Aschheim 1992). Nietzsche was important to the Bruderhof for one main reason: the young Eberhard Arnold wrote his doctoral thesis on 'Early Christian and Anti-Christian Elements in the Development of Friedrich Nietzsche' (Baum 1998). Moving on to the Kibbutz, David Ohana has indicated that Hashomer Hatzair and Gedud

Ha'avoda (Labour Battalion) members studied Nietzsche, and that there was a 'Nietzsche Circle' which functioned with the literary societies of the kibbutzim as late as the 1970s (in Wistrich and Ohana 1995; see p. 55 for the Nietzsche Circle).

Two intellectuals who had some impact upon all three movements considered, Martin Buber and Gustav Landauer, were also strongly affected by the thought of Nietzsche. Michael Löwy has written of Landauer that '[a]part from the Romantic poets – notably Hölderin, whom he compared in a lecture in 1916 to the Biblical prophets! – the author mentioned most in Landauer's writings is Nietzsche' (Löwy 1992, 128; see also Thomas on Landauer and Nietzsche, 1983, 52–56). Buber had an early brush with Nietzsche, as Paul Mendes-Flohr has pointed out. 'In 1895 at the age of seventeen, Buber translated the first part of Nietzsche's *Thus Spake Zarathustra* into Polish, probably his first literary venture' (Mendes-Flohr 1989, 15). He also commented that 'Nietzsche's influence on Buber's pre-dialogical thought . . . proved singular and enduring' (Mendes-Flohr 1989, 15. In this context pre-dialogical means pre-1922. See also Mendes-Flohr's essay in Golomb 1997 for the Buber–Nietzsche relationship.) Aschheim suggested of Buber that '[t]hrough him, above all others, Nietzsche was assimilated into German Zionism' (Aschheim 1992, 105). Are these connections entirely surprising? Arguably Nietzsche put into words in his book *Daybreak* (1881) an important aspect of the practice of the movements we have been considering. 'So it is that, according to our taste and talent, we live an existence which is either a *prelude* or a *postlude*, and the best we can do in this *interregnum* is to be as far as possible our own *reges* and found little *experimental states*. We are experiments: let us also want to be them!' (Nietzsche 1982, 191).

Another intellectual whose thought bears the impress of Nietzsche is Ferdinand Tönnies. Liebersohn commented on a section of the introduction to *Gemeinschaft und Gesellschaft* that '[i]n this passage Tönnies seemed to regard history with the wisdom distilled by Nietzsche from Greek tragedy: humanity shared the natural cycle of Dionysian oneness (*Gemeinschaft*) and Apollonian individuation (*Gesellschaft*), followed by decay and return to oneness with nature' (Liebersohn 1988, 34). Interestingly, according to Liebersohn, in the early 1890s Tönnies extolled the young Nietzsche:

> Tönnies asked the younger generation, which was turning Nietzsche into a cult hero, to return to the Nietzsche of *The Birth of Tragedy*: only Dionysian *Gemeinschaft* could inspire a revival of German culture. As late as the early 1890s, Tönnies preserved his longing for the populist *Gemeinschaft* he had discovered in Nietzsche's first book over two decades before. (Liebersohn 1988, 38)

Tönnies, according to Liebersohn's account, read the early Nietzsche as an 'advocate' of Dionysianism in an era in which the Apollonianism of the Gesellschaft type of social order had triumphed. Arguably, there are considerable similarities at a conceptual level between this Apollonianism and Dumont's 'individual configuration'. Tönnies was certainly not the only reader of Nietzsche to have seen things in that way. One of Nietzsche's first English popularisers, Alfred Orage, is an interesting example. Tom Steele summarises Orage's views, as expressed in a number of his books on Nietzsche that appeared in 1906 and 1907, as follows:

> Orage believed that the decadence of bourgeois democracy was a direct result of the epochal predominance of the Apollonian. It was time historically to redress the balance through the Dionysian principle, in which criticism and destruction of the old order could be achieved, and would be justified by the emergence of a new race of supermen – out of chaos would shine a dancing star. (Steele 1990, 53–54)

The accuracy of Steele's summary can be gauged by the following comment from Orage's *Friedrich Nietzsche, the Dionysian Spirit of the Age*: 'Failing Wagner, he himself [Nietzsche] would be the Dionysian initiator. He would transform Europe, and deliver men's minds from the dull oppression of Apollo' (Orage 1906, 41).

Accordingly, we can suggest that some of Nietzsche's readers felt that there was a sort of programmatic dimension to be derived from the Dionysian–Apollonian dichotomy. Society had become too Apollonian, and there was a need for a Dionysian upsurge. It is in the context of such arguments that the suggestion that the movements examined in this book could (analytically) be seen as part of a Dionysian upsurge against the Apollonian spirit of their times can be seen as less strange than it may have initially appeared. The 'alternative societies' created by the movements could be regarded as embodying the Dionysian impulse. Perhaps, more carefully, what we could suggest is that they embodied a more Dionysian configuration of the two principles. This conceptual schema can arguably afford insights into the movements. The social world of the early Kibbutz, described by Muki Tsur in 'The Intimate Kibbutz' (in Leichman and Paz 1994) is very different from the social world that developed in the later Kibbutz. Changes, as we have seen, have affected all sections of the Kibbutz, and we might describe those changes by suggesting that the 'Intimate Kibbutz' showed a rather different configuration of the two principles than today's Kibbutz, with the Dionysian having become less important. Similarly, with the Bruderhof, we might read Zablocki's argument about the shift from 'Communion' at Sannerz (with its 'funky' quality) to 'Charismatic Community' at the Rhön as a shift in the configuration of the principles, with a diminution of the Dionysian, although a very much less important diminution than that seen at the Kibbutz. One can likewise see elements of the life of the IG as embodying the respective principles, with the feasts, for instance, though far from the Bacchanalia that inspired aspects of Nietzsche's original formulations, embodying a feeling of merger into a wider whole in the context of eating, drinking and listening to talk and music – the Dionysian, in other words.

The Dionysian–Apollonian distinction could also be used comparatively in this context. Consider the accounts in this book of mealtimes at the Bruderhof and the Kibbutz. As was shown, most Bruderhof mealtimes involve sharing a common meal in a large room. All eat the same food. All are involved in singing and praying together. The meal has a distinct start and finish. The Kibbutz meal described by Neil Harris shared some aspects with the Bruderhof meal: a large dining room, a common meal. However, in kibbutzim there may be a choice of food. It appears unlikely that, except perhaps at certain special times, there will be any common singing or listening to a reading. Harris's kibbutzni-kim were split into small groups discussing their own concerns. Is it fanciful to suggest that the Dionysian principle is more evident in the Bruderhof meal than in that of the Kibbutz? What we are calling here the Dionysian aspect of the movements, which can perhaps be seen as manifesting itself in the limita-tion of the personal sphere that is a feature of some of them, has been the focus of criticism. In his bitter attack on the 'New Movements' in Catholicism, the ex-member of the Focolare movement, Gordon Urquhart, focuses on this aspect of their practice (Urquhart 1996). Interestingly, he drew upon some theoretical sources used by Zablocki in his work on the Bruderhof (Zablocki 1980).

At this point we might recall the consideration of Romanticism earlier in this chapter. For Löwy and Sayre, a key aspect of the Romantic critique of the present capitalist reality was that it resulted in social fragmentation and the radical isolation of the individual. This could now be seen as another way of saying that the present reality (over)embodied the Apollonian – or perhaps that it exhibited the features of Gesellschaft, and the 'individual configuration'. We can, accordingly, pull these lines of thought together, and suggest that the Romantic critique shares themes with the 'programmatic' ideas derived by some from Nietzsche's dichotomy. (No suggestion is being made that Nietzsche himself shared, or would have shared, any of these 'programmatic' ideas himself.) Both point to a world in which individualism has gone too far. We have seen that we can find characterisations of the contemporary world that utilise this kind of terminology from sources in the movements examined in this study. We also saw that the Marxist Löwy also expresses a critique of capitalist reality which says something similar, while using a different terminology. Indeed, this type of approach remains extremely common, and can be found in a whole variety of sources. For instance, liberal Catholic Paul Vallely, in a book on Catholic Social Teaching, recently commented that '[i]deologically, the domina-tion of the free market, since the fall of communism, goes universally unchal-lenged. Yet socially there is a growing sense of fragmentation and rootlessness with which most societies seem ill at ease' (Vallely 1998, 132). From a rather different perspective, the leading figure in the North American communitarian school of social thought, Amitai Etzioni, argues a similar point. 'This is the reason communitarians in the United States, who see excessive individualism, call for a return to community. It is not that community is in principle more basic than the individual but that the American I&We is out of balance after decades in which self-interest and expressive individualism have prevailed' (Etzioni 1995, 19). More recently, Robert Putnam's examination of contemporary America, *Bowling Alone*, also pursues this theme, although he paints a picture of recent periods of strengthening as well as weakening of community bonds. That said, he strongly argues that the last few decades have seen a significant period of weakening of such bonds (Putnam 2001, 25), and this is the focus, indeed rationale, of his book. There is evidently a widespread belief that contemporary developed societies exhibit dysfunctional, socially fragmented features, resulting from Gesellschaft-like social orders that, in the terms used here, over-embody the Apollonian principle. Tönnies casts a long, if sometimes unacknowledged shadow, over such arguments.

THE TIME OF THE TRIBES?

In this context, the movements considered in this study are a real alternative. Existing as real communities, they stand out against the supposed social fragmentation of the age. This is the sense in which they can be situated as part of a Dionysian revolt against the spirit of the age, both in their formative period between 1910 and 1948 and today. Their denunciations of present-day society can still be sharply polemical, a good example being the previously noted *A Plea for Purity* by J. C. Arnold. We might suggest that although a distinctly minority trend in their host societies (clearly, less true for the Kibbutz than the others) they will continue to have an appeal. For those who reject an individualised life in a contemporary Gesellschaft type of society, life in one of these movements represents a real alternative, and one that allows for a stand against that type of society (again, less true perhaps now for the Kibbutz, but in this context the Urban Kibbutz may come to have a role).

However, a note of caution needs to be sounded. Just because it sometimes looks as though 'everyone' (except perhaps neo-liberal politicians and newspapers) seems to think that society is becoming more privatised, individualised and fragmented, and that this is a 'bad thing', it does not mean that this is the way things really are. Indeed, it might be suggested that this is not the case at all. Rather, present-day society could actually be going in another direction altogether; it might be seeing a decline in individualism. This argument has been put by the French sociologist Michel Maffesoli in his book, published in France in 1988, *The Time of the Tribes* (Maffesoli 1996b), in which he evoked the symbolic figure of Dionysus. It will not be possible to provide a full account of all aspects of Maffesoli's arguments here. All that will be attempted is a presentation of his thesis as it applies to situating the movements that we have considered. An important starting point for this task is Maffesoli's view of what he calls 'individualism'. He states that

[s]o-called experts, untroubled by caution or scholarly nuance, disseminate a body of conventional, and somewhat disastrous, wisdom about the withdrawal into the self, the end of collective ideals or, taken in its widest sense, the public sphere. We then find ourselves face to face with a kind of *doxa*, which may perhaps not endure but which is nevertheless widely received, and at the very least, has the potential to mask or deny the developing social forms of today. (Maffesoli 1996b, 9)

Maffesoli, in an earlier work *Ordinary Knowledge*, published in France in 1985, has indicated that he believes society stands 'at a time when another new age is beginning' (Maffesoli 1996a, 2). He gives us some indication of the nature of this 'new age' in *Ordinary Knowledge*. 'It seems, however, that the trend is beginning to be reversed. As a result of the first stammerings of ecology, and of the new Dionysian values and the importance they give to space, the principle of identity is crumbling' (Maffesoli 1996a, 67). Later in that book he suggests that '[i]t is tedious to have to say it again, but, no matter where we turn, active collectivities and groups (sports clubs, musical clubs, sexual groups, associations, networks, tribalism) are coming to the fore' (Maffesoli 1996a, 154). That statement perhaps gives some indication of the kinds of phenomena Maffesoli had in mind when he wrote about 'tribes'.

At a theoretical level, Maffesoli argues in *The Time of the Tribes* that the situation society finds itself in can be characterised by a move from the 'social' to 'sociality'. For Maffesoli this corresponds to a move from modernity and a mechanical social structure into post-modernity, with a complex or organic social structure (Maffesoli 1996b, 6). The ambience of the era, presumably the start of the 'new age' referred to in *Ordinary Knowledge*, is built on what Maffesoli calls a fundamental paradox: 'the constant interplay between the growing massification and the development of micro-groups, which I shall call "tribes"' (Maffesoli 1996b, 6). The metaphor of the tribe, Maffesoli suggests, allows for an account of 'the process of disindividuation' (Maffesoli 1996b, 6) that is for him a crucial aspect of the 'new age'. The 'tribes' that Maffesoli suggests are becoming central to life in post-modernity are extremely varied. Referring to the rationality that he sees emerging, he suggests that

> [i]t is organized around a mainspring (a guru, an activity, pleasure, space) which binds people together as well as liberates them. It is centripetal as well as centrifugal, whence the apparent instability of tribes: the coefficient of belonging is not absolute, and anyone can participate in a number of groups, while investing a not inconsiderable part of him or herself in each. This flitting around is surely one of the essential characteristics of the social organization which is becoming apparent. (Maffesoli 1996b, 144)

From this it should be clear that the 'tribes' described by Maffesoli are not necessarily formally structured organisations, though they could be.

Maffesoli's argument extends into many aspects of social analysis. It has a political dimension, with his consideration of power, in which he posits a formal 'power' and a more informal, popular 'puissance', and with his suggestion that popular indifference to politics should not be read as simple withdrawal into the individual realm. (See especially his chapter on 'The Underground *Puissance*'.) The argument has much to say about religion, drawing a lot of its material from the history of religion and analyses produced by Durkheim and others. However, there are two points that can be taken from Maffesoli's work that relate very clearly to the movements that we have been examining. The first of these concerns purpose. Maffesoli argues that 'the "tribes" we are considering may have a goal, may have finality; but this is not essential; what is important is the energy expended on constituting the group *as such*' (Maffesoli 1996b, 96). The rationale for this view can be found in a statement earlier in his account. 'The idea of "keeping warm together" is a way of acclimatizing to or domesticating an environment without it becoming in any way threatening' (Maffesoli 1996b, 42). The movements considered in this study all have goals: the Kibbutz's would be stated – or perhaps would have been stated in the years prior to the crisis – as the creation of a socialist Eretz Israel. The Bruderhof and the IG would state their goals in religious terms, and perhaps even deny that 'they' had any goals other than those of God. However, they embody a clear desire to be part of the building of the Kingdom of God. In this sense the movements initially seem to be poor candidates for being seen as 'precursors' of the 'tribes', given the centrality of goals in their ideologies.

The same was not true of the German Youth Movement. Becker noted that 'virtually every observer of the sects [of the German Youth Movement] comments on what may be called the absence of creed, doctrine, or positively stated ideology. This is what has been hinted at in previous pages by the use of terms such as "aimlessness", "goallessness", "haziness of programme"' (Becker 1946, 95). Rob Shields, in his introduction to *The Time of the Tribes*, writes of the 'tribes', that

> [w]hile they have weak powers of discipline (for example, their only option is to exclude or shun members), they have strong powers of integration and inclusion, of group solidarity. These powers are displayed and actualized in initiatory rituals and stages of membership. As the highest social good, the members of the *tribus* are marked by it, wearing particular types of dress, exhibiting group-specific styles of adornment and espousing the shared values and ideals of the collectivity. (Maffesoli 1996b, xi)

As a description of the three movements examined in this book, this has quite a lot to commend it. Arguably, when we connect it to Maffesoli's point about goals, it can be seen as an acute description of aspects of the German Youth Movement, which accordingly seems a rather better candidate for being a 'precursor' of the 'tribes'.

Maffesoli's point, however, suggests that in looking at the purpose of the movements we may need to go a little further. In Maffesoli's 'new age' of sociality, perhaps the movements are taking on the function of the 'tribes' that he has described. Indeed, perhaps this is a function that they have long had. The movements may perform the function for their members of allowing them to 'keep warm together', in Maffesoli's evocative phrase. Part of the appeal of the movements might be the chance they afford of simply living with like-minded people and, in the case of the children of members, with people that one has grown up with. This connects to Yaacov Oved's arguments about ambiguity in intentional communities. Oved suggested that communes trying to leave the world behind had to develop some ties to the world simply in order to ensure the welfare of their members, whereas communes seeking to change the world had to spend time on building their structures in an atmosphere of seclusion. In world-changing communes this latter aspect of their lives, which could be seen as the 'tribal' function of 'keeping warm together', might perhaps displace the world-changing function as the key goal, in practice if not in theory.

David Merron's analysis of the decline of the Kibbutz appears to suggest that this line of enquiry could well be productive. He points out that '[i]n the inter-war years, the kibbutz movement expanded and was consolidated through a steady flow of highly committed idealists who were the results of a severe selection and self selection process in Central European youth movements' (Merron 2001, 3). However, he continued, following the Holocaust,

> the traditional Zionist youth movements were practically wiped out, cutting off the flow of idealistic reinforcements. After the war, the few members remaining coalesced into new groups but these were augmented by large numbers of survivors heading for Palestine. For most of these, the idea of kibbutz was an attractive option. It offered a surrogate family and community for that which had been destroyed, as well as security in starting a new life in a strange and difficult country. Whilst accepting and paying lip service to kibbutz ideals and way of life, this new membership had undergone very little selection and had no real deeper education of, or commitment to its principles. (Merron 2001, 4)

For Merron this resulted (in the early 1950s) in the rapid expansion of what he called the movement's 'periphery', as opposed to the ideologically committed 'core'. Even when this 'periphery' remained resident at the Kibbutz they were (and presumably are), for Merron, not really concerned with the construction and consolidation of an alternative, communal society. Perhaps they were 'keeping warm together'? No doubt Merron's view will be criticised, and it is only one person's reflection. However, it does indicate some interesting possibilities for this line of enquiry.

The second point that we can take from Maffesoli concerns the environment that the movements move in. Maffesoli's argument suggests that life today is not necessarily lived in an increasingly privatised and isolated manner, characterised by social fragmentation. The suggested more Dionysian nature of life today might mean that this is changing. (Dionysian is one of Maffesoli's favourite words, used as an emblem for the changes he is examining; see Maffesoli 1996b, 9–10, 32.) As society moves from modernity into postmodernity, the inhabitants of the movement's host societies, if Maffesoli is correct, will be living lives in which atomistic individuality is less important than it was in the comparatively recent past. (Need it be pointed out that Maffesoli's vision is greatly different to that of, say, Robert Putnam? A debate between these two social commentators would be, to say the least, interesting.) This suggests that aspects of the appeal of the movements may lose some of their force. The highly moralistic critique of individualism might, in this situation, have a rather hollow ring. If 'tribal' reality becomes more and more important for people, then the radical otherness of the lifestyle of the movements, which may form part of their attraction for some, may diminish. That said, this loss of otherness may also allow some, for whom it represented a barrier, to contemplate the lifestyle that the movements offer more freely. Only time will tell whether Maffesoli's analysis is borne out. What can be said, however, is that if time does bear Maffesoli's analysis out, the situation that the movements will operate in is likely to change radically. Whether the mooted new Dionysian era is one in which the movements will flourish or wither is hard to envisage.

So, Maffesoli's analysis suggests that the 'spirit of the times' is changing. If correct, this will represent a major challenge for the movements that we have been considering. While communal living has a history going back millennia, the Kibbutz, the Bruderhof and the IG are all products of Maffessoli's modern period. This was a period in which he suggested that 'Gesellschaft'-like tendencies dominated, an Apollonian period. The movements were part of a revolt against it. If Maffesoli is correct, and society is moving into postmodernity, a more Dionysian period in which certain aspects of 'Gemeinschaft' start to prevail in social life, then the role of the movements may, as indicated above, change. This is not to say that the beliefs of the movements will alter under the impact of the changes that Maffesoli suggests are happening. Indeed, the IG and the Bruderhof, and sections of the Kibbutz, will find the hedonistic type of Dionysian social life (Maffesoli 1996b, passim, but note p. 143) that Maffesoli appears to envisage as integral to his new era every bit as distasteful as the Apollonian social forms that have preceded it. For the IG, the Bruderhof, and the convinced socialists of the Urban Kibbutzim and the sections of the traditional Kibbutz who still cling to the traditional views of the movement, the task of creating alternatives to bourgeois society will still need to be fulfilled.

Hence, if we return to the questions posed at the start of this chapter, we can perhaps conclude that there is a sense in which the movements are 'backward'-looking. They appear to conform to Löwy and Sayre's judgement that Utopian movements seeking to create a new and better future frequently do so by using possibly unreal, and certainly idealised, images of the past for guidance. This 'Romantic-Utopian' aspect of the movements marks them out as characteristically European. The histories and ideologies of the movements do perhaps illuminate aspects of German thought and experience, with due reservations for the Kibbutz and its specifically Jewish and Israeli features. Their ideologies can be seen in part as variants of Dumont's 'ideal type' of German ideology. A locus of interest here lies in the proximity of aspects of those ideologies to that of Ferdinand Tönnies, clearly, for Dumont, an important figure in the characterisation of German ideology. More generally, we might suggest that the three movements can be seen as embodiments of what we have identified as a Dionysian revolt against an Apollonian era. No claim is made here that they have been successful in this revolt, although they have survived turbulent histories in the twentieth century. Indeed, if the notion of a Dionysian revolt has any value as a tool for understanding recent history, it would have to be said that these movements are by no means the most important aspects of such a revolt. That said, they can be taken as relatively 'pure' examples of Dionysian revolt because of the communal forms they have taken.

References

Allain, Roger, 1992, *The Community That Failed*, San Francisco, Carrier Pigeon Press

Allen, John L., Jr, 2000, *Cardinal Ratzinger*, London, Continuum

Anon, 1999, 'British Habonim Celebrates 70 Years', *Kibbutz Trends* 35/36, Fall–Winter, 71

Anon, 2000a, 'Guardians of the Co-operative Faith', *Kibbutz Trends* 39/40, Fall–Winter, 79

Anon, 2000b, 'An Exodus-Story of Today?', *Community Today*, 10/2000, 20 September, 4

Arian, Asher, 1998, *The Second Republic. Politics in Israel*, Chatham, NJ, Chatham House Publishers

Armoni, Ora, Palgi, Arie, Shakar, Eran, Kanowich, Gregory, and Hayut, Mordechai, 1999, 'The Yavne Conference: Questioning Directions', *Kibbutz Trends* 35/36, Fall–Winter, 40–43

Arnold, Annemarie, 1986, *Youth Movement to Bruderhof*, Rifton, NY, Plough Publishing House

Arnold, Eberhard, 1965, *Love and Marriage in the Spirit*, Rifton, NY, Plough Publishing House

Arnold, Eberhard, 1976a, *Foundation and Orders of Sannerz and the Rhön Bruderhof. Section I. Introductory History: The Basis for our Orders, 1920–1929*, Rifton, NY, Plough Publishing House

Arnold, Eberhard, 1976b, *Inner Land*, Rifton, NY, Plough Publishing House

Arnold, Eberhard, 1976c, *Various Movements and the Way of Unity in the Spirit*, Rifton, NY, Plough Publishing House

Arnold, Eberhard, 1986, *Salt and Light*, Rifton, NY, Plough Publishing House, 3rd edn

Arnold, Eberhard, 1992, *The World Situation and Our Task*, Farmington, PA, Plough Publishing House

Arnold, Eberhard, 1995, *Why We Live in Community*, Farmington, PA, Plough Publishing House, 3rd edn

Arnold, Eberhard and Emmy, 1974, *Seeking for the Kingdom of God*, Rifton, NY, Plough Publishing House

Arnold, Emmy, 1984, *Torches Together*, Rifton, NY, Plough Press, 2nd edn

Arnold, Emmy, 1999, *A Joyful Pilgrimage*, Farmington, PA, Plough Publishing House (a revised edition of *Torches Together*)

Arnold, Heini [J. Heinrich] and AnneMarie, 1983, *Living in Community*, Rifton, NY, Plough Publishing House

Arnold, J. Heinrich, 1994, *Discipleship*, Farmington, PA, Plough Publishing House

Arnold, Johann Christoph, 1995, 'An Open Letter From the Bruderhof', *The Plough*, 41, Winter, 2–6

Arnold, Johann Christoph, 1996a, *A Plea for Purity*, Farmington, PA, Plough Publishing House

Arnold, Johann Christoph, 1996b, 'A Meeting with Louis Farrakhan', *The Plough*, 49, Autumn, 28–30

Arnold, Johann Christoph (ed.), 2000, *Eberhard Arnold*, Maryknoll, NY, Orbis Books

Arnold, Johann Christoph, and Müller, Eckhard, 1995, 'Steps Toward Reconciliation', *The Plough*, 45, Summer, 22–27

Aschheim, Steven E., 1992, *The Nietzsche Legacy in Germany 1890–1919*, Berkeley, CA, University of California Press

Austermann, Isabell, 2000, 'Catholic Integrated Community and Church', *Community Today*, 10/2000, 20 September, 6–8

Avrahami, Eli, 1998, *Kibbutz. An Evolving Community*, Ramat Efal, Yad Tabenkin

Ayala, Rubén, 1995, 'The Million Man March', *The Plough*, 46, November–December, 29–30

Baratz, Joseph, 1954, *A Village by the Jordan*, London, Harvill Press

Barth, Karl, 1969, *Action in Waiting*, Rifton, NY, Plough Publishing House

Barth, Rosanna, and Wardle, Derek, 1993, 'It's Gonna Be Permanent', *The Plough*, 36, Autumn, 14–15

Baum, Markus, 1998, *Against the Wind. Eberhard Arnold and the Bruderhof*, Farmington, PA, Plough Publishing House

Becker, Howard, 1946, *German Youth: Bond or Free?*, London, Kegan Paul, Trench, Trubner

Ben Gurion, Hagai, 2000, 'Communication: Influencing Change on Kibbutz', *Kibbutz Trends*, 37, Spring, 23–26

Ben-Rafael, Eliezer, 1997, *Crisis and Transformation. The Kibbutz at Century's End*, Albany, NY, State University of New York Press

Ben-Shalom, Avraham, 1937, *Deep Furrows*, New York, Hashomer-Hatzair Organization

Beuys, Joseph, 1997, *'Honey is Flowing in All Directions'*, Göttingen, Steidl Publishers/Heidelberg, Editions Staeck

Black, Lawrence, 1999, 'Social Democracy as a Way of Life: Fellowship and the Socialist Union, 1951–1959', *Twentieth Century British History*, 10/4, 499–539

Blumhardt, Christoph, 1998, *Action in Waiting*, Farmington, PA, Plough Publishing House

Bock, Paul (ed.), 1984, *Signs of the Kingdom: A Ragaz Reader*, Grand Rapids, MI, Eerdmans

Bohlken-Zumpe, Elizabeth, 1993, *Torches Extinguished*, San Francisco, Carrier Pigeon Press

Böhner, Hans and Klönne, Arno, 1995, *Was Wißt Ihr Von Der Erde*, Witzenhausen, Verlag Der Jugendbewegung

Bondy, Ruth, 1978, *The Emissary. A Life of Enzo Sereni*, London, Robson Books

Borinski, Fritz and Milch, Werner, 1982, *Jugenbewegung*, Frankfurt am Main, Dipa Verlag, 1982. This comprises a copy of the original English version, *Jugendbewegung. The Story of German Youth 1896–1933*, London, 1945, along with a German translation. The English section reproduces pagination of the original, and does not have a continuous pagination with the German material.

Bramwell, Anna, 1989, *Ecology in the 20th Century*, New Haven, CT, Yale University Press

Buber, Martin, 1958, *Paths in Utopia*, Boston, MA, Beacon Press

Bunker, Sarah, Coates, Chris, Hodgson, David and How, Jonathan, 1999, *Diggers and Dreamers, 2000–2001*, London, Diggers and Dreamers Publications

Catholic Integrated Community (ed.), 1997, *Urfelder Kreis. 'Dedicated to the Urfeld Circle and Our Friends'*, Bad Tölz, Catholic Integrated Community

Catholic Integrated Community, 1998, *The Catholic Integrated Community*, Bad Tölz, Catholic Integrated Community

Catholic Integrated Community (ed.), 1999, *Easter in Israel 29.3.1999–5.4.1999*, Bad Tölz, Catholic Integrated Community

Central Bureau of Statistics, 2000, *Kibbutzim and Their Population* (in Hebrew), Jerusalem, Central Bureau of Statistics

Central Bureau of Statistics and Yad Tabenkin, 2000, *Kibbutzim (Statistical 6)*, unpaginated leaflet, Jerusalem/Ramat Efal, Central Bureau of Statistics and Yad Tabenkin

Coates, Chris, How, Jonathan, Jones, Lee, Morris, William and Wood, Andy (eds), 1993, *Diggers and Dreamers 1994–1995*, Winslow, Communes Network

Coates, Chris, How, Jonathan, Jones, Lee, Morris, William, 1995, *Diggers and Dreamers 1996–1997*, Winslow, Diggers and Dreamers Publications

Cohen, Mitchell, 1987, *Zion and State*, Oxford, Basil Blackwell

Cohen, Rich, 2000, *The Avengers*, London, Jonathan Cape

Community Service Committee (eds), 1938, *Community in Britain*, Ashton Keynes, Cotswold Bruderhof Press

'D., Joel', 1996, Letter to *The Plough*, *The Plough*, 50, November–December, 4

Dalomi, Ezra, 1999, 'It's a Waste of Time, Chaverim' [plus responses], *Kibbutz Trends*, 33, Spring, 25–33

Denzin, K. and Lincoln Y. S. (eds), 1994, *Handbook of Qualitative Research*, London, Sage Publications

Dumont, Louis, 1994, *German Ideology*, Chicago, University of Chicago Press

Durnbaugh, Donald, 1991, 'Relocation of the German Bruderhof to England, South America, and North America', *Communal Studies*, 11, 62–77

Ebeling, Hans, 1945, *The German Youth Movement*, London, New Europe Publishing Co.

Edgell, Derek, 1992, *The Order of Woodcraft Chivalry 1916–1949 as a New Age Alternative to the Boy Scouts*, Lampeter, Edwin Mellen Press (in two volumes)

Eggers, Ulrich, 1988, *Community for Life*, Scottdale, PA, Herald Press

Etzioni, Amitai (ed.), 1995, *New Communitarian Thinking*, Charlottesville, VA, University Press of Virginia

Fiedler, Jeannine (ed.), 1995, *Social Utopias of the Twenties*, Wuppertal, Müller & Busmann Press

Fölling, Werner and Fölling-Albers, Maria (eds), 1999, *The Transformation of Collective Education in the Kibbutz*, Frankfurt am Main, Peter Lang

Fölling, Werner and Melzer, Wolfgang, 1989, *Gelebte Jugendträume*, Witzenhausen, Südmark Verlag

Frank, Manfred et al., 1988, *Gott im Exil*, Frankfurt am Main, Suhrkamp

Frank, Manfred, 1989–90, *Le Dieu a Venir*, Arles, Actes Sud (in five volumes: *Lecons I et II*, 1989; *Lecons III et IV*, 1990; *Lecons V et VI*, 1990; *Lecons VII et VIII*, 1990; *Lecons IX, X, et XI*, 1990)

Freedman, Ralph, 1979, *Herman Hesse: Pilgrim of Crisis*, London, Jonathan Cape

Gardiner, Rolf, 1943, *England Herself*, London, Faber & Faber

Gavron, Daniel, 2000, *The Kibbutz. Awakening from Utopia*, Lanham, MD, Rowman and Littlefield

George, Stefan, 1944, *Poems*, London, Kegan Paul

Gilad, Ayala, 2001, 'Kibbutz: The End' [plus responses], *Kibbutz Trends*, 43/4, Winter, 24–30

Golomb, Jacob (ed.), 1997, *Nietzsche and Jewish Culture*, London, Routledge

Gordon, A. D., 1938, *Selected Essays*, New York, League for Labor Palestine

Gordon, Frank J., 1988, 'Protestantism and Socialism in the Weimar Republic', *German Studies Review*, XI/3, 423–45

Gordon, Haim and Bloch, Jochanan (eds), 1984, *Martin Buber: A Centenary Volume*, New York, Ktav Publishing House [esp. Menahem Dorman, 'Martin Buber's Address "Herut" and its Influence on the Jewish Youth Movement in Germany', 233–51]

Gorni, Yosef, Oved, Yaacov and Paz, Idit (eds), 1987, *Communal Life. An International Perspective*, New Brunswick, NJ, Yad Tabenkin and Transaction Books

Gorringe, Timothy Y., 1999, *Karl Barth: Against Hegemony*, Oxford, Oxford University Press

Guardini, Romano, 1935, *The Church and the Catholic and the Spirit of the Liturgy*, New York, Sheed and Ward

Guardini, Romano, 1998, *The End of the Modern World*, Wilmington, DE, ISI Books

Gur, Batya, 1995, *Murder on a Kibbutz*, New York, Harper Perennial

Halkett, G. R., 1939, *The Dear Monster*, London, Jonathan Cape

Hardy, Dennis, 2000, *Utopian England*, London, E. & F. N. Spon

Hazony, Yoram, 2000, *The Jewish State: the Struggle for Israel's Soul*, New York, Basic Books

Hindley, Marjorie, 1993, '"Unerwünchst": One of the lesser known confrontations with the National Socialist state, 1933–1937', *German History*, 11/2, 207–21

Hofer, Samuel, 1998, *The Hutterites*, Saskatoon, Hofer Publishers

Hoffer, Willi, 1965, 'Siegfried Bernfeld and "Jerubaal". An Episode in the Jewish Youth Movement', *Leo Baeck Institute Yearbook*, X, 150–67

Holler, Eckard (ed.), 1999, *Puls* 22, November, 'Die Ulmer "Trabanten". Hans Scholl zwischen Hitler Jugend und dj.i.ii', Stuttgart, Verlag Der Jugendbewegung

Höss, Rudolf, 2000, *Commandant of Auschwitz*, London, Phoenix Press

Hutterian Brethren (ed.), 1988, *Brothers Unite*, Ulster Park, Plough Publishing House

Hutterian Society of Brothers and Yoder, John Howard (eds), 1984, *God's Revolution. The Witness of Eberhard Arnold*, Ramsey, Paulist Press

Integrated Community, 1996, *'Today – Pro Ecclesia Viva', The Publication of the Integrated Community*, 1, 'About Taking Root again in the Jewish Ground as a Condition for Regaining the Catholic Content', Bad Tölz, Verlag Urfeld

Jackson, Dave and Jackson, Neta, 1987, *Glimpses of Glory*, Elgin, IL, Brethren Press

Kanter, Rosabeth Moss, 1972, *Commitment and Community*, Cambridge, MA, Harvard University Press

Kerbs, Diethart and Reulecke, Jürgen (eds), 1998, *Handbuch der Deutschen Reform Bewegungen 1880–1933*, Wuppertal, Peter Hammer Verlag

Kindt, Werner, 1963, *Grundschriften der Deutschen Jugendbewegung*, Düsseldorf-Köln, Eugen Diederichs Verlag

Klönne, Arno (ed.), 1990, *Puls* 18, October, 'Blaue Blume in Trümmerlandschaften', Witzenhausen, Südmarkverlag/Verlag der Jugendbewegung

Klönne, Irmgard (ed.), 1993, *Puls* 21, November, 'Deutsch, Jüdisch, Bündisch', Witzenhausen, Südmarkverlag/Verlag der Jugendbewegung

Koch, Bernhard, 1999, 'Contemplating the Hour', *Community Today*, 12/99, 2 December, 14

Koch, Bernhard, 2000, 'Ein Segen Sollst Du Sein', *Heute in Kirche und Welt*, 4, November, 3

Kockel, Ullrich, 1999, *Borderline Cases*, Liverpool, Liverpool University Press

Korn, Elizabeth, Suppert, Otto and Vogt, Karl (eds), 1963, *Die Jugendbewegung. Welt Und Wirkung*, Düsseldorf-Köln, Eugen Diederichs Verlag

Krieg, Robert A., 1997, *Romano Guardini. A Precursor of Vatican II*, Notre Dame, IN, University of Notre Dame Press

Landauer, Gustav, 1974, *La Révolution*, Paris, Editions Champ Libre

Landauer, Gustav, 1978, *For Socialism*, St Louis, MO, Telos Press

Laqueur, Walter Z., 1962, *Young Germany*, London, Routledge & Kegan Paul

Laqueur, Walter Z., 1971, *Out of the Ruins of Europe*, London, Alcove Press

Laqueur, Walter Z., 1972, *A History of Zionism*, London, Weidenfeld & Nicolson

Laqueur, Walter Z., 1992, *Thursday's Child Has Far to Go*, New York, Charles Scribner's Sons

Leichman, David and Paz, Idit (eds), 1994, *Kibbutz. An Alternative Lifestyle*, Ramat Efal, Yad Tabenkin

Lejeune, Robert, 1963, *Christoph Blumhardt and His Message*, Rifton, NY, Plough Publishing House

Levi-Faur, David, Sheffer, Gabriel and Vogel, David (eds), 1999, *Israel. The Dynamics of Change and Continuity*, London, Frank Cass Publishers

Liebersohn, Harry, 1988, *Fate and Utopia in German Sociology, 1870–1923*, Cambridge, MA, MIT Press

Lieblich, Amia, 1981, *Kibbutz Makom*, New York, Pantheon Books

Linse, Ulrich (ed.), 1983, *Zurück, O Mensch, zur Mutter Erde. Landkommunen in Deutschland 1890–1933*, München, Deutscher Taschenbuch Verlag

Lohfink, Gerhard, 1998, *Braucht Gott Die Kirche?*, Freiburg, Verlag Herder

Lohfink, Gerhard, 1999, *Does God Need the Church?*, Collegeville, MN, Michael Glazer/The Liturgical Press

Lohfink, Gerhard, 2000, 'Die Kirche – Gesellschaft in der Gesellschaft', *Heute in Kirche und Welt*, 4, November, 1–2

Lohfink, Gerhard and Pesch, Rudolph, 1995, 'Volk Gottes als "Neue Familie"', in Josef Ernst and Stephan Leimgruber (eds), *Surrexit Dominus Vere. Die Gegenwart des Auferstandenen in Seiner Kirche. FS Erzbischof Johannes Joachim Degenhardt*, Paderborn, Bonifatius

Löwy, Michael, 1992, *Redemption and Utopia*, London, Athlone Press

Löwy, Michael, 1993, *On Changing the World*, Atlantic Highlands, NJ, Humanities Press

Löwy, Michael and Sayre, Robert, 1992, *Révolte et mélancolie*, Paris, Éditions Payot

Lunn, Eugene, 1973, *Prophet of Community*, Berkeley, CA, University of California Press

Macmurray, John, 1938, *The Clue to History*, London, SCM Press

Macmurray, John, 1995, *The Self as Agent*, London, Faber & Faber

Maffesoli, Michel, 1996a, *Ordinary Knowledge*, Cambridge, Polity Press

Maffesoli, Michel, 1996b, *The Time of the Tribes*, London, Sage Publications

Magnus, Bernd and Higgins, Kathleen M., 1996, *The Cambridge Companion to Nietzsche*, Cambridge, Cambridge University Press

Manke, Jutta, 1994, 'Relationships', *The Plough*, 38, Spring, 16–18

Margalit, Elkana, 1969, 'Social and Intellectual Origins of the Hashomer Hatzair Youth Movement, 1913–1920', *Journal of Contemporary History*, 4/2, 25–46

Maron, Stanley, 1993, *Kibbutz in a Market Society*, Ramat Efal, Yad Tabenkin

Meier, Hans, 1979, *Hans Meier Tells His Story to a Friend*, Rifton, NY, Plough Publishing House

Meier, Hans, 1990, *Solange das Licht Brennt*, Norfolk, CT, Hutterian Brethren

Melzer, Wolfgang and Neubauer, Georg (eds), 1988, *Der Kibbutz als Utopie*, Weinheim, Belt Verlag

Mendes-Flohr, Paul, 1989, *From Mysticism to Dialogue*, Detroit, MI, Wayne State University Press

Mendes-Flohr, Paul, 1991, 'Rosenzweig and the *Kameraden*: a Non-Zionist Alliance', *Journal of Contemporary History*, 26/3–4, 385–402

Merron, David, 1999, *Collectively Yours*, Bakewell, Country Books

Merron, David, 2001, 'Kibbutz. From Idealism to Pragmatism', unpublished paper presented to the International Communal Studies Association, Belzig, Germany, June

Minion, Mark, 2000, 'Left, Right or European? Labour and Europe in the 1940s: The Case of the Socialist Vanguard Group', *European Review of History*, 7/2, 229–48

Moaz, Eliyahu, 1959, 'The Werkleute', *Leo Baeck Institute Yearbook*, IV, 165–82

Morrison, Sybil, 1962, *I Renounce War*, London, Sheppard Press

Mosse, George L., 1964, *The Crisis of German Ideology*, London, Weidenfeld & Nicolson

Mosse, George, L., 1971, *Germans and Jews*, London, Orbach & Chambers

Mow, Merrill, 1991, *Torches Rekindled*, Rifton, NY, Plough Publishing House, 3rd edn

Neal, Mark Anthony, 1999, *What the Music Said*, London, Routledge

Near, Henry, 1992, *The Kibbutz Movement. A History. Vol. I Origins and Growth 1909–1939*, Oxford, The Littman Library/Oxford University Press

Near, Henry, 1997, *The Kibbutz Movement. A History. Vol. II Crisis and Achievement 1939–1995*, London, The Littman Library of Jewish Civilisation

Nietzsche, Friedrich, 1982, *Daybreak*, Cambridge, Cambridge University Press

Nietzsche, Friedrich, 2000, *The Birth of Tragedy*, Oxford, Oxford University Press

Orage, A. R., 1906, *Friedrich Nietzsche. The Dionysian Spirit of the Age*, London, T. N. Foulis

Orage, A. R., 1912, *Nietzsche in Outline and Aphorism*, Chicago, A. C. McClurg

Oved, Yaacov, 1988, *Two Hundred Years of American Communes*, New Brunswick, NJ, Transaction

Oved, Yaacov, 1993, *Distant Brothers*, Ramat Efal, Yad Tabenkin

Oved, Yaacov, 1996, *The Witness of the Brothers*, New Brunswick, NJ, Transaction

Oved, Yaacov, 2000, 'Anarchism in the Kibbutz Movement', *Kibbutz Trends*, 38, Summer, 45–50

Pachter, Henry, 1982, *Weimar Etudes*, New York, Columbia University Press

Parsons, Talcott, Shils, Edward, Naegele, Kaspar D. and Pitts, Jesse R., 1961, *Theories of Society*, New York, The Free Press

Paul, Leslie, 1951, *Angry Young Man*, London, Faber & Faber

Peck, Robert N., 1987, 'An Ex-Member's Eye View of the Bruderhof Communities From 1948–1961', in G. Beauchamp, K. Roemer and N. D. Smith (eds), *Utopian Studies 1*, Lanham, MD, University Press of America

Peter, Kurt, 2001, 'Mitarbeiter als Mitunternehmer', *Heute in Kirche und Welt*, 5, May, 4–5

Plough Publishing House, 1973, *Eberhard Arnold. A Testimony of Church Community from his Life and Writings*, Rifton, NY, Plough Publishing House, 2nd edn

Putnam, Robert, 2001, *Bowling Alone*, New York, Simon & Schuster

Rapport, Nigel and Overing, Joanna, 2000, *Social and Cultural Anthropology*, London, Routledge

Ratzinger, Cardinal Joseph, 1999, *Many Religions – One Covenant*, San Francisco, Ignatius Press

Regelson, Abraham, 1981, *The Passover Haggadah*, New York, The Press of Shulsinger

Reinharz, Jehuda, 1986, 'Hashomer Hazair in Germany (1) 1928–1933', *Leo Baeck Institute Yearbook*, XXXI, 173–208

Reinharz, Jehuda, 1987, 'Hashomer Hazair in Germany (II). Under the Shadow of the Swastika, 1933–1938', *Leo Baeck Institute Yearbook*, XXXII, 183–229

Repp, Kevin, 2000, *Reformers, Critics and the Paths of German Modernity*, Cambridge, MA, Harvard University Press

Rheins, Carl J., 1978, 'The Schwarzes Fähnlein, Jungenschaft 1932–1934', *Leo Baeck Institute Yearbook*, XXIII, 173–97

Riccardi, Andrea, 1999, *Sant'egidio, Rome and the World*, London, St Pauls

Rideman, Peter, 1974, *Confession of Faith*, Rifton, NY, Plough Publishing House

Rinott, Chanoch, 1974, 'Major Trends in Jewish Youth Movements in Germany', *Leo Baeck Institute Yearbook*, XIX, 77–95

Roseman, Mark, 2001, *The Past in Hiding*, Harmondsworth, Penguin Books

Rosenstock, Werner, 1974, 'The Jewish Youth Movement', *Leo Baeck Institute Yearbook*, XIX, 97–105

Rubin, Julius H., 2000, *The Other Side of Joy*, New York, Oxford University Press

Salinger, Eliyahu Kuti, 1998, *Nächstes Jahr Im Kibbuz*, Paderborn, Kowag/Universität Paderborn

Sayre, Robert and Löwy, Michael, 1984, 'Figures of Romantic Anti-Capitalism', *New German Critique*, 32, Spring–Summer, 42–92

Schatzker, Chaim, 1978, 'Martin Buber's Influence on the Jewish Youth Movement in Germany', *Leo Baeck Institute Yearbook*, XXIII, 151–71

Schatzker, Chaim, 1987, 'The Jewish Youth Movement in Germany in the Holocaust Period (I). Youth in Confrontation With a New Reality', *Leo Baeck Institute Yearbook*, XXXII, 157–81

Schatzker, Chaim, 1988, 'The Jewish Youth Movement in Germany in the Holocaust Period (II). The Relations Between the Youth Movement and Hechaluz', *Leo Baeck Institute Yearbook*, XXXIII, 301–25

Schmalenbach, Herman, 1977, *On Society and Experience*, Chicago, University of Chicago Press

Scholem, Gershom, 1980, *From Berlin to Jerusalem*, New York, Schocken Books

Scholl, Inge, 1983, *The White Rose*, Hanover, NH, Wesleyan University Press

Seeligmann, Haim [Chaim], 1996, 'Haim Seeligmann Reports on His Visit to Europe', *Bulletin of the International Communal Studies Association*, 20, Fall, 15

Seeligmann, Chaim, 1998, *Spuren einer Stillen Revolution*, Hagen, Verlag Urfeld

Siefken, Hinrich, 1994a, *Die Weiße Rose und Ihre Flugblätter*, Manchester, Manchester University Press

Siefken, Hinrich, 1994b, '"The Weiße Rose" and Russia', *German Life and Letters*, 47/1, 14–43

Simons, Tal and Ingram, Paul, 2000, 'Enemies of the State: Competition Over the Supply of Order and the Ecology of the Kibbutz, 1910–1997', unpublished working paper, New York, Columbia University

Society of Brothers (ed.), 1974, *Children in Community*, Rifton, NY, Plough Publishing House

Souchy, Augustin, 1992, *Beware! Anarchist!*, Chicago, Charles H. Kerr Publishing Co.

Stachura, Peter D., 1975, 'The National Socialist Machtergreifung and the German Youth Movement: Co-ordination and Reorganisation, 1933–34', *Journal of European Studies*, 5, 255–72

Stachura, Peter D., 1981, *The German Youth Movement 1900–1945*, London, Macmillan

Steele, Tom, 1990, *Alfred Orage and the Leeds Art Club 1893–1923*, Aldershot, Scolar Press

Steernhell, Zeev, 1998, *The Founding Myths of Israel*, Princeton, NJ, Princeton University Press

Stephens, Susan and Potts, Miriam, 1996, 'From Seeker to Seeker', *The Plough*, 50, November–December, 29–31

Stern, Fritz, 1974, *The Politics of Cultural Despair*, Berkeley, CA, University of California Press

Stötzel, Arnold, 2001, 'On Dr Johannes Joachim Degenhardt, Archbishop of Paderborn, being raised to the dignity of Cardinal on the 21st of February 2001, in Rome', *Heute in Kirche und Welt*, 1, January, 4–5

Stourton, Edward, 1998, *Absolute Truth: The Catholic Church in the World Today*, London, Viking

Strange, Roderick, 1996, *The Catholic Faith*, Oxford, Oxford University Press

Thomas, R. Hinton, 1983, *Nietzsche in German Politics and Society 1890–1918*, Manchester, Manchester University Press

Thomson, George, 1934, 'The Influence of the Youth Movement on German Education' (2 volumes), unpublished PhD thesis, University of Glasgow, Department of Education

Thomson, Watson, 1949, *Pioneer in Community*, Toronto, The Ryerson Press

Thurman, Howard, 1997, *For the Inward Journey: The Writings of Howard Thurman*, Richmond, VA, Friends United Press

Tönnies, Ferdinand, 1955, *Community and Society*, London, Routledge & Kegan Paul

Tönnies, Ferdinand, 2001, *Community and Civil Society*, Cambridge, Cambridge University Press

Tyldesley, Michael, 1994, 'Martin Buber and the Bruderhof Communities', *Journal of Jewish Studies*, XLV/2, 258–72

Tyldesley, Michael, 1996, 'Gustav Landauer and the Bruderhof Communities', *Communal Societies*, 16, 23–41

Urfelder Kreis, 1996, *Urfelder Kreis, 'Dedicated to the Urfeld Circle and Our Friends'*, Bad Tölz, Verlag Urfeld

Urian, Dan and Karsh, Efraim (eds), 1999, *In Search of Identity: Jewish Aspects in Israeli Culture*, London, Frank Cass

Urquhart, Gordon, 1996, *The Pope's Armada*, London, Corgi Books

Utley, Philip Lee, 1999, 'Schism, Romanticism and Organisation: *Anfang*, January–August 1914', *Journal of Contemporary History*, 34/1, 109–24

Vallely, Paul (ed.), 1998, *The New Politics*, London, SCM Press

Vermes, Geza, 2000, *The Changing Faces of Jesus*, London, Allen Lane/The Penguin Press

Walk, Joseph, 1961, 'The Torah va'Avodah Movement in Germany', *Leo Baeck Institute Yearbook*, VI, 236–56

Walker, Lawrence D., 1970, *Hitler Youth and Catholic Youth 1933–1936*, Washington DC, Catholic University of America Press

Wallbrecher, Thomas, 2000, 'Contribution to the Talk about the Youth Diaconate', *Community Today*, 7/2000, 16–30 April, 14–15

Warhurst, Christopher, 1993, 'When Was the End of the Kibbutz? Ein Zivan and All That', *Kibbutz Trends*, 10, Summer, 46–50

Warhurst, Christopher, 1999, *Between Market, State and Kibbutz*, London, Mansell

Wheatcroft, Geoffrey, 2001, 'Death of the kibbutz', *The Guardian*, 14 May, 20

Whitworth, John M., 1975, *God's Blueprints*, London, Routledge & Kegan Paul

Winter, M. and Stötzel, Arnold, 2001, 'Die 68er: Ein Minister denkt nach – wir auch', *Heute in Kirche und Welt*, 2/February, 6

Wistrich, Robert and Ohana, David (eds), 1995, *The Shaping of Israeli Identity*, London, Frank Cass
Yassour, Avraham (ed.), 1995, *The History of the Kibbutz. A Selection of Sources, 1905–1929*, Merhavia
Yassour, Avraham, no date, *Gustav Landauer on Communal Settlement and its Industrialisation. Exchange of Letters Published and Introduced by Avraham Yassour* (translated from *Hakibbutz*, 2, cyclostyled)
Zablocki, Benjamin, 1980, *The Joyful Community*, Chicago, University of Chicago Press
Zerubavel, Yael, 1995, *Recovered Roots*, Chicago, University of Chicago Press
Zimmerman, Christopher, 1998, 'A Visit to Plum Village', *The Plough*, 55, Spring, 2–5
Zuendel, Friedrich, 1999, *The Awakening*, Farmington, PA, Plough Publishing House

WEBSITES

http://207.21.194.249/kvutsatyovel/netscape/strength.htm
http://207.21.194.249/kvutsatyovel/netscape/intimatekibbutz.htm
http://207.21.194.249/kvutsatyovel/netscape/wlzm.htm
http://207.21.194.249/kvutsatyovel/netscape/eshbal.htm
http://207.21.194.249/kvutsatyovel/netscape/haaretzyovel.htm
http://207.21.194.249/kvutsatyovel/netscape/changes.htm
In case of difficulty, all Kvutsat Yovel pages may be accessed via the main page of their site,
http://207.21.194.249/kvutsatyovel/netscape
http://www.tamuz.org.il/english/praxis_join.html
http://www.tamuz.org.il/english/praxis_members.html
http://www.tamuz.org.il/english/faq.html
http://www.tamuz.org.il/english/praxis_housing.html
http://blumagazine.net/closing.htm
http://riftonav.com/
http://www.bruderhof.com/news/news35.htm
http://www.wbenjamin.org/aufbruch.html
http://www.dpvonline.de/hist_4.html
http://www.legionofchrist.org/eng/articles/en99100802.htm
http://www.santegidio.org/en/contatto/cosa_e.html
http://www.perefound.org/KIT4-5_01.html
http://www.schulte-schulenberg.de/logkecic.htm
http://www.theage.com.au/news/2001/03/26/ffxs5faopkc.html

Index

Certain terms appear so frequently that they have not been indexed. These are Bruderhof (see esp. Ch. 4), Kibbutz (see esp. Ch. 6), Integrierte Gemeinde (see esp. Ch. 5), German Youth Movement, Jugendbewegung (see esp. Ch. 2), Wandervogel, and various Wandervogel organisations (see esp. Ch. 2), Freideutsche Youth and various Freideutsche bodies (see esp Ch. 2), Bündische Youth (see esp. Ch. 2)